REAL DEMOCRACY

NOT WESTMINSTER-STYLE BRAWLING, OLIGARCHICAL CAPITALISM & CORRUPTION

G. A. MOHR,

P.E. MOHR & R.S. MOHR

GA Mohr, P.E. Mohr & R.S. Mohr
REAL DEMOCRACY
*Not Westminster-style brawling,
oligarchical capitalism & corruption*

Table of Contents

Preface   i

PART 1: The Evolution of Modern Politics

Chapter 1   Introduction   1

Chapter 2   Brainwashed Consumer Zombies   7

Chapter 3   Religion   21

Chapter 4   The Industrial Revolution   37

Chapter 6   Politics   51

PART 2: Present Problems

Chapter 6   Education   65

Chapter 7   Global Disaster   81

Chapter 8   Big Business   95

Chapter 9   Hierarchical Organizations   117

Chapter 10   War and Terrorism   131

PART 3: The Psychology of Persuasion and Conflict

Chapter 11   Conditioning, Memory and Brainwashing   149

Chapter 12   The Mass Media   167

Chapter 13   Advertising   177

Chapter 14   Attitude Formation and Measurement   193

Chapter 15   Econobabble   207

Chapter 16   The Psychology of Conflict   223

Chapter 17   So, Have You Been Brainwashed?   233

PART 4: Real Democracy

Chapter 18   Real Democracy   241

Chapter 19   Parliamentary Process   251

Chapter 20   Market Research and Referenda   257

Chapter 21   Conclusions   267

References   279

PREFACE

I have long had an interest in politics.

My father was a nuclear physicist who did his PhD in Cambridge and went to some of the meetings run there by the KGB that the (in)famous spy and double agent Kim Philby attended. These were run because, with WW2 in sight, the Russians wanted to recruit students to their cause and encourage them to join the British secret service and become double agents for the KGB.

Perhaps influenced by anti-capitalist rhetoric, my father became a socialist, and after a few post-Cambridge years working at Cape Town University, during which he got married and had 3 children (I was #3), he returned to his birthplace Melbourne to work at Melbourne University.

In Melbourne he joined the Australian Soviet Friendship Society (ASFS) and attended their monthly meetings, once taking me to see a film about Maxim Gorki when I was only about 10.

My father always voted Labor, saying that the (now defunct) Communist Party of Australia had no hope of winning a seat.

Myself, 'Liberal' sounded OK to me when young and I recall suggesting that my mother should vote Liberal, and she did. When I first began voting at 18+ I also voted Liberal.

After stints at consulting engineering, at a technical college, in Cambridge (for my PhD at Churchill College), and then Auckland University, I returned to Melbourne almost 39.

Jobless, having been 'academically crucified' by a new 'bastard boss', I joined the local St Kilda West branch of the Liberal Party to fill in time while endlessly job searching.

Soon after that I contested the preselection to contest the state seat of Melbourne Ports at an upcoming state election.

A year or two later, I contested the preselection for a federal seat in an outer Melbourne area.

In both cases I was unsuccessful, and by the time I was circa 50 I began to vote Labor.

Then, at circa 60+, I began to vote Independent occasionally, eventually doing so on every possible occasion.

Indeed, approaching 70, I gave serious thought to running as an independent myself, but never did.

I also circulated minimally a 'flyer', part of which is shown below:

INVITATION
TO AN IMPORTANT EVENT
The 1st meeting of the ARDA
(Australian Real Democracy Alliance)
AGENDA

1) Opening: G. A. Mohr, PhD Churchill College, Cambridge, world hons mult, CEO of Transworld Research & Innovation (TRI)
2) Call for nominations for election of honorary chairperson.
3) Voting for latter.
4) Call for nominations for election of honorary secretary.
5) Voting for latter.
6) Call for nominations for election of honorary treasurer.
7) Voting for latter.
8) Collection of names of attendees (by secretary).
9) Collection of membership fees (by treasurer) – $2 per meeting or $20 annual.
10) Discussion.
11) Call for agenda suggestions for next meeting:
e.g. (a) $ to keep Holden here; (b) Daylight saving in winter.
(c) The LMS & ISE curves=> int. rates=> inflation. TELL THE RBA.
(d) Profit proportional company tax, not psychopathic Trump's 15%.
(e) Government buy back elec. & gas; (f) Voluntary euthanasia.

I never got around to running this meeting, but perhaps this book is a better idea.

I am grateful to those with whom I have been able to discuss my work from time to time, including, of course, the co-authors.

Special thanks also to the publishers, who have once again done an excellent job.

Geoff Mohr, 2019

PART 1

THE EVOLUTION OF MODERN POLITICS

Chapter 1

INTRODUCTION

> *There is a holy, mistaken zeal in politics, as well as in religion.*
> *By persuading others, we convince ourselves.*
> Junius (18th century). Letter, 19 Dec. 1769.
>
> *As there is no worse lie than a truth misunderstood by those who hear*
> *it, so reasonable arguments, challenges to magnanimity, and appeals*
> *to sympathy or justice, are folly when we are dealing*
> *with human crocodiles and boa-constrictors.*
> William James, The Varieties of Religious Experience, Lectures 14–15,
> *The Value of Saintliness* (1902).

A brief overview of the book

Chapter 2 briefly discusses the evolution of 'tribal man' and religion, and how 'witch doctors' were amongst our first leaders and how they 'brainwashed' their tribal members into believing their ill-conceived and superstitious ideas, thus maintaining a position of power and influence over their tribe.

The agricultural revolution then led, ultimately, to today's *consumer society* in which we are persuaded to buy all manner of products, and believe the waffle and BS of religious and political leaders, Chapter 2 concluding that much of this persistent persuasion could be deemed to be *brainwashing*.

The ninth edition of the Concise Oxford Dictionary has a reasonably flexible definition of brainwashing:

brainwash (v.tr): *subject (a person) to a prolonged process*
by which ideas other than and at variance
with those already held are implanted in the mind.

1

[1] Introduction

The classical Roget's Thesaurus lists brainwashing under *teaching* and *misteaching*. Various other thesauruses suggest synonyms such as:

condition, convert, convince, evangelize, indoctrinate, instill, unduly influence, program, reprogram, persuade, predispose, propagandize, proselytize, soften up, stipulate, tyrannize, work on.

Sometimes referred to in psychology as *thought reform*, 'BW' is an extreme form of *social influence* aimed at changing a person's views without their consent and often against their will, and is discussed further in Chapter 11.

In modern society attempts to persuade us to 'buy' some 'product' emanate from many sources such as:

➢ Often self-appointed and self-serving religious gurus.
➢ Leaders persuading us to engage in ethnic conflict.
➢ Writers and artists trying to influence us.
➢ Scientists pushing their often hair-brained ideas and gadgets.
➢ Industrialists urging us all to buy their new and usually unnecessary, if not downright wasteful, products.
➢ Educators who expect more and more of us to spend longer and longer listening to them regurgitate from one or two books which they themselves hardly understand.
➢ Religious leaders selling their 'brand' of religious BS.
➢ Politicians lying to us to get our vote, for example Western 'pollies' mumbling about so-called democracy when, in fact, we have *oligarchy*.
➢ Big business trying to urge us to become lifelong consumers of products such as junk food, cigarettes, beer, wine, insurance, cable TV, their Internet servers, mobile phone services etcetera.
➢ The big-business-run media selling their pro-capitalist spin on things day and night.
➢ Advertising companies, some of whom employed psychologists a hundred years ago (Eagly & Chaiken, 1993).
➢ Economists mumbling 'econobabble'. No matter which way the economic winds blow they will usually say all is well.

[1] INTRODUCTION

Each of these areas is discussed in this book. Taking on this range of topics inevitably makes the book something of a history of modern man so that the first chapter briefly discusses man's evolution and, in particular, the unscrupulous leaders who have brainwashed us into following their usually misguided bullshit.

Aspects of the science of persuasion are discussed at various points throughout the book, particularly in Chapter 11 which discusses memory, conditioning, and brainwashing, and also in Chapters 12, 13 and 14, which discuss that mass media, advertising, and attitude formation and measurement.

Part 2 of the book discusses some of the many problems that face mankind today, for example:

➢ We have almost exhausted reserves of that very finite 'black gold' oil. Having built our megacities and their massive freeway systems around the car we are faced with having to reverse this trend quite suddenly and soon.

➢ Consider also the AIDS epidemic in Africa and the continuing turmoil in the Iraq, Syria, Afghanistan, Libya and much of Northern Africa where dozens of Islamic terrorist groups control large areas, resulting in continuing and bitter conflict and mass migrations greater than those of the Second World War.

➢ The largest industries in the world are those of arms and drugs, an unacceptable situation. Millions starve in some poor countries while children in the more affluent West are being turned into brainwashed zombies carrying a drink bottle in one hand and a mobile phone in the other while dressed in increasingly ridiculous and impractical clothes and behaving as badly as their screen and pop music idols.

➢ In his interesting book *Paper Money* Adam Smith bemoans the million dollar house prices in California in the early 1970s (Smith, 1981). That situation has spread to most of the major cities of the Western world so that in Australia the "Great Australian dream" of owning one's house is now beyond most of today's young people.

If this is so-called democracy then it is not good enough.

At least socialism, usually referred to by propagandists using the more emotive and incorrect term communism, might give your children a roof over their heads and some certainty of being able to have a sensible career.

They might also hope to have a lasting marriage and bearable standard of living in which they are not addicted to Coke, junk food, drugs, booze, cigarettes, mobile phones, the 'gee whiz' but largely useless Internet, ridiculous clothes, gambling, etcetera, all symptoms of a sick amoral society in terminal decline as Rome was nearly two millennia ago.

God is not the answer but an invention that has had few positive results but many bad ones such as interminable wars. At best, religion is a waste of time, at worst it is preached by paedophiles and used as an excuse by politicians and terrorists for war.

The answers lie within ourselves.

Human beings are only animals, but we were clever enough to invent antiseptics, anaesthetics, antibiotics and nuclear power. At least a *few* of us were.

Then there are the unscrupulous arms dealers, pharmaceutical industries that peddle such addictive things as tranquilizers and antidepressants, the medical industry which puts you on blood pressure medication for years rather than treat the root cause (atherosclerosis), and then carves you up to put in heart bypasses which prolong life no more than careful diet and exercise (Cooke & Zimmer, 2002).

The education business has grown out of all proportion. Twelve years at school is too long, let alone a few more in day care centres, and then countless years can be wasted studying such ludicrous courses as postgraduate diplomas in Sexology and Puppetry.

Over 50 years ago it was found that average IQ in the UK had decreased and continuing decline was predicted. Recent studies confirm that this *reverse evolution* is actually happening globally.

The picture is bleak to say the least and World War 3, thanks to widespread Islamic terrorism, is happening on a grand scale right now (Mohr, Fear & Sinclair, 2015).

Part 3

Part 3 of the book begins by discussing conditioning, memory and 'brainwashing' (Chapter 11), Chapters 12 and 13 then discussing the how the mass media and advertising persuade us into becoming 'consumer zombies' and believing most, if not all, the BS religious and political leaders spout at us.

Chapter 14 then discusses the psychology of attitudes, including expectancy-value and information integration models of attitude formation, the contact hypothesis model of ethnic conflict, 'mere exposure research', Likert's widely-used method of summated ratings, Guttman scaling and Bogardus' social stimulus scale.

Chapter 15 discusses the 'econobabble' ignorant economists and misguided politicians constantly indulge in, for example almost all of them saying that increasing official/government interest rates increases inflation when, as intuition would suggest, and as is demonstrated mathematically in Chapter 15, the reverse is the case.

Chapter 16 discusses the psychology of conflict, presenting a simple 'summation model' to evaluate the attitudes of a group of people to another group of people which is different in some way such as ethnically, religiously, politically etcetera.

Finally, Chapter 17 gives an example of Likert scaling to evaluate whether one has, indeed, been 'brainwashed' into becoming a 'consumer zombie'.

Part 4

Part 4 of the book begins by discussing our basic proposal of how *real democracy* should work (Chapter 18), then Chapter 19 and 20 discuss further details of how this 'real democracy' should work in practice, Chapter 21 concluding with brief summary discussion of some key issues discussed in the book, in particular that of Real Democracy.

[1] Introduction

Chapter 2

BRAINWASHED CONSUMER ZOMBIES

> **zombie** 1. Orig., the snake-deity of voodoo cults in W. Africa, Haiti
> and the southern U.S.; hence, a supernatural power that may
> reanimate dead bodies or a body so reanimated.
> 2. *colloq.* A person resembling a revived corpse;
> a dull or slow-witted, or apathetic person 1941.
> *The Shorter Oxford Dictionary,* 3rd edn, Oxford University Press 1973.

A long history

Men have used pretentious bullshit of one kind or another throughout history to persuade, if not brainwash, others into doing as they want, for example:

➤ Witch doctors or *shamans* claiming mystical powers over illness.

➤ Religious leaders claiming knowledge of some god or other.

➤ Throughout history the building of religious and other monuments has enslaved millions.

➤ Throughout history leaders have led us like lemmings into disastrous wars for little or no reason using religio-political rhetoric.

➤ Political leaders periodically try and persuade us to vote for them.

➤ Economists spout 'econobabble' to constantly assure us that, no matter which way the economic wind blows, its direction is favourable.

➤ Since the industrial revolution, especially, we have been persuaded to rush en masse to buy the latest model of every type of contrivance.

➢ Advertising companies, some of whom employed psychologists a hundred years ago (Eagly & Chaiken, 1993), are often able to ensure that their marketing campaigns target consumers of all ages to the point at which they end up spending most of their lives and all their money buying products they can't really afford, don't really need, and which in many cases are downright harmful one way or another.

The sorry truth is that mankind has been inveigled into 'buying' all manner of 'products' almost at the will of the 'seller' throughout its history. Thus we have, as often as not, been led like lemmings from one disaster to another, these tending to grow in magnitude like our now excessive population:

lemming n. 1 any small vole-like Arctic rodent of the genus Lemmus
and related genera, including L. lemmus of Norway
which is noted for mass migrations during which
it attempts to cross large bodies of water.
2 a person who unthinkingly joins a mass movement,
esp. a headlong rush to destruction.
The Concise Oxford Dictionary, 9th edn, Oxford University Press 1997.

Consumer zombies

The result is that our consumer societies have evolved to the point at which we have been reduced to brainwashed zombies shuffling along with a mobile phone in one hand, a drink bottle or cigarette in the other, and wearing jeans once intended for farm workers but which we have been led by the nose for nearly 50 years to believe are 'trendy.'

In more affluent countries we drive tank-like four wheel drives down the freeway just to go shopping and live in or aspire to live in a 'McMansion' with a heated swimming pool and sauna.

Regardless of the climate or weather houses and offices are open plan and air conditioned, requiring massive energy usage, increasing the rate at which we use up the fast vanishing oil reserves on the planet.

Worse still, nothing is built to last, most products have built-in obsolescence, and many others are 'disposable' after first use.

Belatedly we are becoming aware that this is a recipe for disaster and that we are fast exhausting some of the planet's most precious resources and polluting it terribly in the process.

What led to us becoming such gullible consumer zombies? - to understand what then led us to this sorry state we should, of course, begin at the beginning.

Evolution of tribal man

Chimpanzees, with which we share 96% of the same genes, are quite sociable animals and live in groups of 20 to 60, forming into subgroups of adults (male and female), all-male groups and groups of mothers and offspring. African gorillas also live in bisexual groups of between 2 to 30 but which do not comprise smaller subgroups.

The best known studies of chimpanzees were conducted by Jane Goodall and associates in the Gombe National Park on the edge of Lake Tanganyika in Tanzania (van-Lawick Goodall, 1971).

Ultimately, Goodall was quite disillusioned to find that *tribes* of chimps were led by an alpha male and would occasionally have small wars with neighbouring tribes, these resuming at intervals over periods of many years. She concluded that they were all too much like humans!

Comparisons of blood proteins and the DNA of the African great apes with that of humans indicates that the line leading to modern people did not split off from that of chimpanzees and gorillas until comparatively late in evolution, perhaps 6 million to 8 million years ago.

Fossils of the first *hominines,* the *australopithecines*, have been discovered dating to 5 million years ago. This genus seems to have become extinct about 1.5 million years ago, but before doing so one of seven species of australopithecines, *Australopithecus africanus*, evolved into the genus *Homo* between 1.5 and 2 million years ago.

The earliest evidence of stone tools comes from sites in Africa dated to about 2.5 million years ago. These tools have not been found in association with a particular hominine species.

9

Around 1.7 to 1.9 million years ago two new species of large brained, small-toothed hominines emerged, *Homo ergaster* in Africa and *Homo erectus* in Asia. Later *H. erectus* skulls possess brain sizes in the range of 1100 to 1300 cc (67.1 to 79.3 cu in), within the size variation of *Homo sapiens.*

A number of archaeological sites dating from the time of *Homo erectus* reveal a greater sophistication in tool-making than was found at the earlier sites. Evidence found at the cave site of "Peking Man" in northern China, suggests that *H. erectus* used fire.

The remains of the foundations of an oval structure built by a *Homo erectus* group were found at the Terra-Amata site in France, and within this structure there was a fireplace (Weiss & Mann, 1978).

The *Homo* species spread widely and by 350,000 years ago planned hunting, fire making, wearing of clothes, and probably burial rituals, were well established.

Between 200,000 and 300,000 years ago, *Homo sapiens* evolved.

The Neanderthals or *Homo sapiens neanderthalensis* had similar DNA to modern man and occupied parts of Europe and the Middle East as early as 120,000 years ago. They lived only in family groups, the men being hunter-gatherers to feed the family.

The Neanderthals left cave paintings which were an important evolutionary advance. These often depicted a simple activity, perhaps a precursor to the highly pictorial hieroglyphic script of the ancient Egyptians (Egerton Eastwick, 1896).

Though Neanderthals had 10% larger brains than modern man, there is some evidence that the part of the cerebral cortex devoted to language and thinking in modern man was underdeveloped in Neanderthal man, casting some doubt on whether Neanderthal man was capable of modern spoken language. Thought by some to be a different evolutionary branch, the Neanderthals disappeared from the fossil record about 30,000 years ago.

Differing in appearance, modern humans or *Homo sapiens sapiens* evolved in southern Africa or the Middle East perhaps 90,000 to 200,000 years ago and 70,000 years ago began to spread to all parts of the world, reaching Europe about 40,000 years ago, soon outnumbering, perhaps interbreeding with, and finally supplanting the local, earlier *Homo sapiens* populations.

Like chimpanzees, Homo sapiens sapiens formed tribes and there is evidence of religion, recorded events and art dating from 30,000 to 40,000 years ago implying the advanced language and ethics required for the ordering of social groups.

Evolution of religion and the 'brainwashers'

Around the same time Homo sapiens developed cave art, about 100,000 years ago, he would have developed language and, eventually some form of 'pictorial' communication which eventually evolved into hieroglyphic script, then cuneiform script, and finally the symbolic writing we now use.

Typically each tribe had a leader, a religion, and a common language and culture.

The first forms of religion involved such beliefs and practices as

(a) *Animism*, a belief that plants, inanimate objects and natural phenomena had souls or spirits.

(b) *Polytheism,* a belief in multiple Gods, sometimes attributing certain acts of nature to each.

(c) *Ancestor Worship* teaching that a tribe's people were descended from a common ancestor.

(d) *Immortality* or belief that the dead live on as spirits.

Eventually these religions evolved into the *monotheism* that dominates the world today. At the outset, however, it was the tribal elders who passed on tribal beliefs from one generation to another. Along the way *shamans* or 'witch doctors' claiming some special connection with the spirits appeared, along with religious rites and ceremonies.

In groups of hunter-gatherers, as with many other species of animals, the 'dominant' males were, of course, responsible for protection of the group from external threats which, just as with chimpanzees, often took the form of other 'tribes' or groups.

11

At the same time, however, the supposedly wiser elders still indoctrinated the young into religion and had considerable influence, if not control, over the 'dominant males.' Their weapons for control ranged from rhetoric to dire threats of a vengeful spirit or God.

Thus from the ancient Greeks through to the middle ages a study of *rhetoric* was considered important because of its use to bullshit people into doing as political and religious leaders wished. Francis Bacon (1561 - 1626), for example, studied Elizabethan logic and rhetoric at Cambridge University for two years, leaving at the age of 14, a point we return to in Chapter 6.

The agricultural revolution and the consumer society

About 12,000 years ago the agricultural revolution, in part enabled by development of primitive forms of permanent housing, led to the growth of human societies from small tribes to those of settlements of hundreds and eventually, as farming became more productive, thousands of people.

More efficient farming allowed more specialization, for example millers, bakers and weavers. Such people were *producers* of a particular product so that the rest of the society became *consumers*.

The agricultural revolution, then, was the beginning of the *consumer society*. In these growing societies religion became increasingly important as a means of imparting ethics and standards.

These larger societies now had houses and farms to defend, however, so that the need for stronger males for territorial defence grew and with it the influence that military leaders had upon society. This may have led to the appearance of leaders of towns or regions involving a few nearby towns and, eventually, monarchs.

In some societies, however, priest kings emerged, but generally 'church' and 'state' have remained separate entities to this day, both doing their utmost to control their societies.

These growing societies and the organizations within them, especially the army and the church, took on hierarchical forms and the main weapons of control ranged from verbal *persuasion* to threats throughout a chain of command to see that the rest of the population towed the line.

Unfortunately, however, the ambitious/aggressive/assertive people who literally fight their way to leadership positions through impatience, stupidity and deceit have done far more harm than good and our unending history of war, practically useless temples and other monuments to stupidity attests to this, a point revisited in following chapters.

These wasteful leaders were *consumers* of, in particular, the *good*s provided by builders and the *services* of large numbers of domestic slaves and large armies of soldiers.

In the rest of society the mercantile infrastructure of the consumer society that we have today began to evolve with open air markets largely giving way to shops and barter systems giving way to currency.

The modern consumer society

Our highly structured modern consumer societies do not have the problem of one all-powerful leader but countless little Hitlers:

Capitalism tends to produce a multiplicity of petty dictators each in command of his own little business kingdom.
State Socialism tends to produce a single, centralized totalitarian dictatorship, wielding absolute authority . . . through a hierarchy of bureaucratic agents.
Aldous Huxley, *Ends and Means* (1937).

These psychopathic little Hitlers make life miserable in every area of human activity, for example:

➢ Hypocritical religious leaders whose choir boys have all too often been asked to do much more than sing.

➢ Military officers, particularly NCOs, who bully troops to the point at which death is preferable to marching out of step.

➢ Artists who often earn indecent amounts of money inflicting atrocious art, movies and music on us.

➢ Scientists whose every invention is marketed to the point at which everyone has to have one.

➢ Industrialists whose factory slaves resemble automatons and zombies forced to work harder than animals would be allowed to.

➢ Educators who imprison children in school far longer than necessary to simply brainwash them into routine until they are more than old enough to join the work force.

➢ Politicians who lie through their teeth during each election campaign to try and win enough votes and then, if elected, continue to assure us that their mistakes are not mistakes and that they are actually improving things when, quite obviously, the human race is racing towards catastrophe.

➢ Business leaders whose gigantic salaries dwarf those of their employees and whose gullible shareholders accept usually minuscule returns on their investments.

➢ Electronic and print media executives who ensure that we are fed trivia and follow the official line that glosses over the increasingly wide cracks in our corrupt and decaying society.

➢ Economists who constantly bleat about the exchange rate, inflation, unemployment and other numbers in much the same way as do news readers reporting on the weather. No matter what new disaster occurs they always assure us that all is well when often the country may be virtually bankrupt.

➢ Advertising gurus who are so good at brainwashing us that, for example, many people are turned into zombies wearing uncomfortable jeans and baseball hats and carrying a mobile phone in one hand and a cigarette or drink bottle in the other.

So it is, therefore, that in modern society we have leaders in all walks of life ranging from religious, educational, business and political leaders, to those in the arts and sciences, who spend a good deal of effort in brainwashing us with repetitive bullshit so we will 'buy' their product which may be anything from fast food to one side or other of a political fence.

How we are persuaded

Effective persuasion of people en masse involves several key factors including:

➤ Simple messages are more effective that complex ones and these should target the appropriate *segment* of the population.

➤ From early in our evolution we *Homo sapiens sapiens* have been talked down to by tribal and religious leaders that pitch to us from 'on high.' Today, however, the pulpit has been largely replaced by the TV screen but it is still important to remember that effective ads take the high ground by having an air of authority and confidence.

➤ Messages should be structured to ensure (Robertson, 1970):

(1) *Cognitive response* to the message involving
  (a) *Awareness* of the product's existence.
  (b) *Knowledge* of the product's features.

(2) Positive *attitudinal response* to the message, that is
  (a) *Liking* of the product.
  (b) *Preference* for the product.

(3) The desired *behavioural response* to the message, that is
  (a) *Conviction* that the product is worth buying.
  (b) *Purchase* of the product.

➤ This *cognitive/attitudinal/behavioural* or 'CAB' approach to advertising is *conditioning,* where now an advertisement is a *stimulus,* and conditioning is discussed in some detail in Chapter 13.

➤ The proportion of the target population that remembers a message increases with the number of repetitions and thus follows a *learning curve.* The learning curve for populations is quite likely to take a hyperbolic form and the Mohr Plot of Fig. 6.1 can be used to establish the asymptote of such hyperbolae.

➤ Frequency of messages should be limited to avoid *advertising wearout.* The *three-hit theory* is that only 3 ads are needed to make consumers aware of a product, make them perceive its relevance to their needs, and inform them of its benefits, but it needs to be realized that more like a dozen ads will be needed to ensure that a substantial proportion of the population will see the advertisement.

➢ Consumer memory follows the *forgetting curves* of Fig. 13.3 so that advertising campaigns must be periodically renewed.

➢ Appealing to people's secondary *psychological needs* such as achievement and beauty, rather than their primary and regular 'anything will do' *physical needs* such as hunger and thirst.

➢ Pitching messages at those with a relatively low 'consumer IQ' because high 'CIQ' increases likelihood of messages being understood but reduces likelihood of being influenced by them. This *reception-yielding* situation is illustrated in Figure 13.2 and the 'get em young' notion that this suggests is well illustrated by the quotation that opens Chapter 13.

➢ Taking advantage of the fact that for brainwashed modern man his car and the brand of soft drink or beer he drinks is an important part of his *identity*. Similarly, for a woman the way she does her hair and makeup, and the way she dresses are part of her identity. In other words, just as we describe different species of animals by their appearance and habits, we view other people in the same way.

➢ We humans are suckers for anything new and effective advertising need not appeal to our higher instincts or the advancement of mankind. For example, supposedly civilized societies happily copied people their explorers thought 'savages' by taking up tobacco en masse.

➢ We are not simply persuaded as individuals, however, but also en masse or sociologically. The key to this is *imitative* and *social learning* so that just one or two of a particular group of people need to be persuaded to a buy product and then, one by one, others in the group will follow their lead.

➢ We often *imprint* upon a particular type or group of people and adopt their behaviours and imprinting, imitative learning, and modeling play important roles in our learning.

➢ Finally, it is important to realize that our memories are 'hard wired.' That is, unless neurons are damaged physically, memories that have been stored in long-term memory are permanent. This is why it is we remember some of our earliest childhood experiences and why we find it so hard to give up some of our habits.

Persuasion or brainwashing?

Today advertising is so repetitive and effective in reducing us to consumer zombies that the results are comparable to those of conditioning of laboratory animals.

In other words, it goes a little, if not a long way beyond just *persuasion*.

Colloquially, at least, most would agree that it would be fair to use the term *brainwashing* but, strictly speaking, this originated in connection with 'conversion' of American prisoners by the Communists during the Korean War in the early 1950s (the Three D's method they used is discussed in the last section of Chapter 11).

Sometimes referred to in psychology as *thought reform*, 'BW' is an extreme form of *social influence* aimed at changing a person's views without their consent and often against their will.

To this end BW combines three approaches:

(a) The **coercive** or 'just do it' approach which is concerned only with *compliance* and not with your attitudes and beliefs.

(b) The **persuasion** or 'do it because it will make you feel good, happy, healthy or successful' approach.

(c) The group-based **education** or 'do it because it's right' approach which is much used for *propaganda* campaigns.

The 1999 Encyclopedia Brittannica describes brainwashing as **coercive persuasion**, noting its origins as a means of political or religious indoctrination. It also notes that it is a *"colloquial term"* usually *"applied to any technique designed to manipulate human thought or action - -."*

The third edition of the American Heritage Dictionary of the English Language gives two definitions of brainwashing:

1. *Intensive, forcible indoctrination, usually political or religious, aimed at destroying a person's basic convictions and attitudes and replacing them with an alternative set of fixed beliefs.*

2. *The application of a concentrated means of persuasion, such as an advertising campaign or repeated suggestion, in order to develop a specific belief or motivation.*

WordWeb 6 defines the adjective 'brainwashed' as:

1. *Subjected to intensive forced indoctrination resulting in the rejection of old beliefs and acceptance of new ones*

"*brainwashed prisoners of war*"; "*captive audiences for TV commercials can become brainwashed consumers*"

Indeed, most of us now associate brainwashing with persuasive advertising, political campaigns, mass media, and perhaps education. In fact BW is perceived to be so widespread that it is a major concern for many people and a search for 'brainwashing' on the Internet gives over 2 million results for *media brainwashing*.

Just three examples are:

[1] A 1995 report that "hard-up" schools in the UK used free educational packs provided by McDonald's which were littered with references to McDonald's and its products.

(www.mcspotlight.org/media/press/brainwashing.html)

[2] Claims that, because it supposedly misled the public over the 9/11 attacks, the American news media "*is the largest, most expensive, mass-brainwashing machine ever assembled in human history. It is a machine that so completely brainwashes the nearly 300 million Americans, that the Nazis' infamous Propaganda Minister Josef Goebbels would be envious*" (Wolfe, 2001).

[3] Claims that after WW1 psychological warfare research at the Tavistock Centre in London resulted in "*a theory of mass brainwashing, involving group experience, that could be used to alter the values of individuals, and through that induce, over time, changes in the axiomatic assumptions that govern society*" and that this work found application in both the UK and the US media (Wolfe, 1997).

US journalist Walter Lippmann was involved in Britain's WW1 'psywar' effort and was first to translate Sigmund Freud's work into English. In his 1922 book *Public Opinion* he wrote of the brainwashed masses:

". . *the mass of absolutely illiterate, of feeble minded grossly neurotic, undernourished and frustrated individuals is very considerable, much more considerable, there is reason to think, than we generally suppose. Thus a wide popular appeal is circulated among persons who are mentally children or barbarians, whose lives are a morass of entanglements, people whose vitality is exhausted, shut-in people, and people whose experience has comprehended no factor in the problem under discussion.*"

Some of this is a bit 'over the top' but, if we consider that advertising has reduced most of us to brainwashed zombies wearing uncomfortable if not ridiculous jeans and carrying a mobile phone in one hand and a drink bottle or cigarette in the other, then 'brainwashing' is a serious issue.

And make no mistake, it must certainly be fair to call today's high pressure TV and radio advertising brainwashing. After all, in line with the original brainwashing of POWs, the victims are seated in a room and screamed at for hours each day with up to 10 ads blaring at them in each of all too frequent ad breaks (make that up to 50 ads per ad break in Brazil, according to Cateora (1996)).

After all, 50+ years ago advertising managed to make about half the adult population take up smoking, a downright unpleasant practice in reality. If advertising can do that then it can make us do just about anything short of eating shit.

For this reason, therefore, the term *brainwashing* is used frequently in this book because no other single word exists to convey just what religious mantras and rituals have done for millennia and what increasingly ubiquitous, repetitive and persuasive advertising does today.

Conclusion

The extent to which man has been brainwashed, one way or another, to adopt countless religions, periodically fight wars over them, and in modern times become mindless consumer zombies is regrettable.

We should all hope that we will never be subjected to *coercive persuasion* or *brainwashing* in its 'original' form but few of us would disagree that we are perhaps now subjected en masse to something far more subtle, far more effective and sometimes, at least, far more sinister and detrimental to both ourselves and, in turn, the world we live in.

.

Chapter 3

RELIGION

> *Where questions of religion are concerned,*
> *people are guilty of every possible sort of*
> *dishonesty and intellectual misdemeanor.*
> Sigmund Freud, *The Future of an Illusion* (1927), ch. 6.
>
> *Religion has always been the wound, not the bandage.*
> Dennis Potter (1935 – 1994), British playwright,
> *Observer,* London, April 10, 1994: 'Sayings of the Week.'

Introduction

To begin with, let us quickly gather some logical thinking apparatus:

[1] The algebra of sets in which, for example, if the set of integer numbers is denoted as N, then the number 3 is a member of N which we denote $3 \in N$. Then, if we call the set of prime numbers P, this is a *subset* of N which we denote as $P \subset N$.

[2] Propositional calculus is one in which simple statements or propositions are either true (T) or false (F) and these simple statements are connected by:

(a) The *conjunction* 'and', denoted as $\wedge$.
(b) The *disjunction* 'or', denoted as $\vee$.
(c) The *conditional* 'if ... then ... ', denoted $\rightarrow$.
(d) The *biconditional* 'if and only if', denoted $\leftrightarrow$.

$\rightarrow$ is sometimes called *implication* and $\leftrightarrow$ is sometimes called *mutual implication*. Negation is denoted as $\sim$ so that, if a proposition $p = $ T then $\sim p = $ F.

Now we are ready to tackle the question of the existence of God with a little logical thinking.

The invention of God

Some of us belong to the set of Christians C, others are Buddhists B, others Muslims M, another lot are Hindus H, others might still subscribe to the polytheist ideas of the Greeks and Romans, and some of us are atheists A who might believe in another ridiculous idea - that the Universe U began with the Big Bang BB (Mohr et al., 2014).

For the first author GM we can say $GM \in A$, except when having his weekly nervous breakdown, when he believes that it was all started by somebody or something (he's not sure which so you'd better place an each way bet rather than go to war over it) called *Number One*.

This is proved as follows (not in order):

If God existed (G) then he created the Universe (U): $G \rightarrow U$

If the Big Bang occurred then it created the Universe: $BB \rightarrow U$

On day one U existed: $U \rightarrow (\sim G \wedge \sim BB)$

If nothing existed on day one (N): $N \rightarrow \sim GM$

Geoff Mohr does exist: $GM = T$

There you have it already!

Note that, as in Finite Element Method analysis of a simple network in Chapter Nine we need a *datum* or 'break in point' in the foregoing list of propositional calculus statements. Here it is GM is true and then we can work backwards to see that $\sim$ N, so U and thus $\sim$ G and $\sim$ BB from the third last statement.

Rather pointlessly, we can also add the exclusive disjunction:

$$(U \vee N) \wedge \sim (U \wedge N)$$

That is, U or N but not both.

So who invented the *idea* of God?

Godlike properties were an early 'tribal' *polytheistic* belief used to explain phenomena that early man could not understand such as lightning, the stars and so forth.

Early on some desperate witch doctor hit on the *monotheistic* idea of praying to an ethereal God to cure some sick person, perhaps the chief. That puts the witch doctor in a position of some power and influence. If, by chance, the chief gets well then no doubt the 'WD' would make a great song and dance of it. I'm sure he did just that.

One of the worst results is that a large proportion of the world's population wastes its time praying to some nonsensical God rather than talking to each other. If that time were spent being friendly to other people then, perhaps, there would be far less conflict in the world.

All over the globe we are still slogging it out over this religion crap like children fighting over whose doll is nicest but childish would be too kind a word for it. *Criminal* is the word that should be used and the priests and politicians who provoke wars in the name of God, or so-called democracy for that matter, should be shot and that would save a lot of lives in the long run.

Motivation

Aristotle was first to assert that our goal was to become more nearly what we were intended to be. Psychologists refer to this is as *self-actualization* and Maslow viewed this as striving to reach our potential (Robertson, 1970; Lindzey at all, 1978). He defined two kinds of needs:

(a) *Basic needs* such as hunger, thirst, sex and security.

(b) *Metaneeds* such as achievement, beauty, goodness, justice, order and unity.

Maslow defines achievement as a basic need but the present authors prefer to classify it as a 'higher' or more human metaneed.

First, we must meet our basic or 'animal' needs. That done, we can turn our attention to the higher 'human' metaneeds and thence self-actualization as a human being. These needs provide *primary goals* that may motivate us towards *secondary goals* such as money in order to achieve them.

Most of our basic needs are *intrinsic motivations*. Of these, *competence motivation* is perhaps the most basic and is learnt by infants challenged by goals such as standing up in their cot or walking.

Most of our metaneeds are *learned goals*. Achievement motivation, for example, can be inculcated by parents or teachers. *Social motivations* such as justice are also acquired in this way.

The authors conclude from this that we are, basically, *animals.* Nothing demonstrates this more than the incredible success which advertising, with the help of the 'pyramid effect' provided by social and imitative learning, has had in reducing millions of people into zombies wearing jeans and carrying a drink bottle in one hand and a mobile phone in the other.

Like conditioned rats they are in a great hurry going nowhere down a tunnel of despair in search of rubbish that they have been brainwashed into believing to be desirable, trendy and having the appropriate image.

The same could be said throughout history of the countless armies of brainwashed young men fighting for their God, king and country.

The extent to which we are human we might be the degree to which we have self-actualized in terms of meeting the more aesthetic and social metaneeds compared to the extent to which we have succumbed to advertising and some of the more animal or basic needs such as greed for money.

We might define this as the *net social achievement* or NSA. This we can evaluate using Mohr's 10th Law which is that we should judge things out of 10 and not as black or white and right or wrong. Thus we could judge a person's humanity by their value of this NSA measured on the Mohr Scale which is sometimes limited to 0 to 9, for example in the case of health when 0 = dead, and 10 or perfection is deemed impossible.

Then, for example, we might rate Jesus Christ very highly in terms of his NSA because he did great good though he was poor.

A filthy rich capitalist who gave but a tiny fraction of his great wealth to a charity, on the other hand, we might rate poorly. In fact we might give them a negative rating because their great greed must have deprived countless needy people of desperately needed money whereas their comparatively small benefactions would do comparatively little good. In other words, on balance, their net social achievement would be a large negative number.

Such robber barons we might describe, therefore, as 'not long out of the tree', an expression that reminds us of our animal origins, a consequence of which is that we still are animals, though some of us more so than others!

What then is the motivation involved in religion? Clearly it is a metaneed and ideally it would provide us with the social motivation to do the right thing by our fellow man.

Usually, however, church and state go hand in hand, especially when wars are begun when priests are always happy to condone the slaughter because they have God on their side. So does the enemy, of course, so what the hell are they really fighting for?

Pomp and circumstance

The propagation of religion is firmly based on the usual tools of brainwashing, that is pitching the message repetitively and strongly from on high and 'getting them young'.

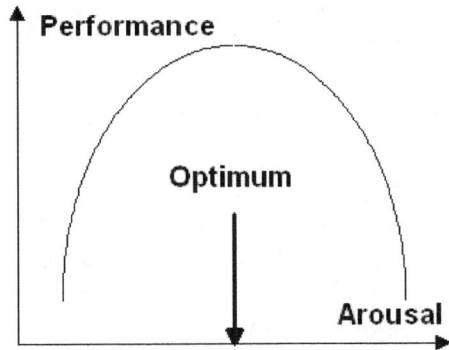

Figure 3.1. Performance variation with level of arousal.

As shown in Figure 3.1, with greater 'arousal' or motivation, performance improves and there is an optimal level of performance. Certainly, the rites, rituals and bible bashing of all religions are designed to put the fear of hellfire into you and, should the national leader desire it, make you march off to war.

In peacetime, however, religion is, as Karl Marx said, *"the opium of the people"* so that, as Napoleon Bonaparte put it:

Religion is what stops the poor from killing the rich.

This reminds us that religions impart some morality, for example the Ten Commandments of the Christian Bible, the sixth saying we should not kill one another yet Christians have been crusaders and imperialists on a grand scale for centuries.

The Koran contains countless statements urging Muslims to jihad and to behead etc. evil unbelievers, in part why there is so much Islamic terrorism around the world, much of it seeking to overtake whole countries to establish Islamic caliphates.

As for the other Christian commandments, Western society is now so decadent that one cannot help but wonder if Armageddon is indeed due.

Religion and education

In Western Civilization our recorded history of education centres around the Greek and Roman civilizations, in which monastic education had a parallel with Buddhist training.

From those early times until today there remains for the teacher a social obligation to search for 'pure' knowledge and to impart practical knowledge and skills needed for specific roles in society.

Both Greek and Roman higher education placed much emphasis on equipping young men for roles as soldier-citizens able to play a part in and protect the state. Much of our modern philosophy and science, however, we owe to the teachers of those periods.

The final stages in classical Roman education were the Trivium (grammar, rhetoric, logic) and Quadrivium (music, astronomy, geometry, arithmetic) and these were the basis of the medieval arts course in Europe centuries later.

Elsewhere in Europe, before the medieval period academic pursuits were largely limited to clerical education in monasteries.

By the twelfth century, however, a few *cathedral schools* had been established and these began to place more emphasis on lay education by studying law, albeit mainly clerical law.

Gradually small schools were established in most towns where basic education in reading and writing was given for a few years. Few families could afford to pay for such education, however, and much of the population was semiliterate at best.

The thirteenth century saw the development of the first Universities, in Paris and Oxford, and the fourteenth and fifteenth centuries saw many new Universities established in Europe, increasingly with a more localized emphasis. In these training was based on the three stages of membership of the craft-guilds: apprenticeship, journeymanship and mastership.

The ancient Trivium and Quadrivium, however, were still the framework of the arts course that all had to take before moving on to the higher courses of Theology, Medicine and Law.

To this day, therefore, such landmarks as King's College Chapel in Cambridge remind us of the key role religion played in education.

Thanks to the role of religion in education at countless schools, and still in some Universities, countless millions are still brainwashed almost daily for much of their lives.

Religious imperialism

"The oldest and most repeated justification for imperial activity was the Christian mission to go into the world and preach the Gospel, bringing salvation to the 'heathen'. Early imperialist activities by the Spanish and Portuguese carried the pope's blessing for this endeavour" (Cowie et al., 1994).

Rudyard Kipling extolled the virtues of such imperialism as being a responsibility:

Take up the White Man's burden -
Send forth the best ye breed -
Go, bind your sons to exile
To serve your captive's need;
To wait in heavy harness,
On fluttered fold and wild -
Your new-caught, sullen peoples,
Half-devil and half-child.

R. Kipling, *Rudyard Kipling's Verse,* Inclusive edn.
Hodder & Stoughton, London (1949) pp 371-372.

So it was that England, France, Germany, Portugal and Spain sailed the high seas and colonized much of the world. In the process they usually decimated the heathen natives, in some cases such as in Tasmania, extinguishing them altogether.

These Christian imperialists also plundered the countries they colonized, at first of gold and silver and later of oil. They were also able to farm these countries, for example the British tea and cotton plantations in India and North America. To top it all off, of course, they had slave labour to work the plantations.

In addition, the imperialists were able to create new assured markets for their industrial products in their colonies. To keep the slaves in the colonies in line, of course, they were brainwashed with religious propaganda.

Marketing religion

In the USA Christianity has been so heavily marketed that it has been desacralized, for example by:

➢ Religious symbols such as stylized crosses in the jewelry business.

➢ Religious holidays, particularly Christmas, have become materialistic occasions devoid of the original meaning.

➢ Christian sects increasingly market their message on TV to insomniacs.

➢ The Catholic Church hired a prominent public relations firm to promote its anti-abortion campaign (Solomon, 1992).

➢ The Mormons spent $US12M on a campaign in *Readers Digest* and *Newsweek* called *On Campus* to recruit college students as clergy (Solomon, 1992).

Perhaps more than most advertising religious advertising is fairly blatant brainwashing seeking to modify beliefs.

Ethnic conflict

To try to understand ethnic conflict, consider only two ethnic or linguistic groups *A* and *B* separated by a boundary. The amount of contact or 'social exchange' between them is obviously the same for both groups.

Now define the term *ethnocentrism* (Forbes, 1997) to represent the segregation, discrimination and prejudice that so often exists between ethnic groups.

The level of ethnocentrism in each of the two groups will depend upon its situation, traditions, and institutions, and upon its level of contact with outsiders.

Forbes postulates that the ethnocentrism in the groups is increased by contact. His *contact hypothesis* is discussed in Chapter 14 and is the opposite to the expectations of most people because it is assumed that the contacts are 'negative' in nature, ranging from dress and behaviour differences construed as impolite or 'foreign' to acts of violence or even terrorism.

Conversely, ethnocentrism in the groups will diminish during the intervals between contacts.

Theories of ethnic conflict, therefore, borrow a little from those of learning and advertising where attitudes and forgetting curves are important, and these are discussed in Chapter 16.

For the present, however, one cannot help but think of the tribal conflicts that Jane Goodall witnessed amongst chimpanzees and wonder whether the contact hypothesis might apply equally well to our evolutionary cousins!

The chimpanzee groups, however, have only different physical location and their conflicts may be largely acts of territorial defence, albeit one suspects, with some measure of 'foreigness' or ethnocentrism involved as well.

With humans, however, we have different races, religions and political creeds to fight over before we even get down to business, another area of considerable competition and, sometimes, conflict.

Through much of our catastrophic history it is the *brainwashing* that we are subjected to by religious and political leaders that has been largely responsible for the endless imperialism and war that has ravaged mankind so greatly.

Global terrorism

One of the best examples of conflict between religious sects is that of Northern Ireland where Catholics and Protestants have been at loggerheads for almost a century with thousands of innocent people being maimed or killed (Holland, 1999).

The release of deadly sarin nerve gas in the Tokyo subway by the religious cult Aum Shinrikyo was, from the point of view of world publicity, a relatively isolated event.

This small group isolated its converts and brainwashed them for long periods and had ambitious plans which included obtaining nuclear weapons (Lifton, 1999).

Osama Bin Laden, of course, had been on the side of the Americans in helping the Taliban fight the occupying Russian forces in Afghanistan in the 1980s (Nojumi, 2002).

In the 1990s he and his associates in Al Qa'ida turned their attention to the Americans with the bombing of several US embassies in the Middle East and Africa, culminating in the spectacular plane attacks of September 11, 2001.

Besides the Taliban and Al Qa'ida there are numerous other Muslim organizations around the world such as Islamic State (IS), Jemaah Islamiah (JI), Hamas, Hezbollah, and other fundamentalist Islamist groups in Libya, Chechnya, Indonesia, Pakistan and the Philippines.

The famous economist Keynes said that war was like digging a hole and pouring money into it, a phenomenon we like to call the *Keynes hole.*

Trying to run the world is an expensive business and people used to joke not long ago that England was still paying off the Napoleonic wars. The US is now in that sort of position with its debts still mounting to the point that the World Bank is considering taking action. Worse still the US economy is in great trouble. The Enron disaster and Chinese takeover of IBMs PC business may have been early warnings, but the GFC saw major banks collapse and major bailouts being required for others and for both GM and Chrysler (the latter has now been taken over by Fiat).

The US already has bases all over the world and a massive peacetime defence budget. In addition, for about a decade Al Qa'ida and other groups have had over 100,000 US troops tied down in Iraq and then Afghanistan and elsewhere in the Middle East.

There have been countless military intelligence blunders in modern times (Hughes-Wilson, 1999) and Iraq was yet another. Removal of Sadam Hussein is exactly what Bin Laden, and perhaps the Saudis, who now own much of the USA as well as the UK, would have wanted.

An article in *The Australian* newspaper on 3 November 2004 reported that Bin Laden had vowed in one of his regularly released videotapes to send the US broke. He claimed that every dollar spent by al Qa'ida on terrorist strikes had cost the US $1 million in economic damage. He estimated the US deficit at more than $US 1 trillion.

In reality the US deficit for that year was just under $0.4 trillion but the US national debt was close to the $US 7.4 trillion statutory limit. In 2011, after a tense holdup in Congress, it was increased to $US 15 trillion.

Elsewhere terrorism has continued, for example the bombings in Bali, England and Spain in recent years.

In the Western world we were brainwashed with constant pictures of Sadam Hussein holding a rifle and misguided innuendo about weapons of mass destruction (WMD) long before the most recent US-led invasion. We ourselves began to feel that we would scream if we heard the term WMD once more. It was an orchestrated litany of lies, of course, as usual in the case of drumming up support for a war, or almost any other cause for that matter.

Islamic terrorists, however, willingly go to the extreme of suicide bombers, statistically a very effective weapon because their own losses are a small proportion of those of their opponents.

As in most military training, doubtless the training used by terrorists to turn people into suicide bombers involves a good deal of brainwashing and does away with the pointless parade ground drills of traditional armies.

The sham of religion

Using religion as a pretext for war is old hat. Bin Laden and associates, for example, are fighting to get Americans out of the Middle East where they have had most of the oil leases since the 1930s.

Back then there was no Israel, just the quite large country called British Palestine. With oil already of great strategic importance Jack Philby went to Saudi Arabia. Jack had been in MI6, then called the SIS, and (supposedly) been discharged from it.

Jack was the father of the famous counterspy Kim Philby who was recruited around the same time by the KGB in Cambridge, along with Guy Burgess, Anthony Blunt and Donald MacLean.

It is said that Jack Philby helped found the kingdom of Saudi Arabia and then, disgruntled with England, set about giving most of the oil exploration leases to American companies, a reason why Bin Laden and associates belatedly want the US out of that country.

For Syria, whose oil reserves have been exhausted by foreign companies, it is too late, but this is one of a number of countries that will long harbour a grudge against such economic imperialists as the UK and US.

Another sham is that of Christmas where the image of the jolly Santa Claus is used to promote consumer mayhem during what was once a religious festival. The image dates back to a 1881 cartoon by Thomas Nast in which the jolly figure is a caricature of a man who has accumulated a wealth of worldly possessions (Solomon, 1992):

"- our contemporary image of Santa Claus was shaped by the famous nineteenth century cartoonist Thomas Nast, whose rendering of Santa was related to other drawings related to 'fat cats' like Boss Tweed and the Robber Barons, greedy capitalists who exploited the poor and lived in useless luxury. Santa stands in opposition to Christ as a God of materialism. Perhaps it is no coincidence, then, that he appears in stores and shopping malls - secular temples of consumption.

Christianity is based on the absurd belief that Jesus Christ rose from the dead. This is definitively impossible: *when you are dead you are dead.* The Romans crucified thousands of people, however, and it was not uncommon for some of them to hang around alive for days. In fact, JC was drugged but still alive when taken down from his cross by disciples, his later appearances confirming this (Mohr & Fear, 2015).

That there were few such appearances then suggests that he left the region, no doubt to escape capture by the Roman authorities.

As Mohr and Fear (2015) show, all religions are, of course, BS invented to gain influence, status, power and money.

What seems certain is that we are the result of evolution occurring on a tiny planet in an incredibly large Universe (Mohr, Sinclair & Fear, 2014). Just one elliptical galaxy named NGC 4261 is 100 million light years away. It contains the mass of 100,000 suns spiraling towards a black hole 1.2 billion times heavier than the Sun (Goodwin, 1996).

The galaxy cluster known as Abell 2218 is located in the constellation Draco and is 1 to 2 billion light years from Earth. Its total mass is 50,000 billion times that of the Sun.

Countless stars are millions of times brighter than the Sun and have surface temperatures several times greater than that of the Sun (which is approximately 6,000 °C).

These sorts of numbers make talk of God creating the Universe and then having some special interest in us quite absurd. No ethereal spirit with the psychological characteristics of a person could create anything, let alone something so mind bogglingly huge as the Universe.

As an exercise in the Peter Principle,[1] the authors wrote the book *World Religions* (Mohr & Fear, 2015). This proposes the new religion Mohronism which has 10 laws, the ninth being that God's prophet is the famous *Murphy* of the renowned Murphy's Law[2] which explains human history so well.

---

[1] *In a hierarchy every employee rises to his own level of incompetence.* A corollary is: *In time every post tends to be occupied by an employee who is incompetent to carry out his duties.*

[2] *Everything that can go wrong will go wrong.*

Another Irishman Jonathan Swift gets it halfway right with:

We have just enough religion to make us hate,
but not enough to make us love one another.
Thoughts on Various Subjects (1711).

The authors consider the first half of that statement right but believes that, as all the evidence in the world today suggests, people brainwashed with higher doses of religion or religious fundamentalism seem to develop even stronger prejudice and hatred for others.

Finally, perhaps the greatest sham is the blatant hypocrisy of religion, the most disturbing example in modern times being the many Christian priests in many countries found guilty of paedophilia and pederasty. Similar sins have been found to be committed by Muslim clerics.

The sheer hypocrisy of these dirty old men beggars belief, as do such silly stories of people doing the definitively impossible and rising from the dead. If you really do believe in zombies, i.e. the living dead, then perhaps you have been brainwashed to the point of being one yourself!

Islam is a Satanic religion

Many now believe that Islam is a harmful, evil religion, Theodore Shoebat saying:

Islam is a form of Satanism. - - - Islam being a religion that was founded to deliberately to destroy the Church, is a religion of Satan, and is thus Satanism. Both Muslims and Satanists have burned down churches, and that is because they are both enslaved by the dark power of demons.
(www.shoebat.com/2014/18/24)

In another article entitled *Why Islam, And Every Satanic Religion, Must Be Banned,* he reports:

A Muslim man named Ibrahim in New Jersey beheaded and dismembered two Coptic Christians and buried their bodies in a backyard.

A British man who converted to Islam beheaded an 82 year old woman with a machete.
(www.shoebat.com/2014/09/08).

Another article posted on the internet says:

Islam, as a religious system, is entirely of Satanic origin. The Devil is behind every aspect of it. It is a "monotheistic" form of the ancient moon worship that Abraham left in Iraq 2000 BC, but his descendants through Ishmael have continued. When Muslims circle the Kabah on mass, the Devil is the true object of their worship.

(www.bible.ca/islam/islam-encyclopedia-westerners-need-to-know-list.htm).

Another internet article headed *The Qur'an's Deception Passages* says:

the Islamic god is called "The Greatest Deceiver" (Qur'an 3:54).

Unfortunately because there are over 1.6 BILLION Muslims on the planet, even a SMALL fraction of this number can equate to 70 Million People who are in support of Islam's radical ideology!

(www.deonvsearth.com/who-is-allah-evidence-discovered)

Yet another internet article says:

I am an ex-muslim *and one time staunch defender of Muhammad and Islam. It is my sincere hope to save as many Muslims as I can from the curse of Islam. It is an evil and barbaric ideology which has no place in 21ˢᵗ century civilized world. I will prove here without any doubt that Islam is a bogus religion and Muhammad and Quran have nothing to do with any god* (www.falseislam.org).

The Hindu philosopher Vivekananda said of Islam:

Now, the Muslims are the crudest in this respect, and the most sectarian. Their watch-word is: there is one God (Allah), and Mohammed is His Prophet. Everything beyond that not only is bad, but must be destroyed forthwith, at a moment's notice, every man or woman who does not exactly believe in that must be killed; everything that does not belong to this worship must be immediately broken; every book that teaches anything else must be burnt. From the Pacific to the Atlantic, for five hundred years blood ran all over the world. That is Mohammedanism.

Conclusion

A study by social scientist Gregory Paul published in the *Journal of Religion and Society* in 2005 used data from international surveys and research organizations to find much evidence that religious beliefs can, on balance, do society more harm than good:

"In general, higher rates of belief in and worship of a creator correlate with higher rates of homicide, juvenile and early adult mortality, STD infection rates, teen pregnancy and abortion in the prosperous democracies."

He found the US the most "dysfunctional of the developing democracies, sometimes spectacularly so," with rates of gonorrhea in adolescents up to 300 times those in less devout democracies.

The authors, in the current light of endless global terrorism and conflicts in the Middle East and elsewhere, find a good many people are disillusioned with religion, believing it has done more harm than good.

Chapter 4

THE INDUSTRIAL REVOLUTION

> *It is brought home to you ... that only because miners*
> *sweat their guts out that superior persons can remain superior.*
> George Orwell, *The Road to Wigan Pier* (1937).
>
> *The selfish spirit of commerce, which knows no country,*
> *and feels no passion or principle but that of gain.*
> Thomas Jefferson, letter, 15 April 1809.

Introduction

In the present chapter the innovations of mechanical and electrical engineering that led to the industrial revolution are discussed, this in turn leading to advances in the construction and arms industries.

The agricultural revolution led to man living in small communities and towns (Cipolla, 1974). As far back as the ancient Egyptians, however, priests and military men held the highest positions in the country and the king was always from one of these two backgrounds (Egerton Eastwick, 1896). Ruled by monarchy supported by a host of priests and military men, the common man through much of history since that time has been condemned to serfdom.

With the advent of the industrial revolution these peasants moved to the cities to work as little more than slaves in factories, a process that has been taking place in modern China in recent times.

Machines for agriculture

Bulls were tamed by castration around 4500 BC in Western Asia and horses were tamed in India around 2500 BC (Cipolla, 1974). In Europe the steppe horse was tamed somewhere between 2000 BC and 1500 BC in the Lower Volga and Hungarian regions of Europe.

These horses and oxen were harnessed for plowing, originally using the throat-and-girth harness and later the modern collar harness.

Wheeled vehicles were used in Sumeria and in the Indus Valley circa 3000 BC and their use spread into Egypt, and possibly China, before 1500 BC. The earliest wooden cartwheel found in Europe was estimated as dating back to 1900 BC and was found in a Neolithic roadway in the Netherlands.

The horseshoe is thought to have been invented by Celtic inhabitants of the Alps circa 400 BC and prolonged the working life of horses and oxen considerably.

Jethro Tull made the first seed-drill about 1701 and used it on his own land despite much opposition from his labourers (Odle, 1966). He did not patent it until 1733.

Water and wind power

Sailing boats are depicted on Egyptian vases dating 3500 BC and were plying the Eastern Mediterranean by 3000 BC (Cipolla, 1974).

Water-mills appeared at around the same time, in the first century BC, in Europe and China (Cipolla, 1974). In China they were first used to blow metallurgical bellows whereas in Europe they were used to grind grain and press olives. In medieval times their use was extended to producing cloth, paper and iron.

Windmills date back to Persia in the 7th century AD and appeared in Europe and China in the 12th and 13th centuries respectively.

Until the industrial revolution, however, man's use of water and wind power was limited.

Power for textiles

James Hargreaves, who had worked as a carpenter and hand-loom weaver in Blackburn, Lancashire, was asked by his employer to make an improved machine for carding wool (untangling the fibres) in their raw state. Observing an ordinary spinning wheel he hit upon the idea of a spinning jenny which could spin several threads at once. His first spinning jenny was made in 1764 (Odle, 1966).

In 1768 a mob of angry cotton labourers gutted Hargreaves' house and destroyed his machinery. He moved to Nottingham and, with a partner, took out a patent for his machine in 1770.

In 1769 Richard Arkwright took out a patent for a horse-powered spinning-frame. In 1775 he patented a carding machine and made other machines for drawing and roving cotton, reducing it to thinner strands for feeding to the spinning-machine.

In 1789 a mob smashed up his mill but he continued his work regardless and in 1790 he applied steam power to his spinning frames. In that same year he heard that a mob was preparing to march on his Derbyshire mills and he organized a battery of guns and issued 1500 small arms and 500 spears to all able-bodied men in his employ. The would-be attackers dispersed before reaching any of his mills.

Steam power for industry

Thomas Savery patented one of the first steam engines in the late 17th century. His device worked by pouring cold water into a steam filled vessel to create a vacuum which then drew up water from mines (Odle, 1966).

IN 1712 Thomas Newcomen invented a steam engine for the same purpose using the same 'condensation-vacuum' principle but which used a piston working within a cylinder that could be linked to other equipment, the greatest single advance in the history of steam power.

In 1769 James Watt patented a design which dramatically improved the efficiency of the steam engine by using a stop cock to pass the steam from the cylinder into a separate condenser.

Watt's engines used steam at a pressure of only 5 lb per square inch (5 psi) but by 1812 Richard Trevithick was making much more efficient steam engines with pressures of 40 psi, sometimes extending this to an unheard-of 150 psi.

In 1840 James Nasmyth built a steam hammer to press steel plates for ship building. His design was adopted in Europe for various metal forming processes and steam power and the industrial revolution had begun in earnest.

Steam power for transport

In 1788 Scottish engineer William Symington built the first steam boat, a small pleasure craft. By then he had already build steam road locomotives and fourteen years later he built a steamboat which towed two 70-ton barges (Odle, 1966).

In 1801 Richard Trevithick built a steam road locomotive and in 1804 he built the first steam locomotive to draw a load on rails, carrying 10 tons of iron and 70 men in 5 wagons at 5 miles per hour.

In 1825 a locomotive designed by George Stephenson pulled 12 wagons of coal and 21 wagons of passengers for ten miles at speeds of up to 12 miles per hour, taking 65 minutes for the journey. This success led to the construction and opening of the Liverpool-Manchester Railway in 1830.

In 1837 Isambard Kingdom Brunel built the 1340 ton steamship *Great Western*, the first true Atlantic steamship. It had 750 horse power (HP) but his third and last great ship, *Great Eastern*, had a massive 8300 hp.

Later the Parsons steam turbine was adapted for use in ships. It did not prove economical for low-speed ships but was used successfully for naval vessels which it drove to speeds of up to 35 knots.

Electric power and light

In 1819 Danish scientist Oersted discovered electro-magnetism. In England only two years later Michael Faraday showed that electric current could be turned into continuous mechanical motion, the principle behind the electric motor. Ten years later Faraday made the first experimental dynamo which turned mechanical energy into electrical energy (Odle, 1966).

In 1884 Charles Parsons built his first steam turbine. It span at 18,000 RPM to produce 75 amperes of current at a potential of 100 volts. This was the forerunner of the massive hydroelectric and coal-fired power-stations of today.

William Murdock piped gas into his cottage in Cornwall in 1792 to illuminate it. Prior to that time oil lamps had been used for artificial lighting.

In 1798 he began work on providing lighting for the Soho works of Boulton & Watt which manufactured steam engines for dewatering mines. By 1804 the firm was ready to start selling Murdock's primitive lighting equipment.

Early in the 18th century Humphry Davy invented the electric arc-lamp which was used in mines but was too hot and costly for use in houses. In these two sticks of carbon almost touched and the arc closed the circuit.

Joseph Swan began experiments to develop incandescent electric lights in 1848. By 1860 he had developed carbon filaments with the strength and flexibility of metal. These he placed in glass bottles from which the air had been exhausted but he was not able to develop a good enough vacuum to prevent the filaments simply burning up.

Five years later an air pump that created much better vacuums was developed in Germany by Sprenger. It was a further ten years later, however, before Swan met Charles Stearn, a bank clerk familiar with the Sprenger pumps. They repeated Swan's 1860 efforts using a Sprenger pump with better results and, after further work, Swan's lamp was demonstrated in public in 1878. In 1881 he formed a company to make and install lamps and in that year his lamps were installed in the Savoy theatre, on a passenger ship and in the House of Commons.

In 1879, working along similar lines to Swan, Thomas Edison made a successful electric light bulb and patented it in Britain, Swan having patented his procedure for evacuating his bulbs a few months earlier. Fortunately, dispute was avoided by forming a joint company.

The electric telegraph

The electric telegraph was developed by Charles Wheatstone and William Fothergill Cooke and first used in 1837 between the Euston and Camden Town railway stations, some two miles apart (Odle, 1996).

In 1839 their telegraph was installed between Paddington and West Drayton railway stations, a distance of 13 miles apart. By 1868 over 16,000 miles of telegraph line had been installed in England.

In 1851, after a first unsuccessful attempt in 1850, the Brett brothers laid and successfully tested an undersea cable between Dover and Calais.

The service was immediately opened to the public and was the forerunner of the intercontinental cables spanning the oceans that we have today.

In 1867 Alexander Graham Bell patented the telephone which became the massive global telecommunications industry of today.

It was Edison, however, who invented the word 'Hello' for use in answering the telephone, whereas Bell favoured the word 'Ahoy'.

Indeed, with the advent of the mobile phone brainwashing of people into becoming consumer zombies strolling the streets with a phone on the ear, seems to have reached an unsurpassable level!

New materials

The Romans used cement-lime blended with silica to produce the first really weather-resistant cement but it was not until the 18th century that inventors began trying to produce artificial cements (Odle, 1966).

It was Joseph Aspdin, a Leeds bricklayer, who in 1824 patented Portland cement, naming it after the stone which he thought it resembled. His cement was made by mixing finely ground chalk and clay and burning it at high temperature to produce clinker which, when finely ground, produced cement far superior to any before.

In 1839 John Bennet Lawes, after three years of experiments, found that calcium phosphate was an effective crop fertilizer. He had produced 'superphosphate' by using acids to decompose bones and mineral phosphate. He soon found it cheaper to use mineral calcium phosphate, large deposits of which had been found, and thus the fertilizer industry began.

In 1856 Henry Bessemer developed the steel-making process named after him. Before then, steel-making was slow, inefficient and expensive. In the Bessemer converter fine jets of air are forced through the crude iron. This oxidizes impurities such as carbon, phosphorus, silicon and sulphur, in turn creating intense heat well above the 1500 °C melting point of steel.

The result was that in the next 40 years the production of steel in Britain went up 30 times and the cost of steel was reduced by 80%. Everywhere cast iron was replaced by steel and in 1883 the first steel ship was launched.

Polythene was discovered in 1933 at ICI. It is made by compressing the gas ethylene and extruding the resulting solid. In 1938 the first ton of polythene was made by a commercially viable plant.

Highly flexible and waterproof polythene is used in a wide variety of ways, for example for packaging consumer goods. More important, it was the first of many man-made plastics.

The synthetic fibre Terylene was discovered by J.R. Whinfield and J.T. Dickson in Lancashire in 1941. Subsequently it was developed commercially in collaboration with ICI and widely used for clothing.

The motor car

In the 1850s, James Young, a Scottish chemist established the basis for oil refining. In 1851 E.L. Drake drilled 70 feet through bedrock in Pennsylvania and began the development of the American oil industry (Cipolla, 1974).

In 1860 a French engineer J.E. Lenoir patented a gas engine. In 1884 Dr N.A. Otto made a gas engine with a four-stroke cycle. A year later Daimler-Benz cars took to the road successfully using petrol engines and the Otto cycle.

The rest is history, as they say, and reciprocating engines were used in the first aircraft engines until the first jet airplane was designed by Frank Whittle and flown successfully in 1941.

Vance Packard entitled a chapter of a book *America's Toughest Car - and Thirty Models Later* (Packard, 1960). For a similar reason Ralph Nader rose to prominence in the USA during the 1960s with his book *Unsafe at Any Speed,* the point of which was that cars are more of a fashion statement than anything else and, therefore, just another example of the almost universal practice of *planned obsolescence.*

With the current fad for four-wheel drive cars with massive engines which are driven on sealed roads in perfect condition to go shopping we encounter another of the finest examples of brainwashing.

Megacities

Worse still, our major cities have become bloated by building them around the car. The result is city centres filled with unsightly high rise office buildings which resemble massive filing cabinets in which multinational companies make their offices.

Workers in these miserable offices often commute absurd distances back and forth each day along choked freeways while, all the while, the planet's finite oil reserves are rapidly running out.

It suits the transnational companies, of course, to have their offices and factories in a limited number of such megacities around the world. That is the way of globalization.

It cannot be more economic, however, to ship cars from one side of the world to the other. The high cost of this must inevitably be borne by the consumers.

It cannot be best to develop a nation around one or two megacities and at the whims of transnational companies and this has long been realized by many people who are often called 'left-wing', the usual propaganda of big business.

An underdeveloped nation, and Australia could be deemed an example because of its comparatively low population density, is surely better developed by building larger numbers of cities with no more than a million people in each.

Austin, the capital of Texas, one of the richest states in the USA, for example has a population of around half a million. In the same state Dallas and San Antonio have populations around a million, Forth Worth about half a million and Houston approaching two million, presumably because it is on the coast.

In Australia we have more than 40% of the total population crammed into Sydney and Melbourne, an insane situation no doubt brought about in part, at least, by transnational companies usually basing themselves in these two cities.

Radio and TV

In 1896 the Italian physicist Guglielmo Marconi patented the first wireless telegraph. In 1901 he successfully sent signals between Newfoundland and Cornwall and in 1914 he began experiments which led to the 'beam' system of directed long distance transmission.

In 1889 the English photographer William Friese-Greene, after much experiment, patented sensitized celluloid for fixing photographic images and the same year successfully took his first moving pictures on it.

In 1925 John Logie Baird was first to transmit pictures from one room to another. He showed his system to the Press and a scientific society and a company was formed to develop it. Eleven years later, the BBC began regular transmissions using his system but eventually chose to use the Russian-American Zworykin's system because it was able to obtain better definition by using more lines (Odle, 1966).

Both radio and TV have had a great effect on our lives, providing and endless source of free entertainment and communication to people all over the world. The downside of this is the endless brainwashing new programs and advertisements subject us to and we shall discuss these subjects further in Chapters 12 and 13.

The PC

The digital computer was an important invention but early devices were large and very expensive and affordable only to large companies, government organizations and Universities.

In the 1970s 'minicomputers' were developed which were about the size of a refrigerator and these were typically able to handle a dozen or more computer terminals. These terminals began in the mid 1970s to switch from teletypewriters to 'video display units' (VDUs) which are now called monitors.

Minicomputers usually used BASIC, a simplified version of the powerful but unwieldy FORTRAN computer language which had been designed for use with punch cards. BASIC was developed by Kemeny and Kurtz at Dartmouth College (New Hampshire) in the early 1960s and early versions required only 16 kb of RAM.

In 1975 the first microcomputer was sold, a clumsy box + switches affair with storage of only 256 bytes. In the same year Tiny BASIC, consisting of just 20 pages of code, was written and many versions of this quickly appeared and, also in 1975, Gates and Allen launched Microsoft Corporation with their version, this being marketed with the Altair microcomputer.

A flood of microcomputers with as little as 16 kb of RAM then appeared, the Sinclair ZX80, the Apple, the Commodore 64, the Spectravideo, the HP85 and many others, all having their own version of BASIC.

In the early 1980s IBM quit their near monopoly of the electric 'golf ball' typewriter market, switching to production of *PCs* with about a MB of RAM. Now there was a flood of PCs, Apple, IBM, ICL, NEC, Olivetti etc., as well as many IBM 'clones.'

With the advent of a MB of RAM or more Chris Cochran and American Planning Corp's MegaBasic appeared to make full use of it. Then came Visual Basic (VB) which was used to produce the Windows operating system.

The downside of this was the great amount of *value adding* that occurred in developing PC software. Originally the DOS operating system and its predecessors were given free with every PC, along with a version of BASIC.

The latest versions of Windows, however, have become increasingly expensive. So too have the latest versions of VB and Microsoft Office. As a result, if you now want VB to learn BASIC as well as a word processor, a DB program, and a spreadsheet program, then you will have to pay a lot more than the price of a perfectly good PC!

This is a somewhat radical change from buying a computer with startup software free in the early days of the PC business and it is not surprising that many people regard Bill Gates as something of a robber baron.

Conclusions

So what has all this to do with brainwashing and consumer zombies? A brief history of the industrial revolution allows a brief look at examples of people inventing new things. The point is, perhaps, that overnight somebody might invent a new, useless and possibly harmful type of drink, say Choke a Cola. Are you going to feel impelled to buy it?

In the same vein here is a list of examples, most of them relating in some way to the inventions discussed in this chapter, of how the advertising industry might make a sucker of you:

[1] Inventions for agriculture were fine, but how about more recent inventions in the food business such as:
(a) Coke: why on earth won't people support the local brand?
(b) Junk food: 50 million people eat junk food every day,
a very sad commentary on just how brainwashed we are.
(c) Kellogg's: ditto (even we can add sultanas to cereal).
(d) Confectionary: addicting young children to sugar is criminal.

[2] Wind power? That reminds us a little of the countless unnecessary and often ridiculous sports, including sailing.

[3] Clothes? They used to say fashion goes in cycles. Now the girls try to look and act like boys and the boys try to look and act like apes. We therefore think we are in a cycle with a much larger 'time diameter', namely reverse evolution.

[4] Trains and ships? The travel industry is certainly one of the most wasteful and pointless. Generally people spend a lot of money to spend their time in foreign bars and restaurants. My father used to call tourists rubber necks which is appropriate.

[5] Electrical goods? When the first author was young simple yo-yo's where a craze. More recently portable CD players and Ipods are the craze.

[6] How ubiquitous the mobile phone has become as a result of marketing and the pyramid effect of social and imitative learning is hard to believe.

[7] New fabrics? Yes, the first author is old enough to remember buying clothes in new fabrics such as Dacron and Terylene because they were new.

[8] Cars? As said earlier, another fine example of how gullible we are and how corrupt big business is. As discussed in Chapter 12, Clive Sinclair built a halfway credible electric car for about 25% of the petrol car price in the mid 1970s.

[9] Megcities? When big biz expects people to work longer hours and some of them have to commute for 2+ hours a day they might be tempted to buy an inner city apartment and live in a filing cabinet for people as well as work in one. They might as well have a brain transplant with a dog as donor to complete the happy picture.

[10] Radio and TV? Try counting (in Australia) the number of ads in a bracket sometimes, and then note how many of them are for foreign products. Why should we worry about the commies when these crooks have taken over the country already?

[11] The PC? The way we were pushed into using the Internet is one of the finest examples of treating people like rats in a Skinner box that we have seen.

The bottom line is that workers of the industrial revolution in England in the 19th century rented a house in a row of look-alike houses and worked in a factory at the end of this depressing street. On Saturday nights they could scarcely afford a couple of pints of lousy beer from the pub at the end of the street, all of which was no doubt owned by the man who owned the factory. Thus this lifestyle was comparable to that of slaves in Rome who lived in the bowels of a very large house.

Today workers live in a somewhat comparable way, housing being increasingly unaffordable and there is no security in marriage, employment or anything else.

In Australia company taxes have roughly halved in the last 20 years which means that the workers are footing most of the tax burden. In any case even the smallest companies can write off assets and use such artifices to escape tax all together.

In like fashion executives with exorbitant salaries, bonuses and share options are able to minimize tax.

The workers are not. If they beat the odds and manage to pay off a house the increasingly privatized health care business will take it away from them if they live to any great age.

The reality is that in a capitalist society you have to be born rich. Many of the greatest inventors during the industrial revolution were examples of that, often having to work in poverty to develop their ideas and then sell them for a pittance to large companies.

So, if you can't beat them, join them and make/import and/or sell some simple product(s). It's easier than making them and a hell of a lot easier than inventing them! The problem is you might need some startup capital which we can't help you with, and that brings us back to the problem of capitalism really stifling human life far more than providing anything like freedom for most people.

The <u>bottom line</u> is that most people in the world are now condemned to being little more than slaves, if they can even get a job that is, and they are thus *deprived by the depraved* executives who make up to $1,000 a minute for making sure businesses are more profitable, a result being that ordinary people stand longer in queues like brainwashed sheep waiting to be fleeced.

Chapter 5

POLITICS

> *A democracy exits whenever those who are free and are not well-off,*
> *being in the majority, are in sovereign control of government,*
> *an oligarchy when control lies with the rich and better born.*
> Aristotle, *The Politics* (343 BC)
>
> *Just as Darwin discovered the law of evolution of organic matter,*
> *so Marx discovered the law of evolution of human history.*
> Friedrich Engels, said at the funeral of Karl Marx (1883).

Introduction

Man's first leaders were tribal elders who passed on learning and wisdom to the young. It is probable that most practical learning came from their parents, however, and that leaders simply brainwashed tribes with religious and other bullshit, as they still do today.

In many parts of the world tribes were polytheistic and often believed in *animism*, that natural objects possess a soul (Bell & Hall, 1991).

With the coming of the Agricultural Revolution small communities and towns were built up and *pantheism,* the belief that God and the universe are the same, become widespread in Asia. A little later monotheism emerged in the Middle East.

Some of the preachers of these religions eventually became 'priest-kings' with secular as well as religious authority. This in turn led to the form of monarchy that prevailed throughout much of the world from the time of the ancient Egyptian civilization circa 3000 BC.

Imperialism

Man's imperialism first assumed grand proportions in the Egyptian Empire. Alexander the great is so-called because he founded the great Greek Empire. The most impressive of the ancient empires was the *Pax Romana* which dominated Europe from circa 30 BC until 476 AD (Cowie et al., 1994).

In the seventh century the Islamic empire began to develop and early in the eighth century it had spread to Spain and threatened France.

From this Islamic zeal sprang the Turkish Ottoman Empire which established control over Asia Minor, captured Constantinople in 1453, and over the next 200 years conquered the whole of the Balkan Peninsula and Hungary. The Ottoman Empire survived until 1919.

In the Renaissance of the 14th and 15 centuries came Portuguese exploration of much of the world, and this was followed by exploration and colonization of much of the world by several European nations.

This imperialism had a strong economic motive because it provided new sources of raw materials needed for the industrial revolution and created new markets for industrial products.

As noted in Chapter Five, however, European imperialism had the religious pretext of 'civilizing' heathen natives. The truth is that it was monarchs who encouraged exploration and colonization for nationalistic and economic reasons.

Democracy

Aristotle's remark about oligarchy which opens this chapter is an important reminder that, as then, we do not have *real* democracy today.

The populations of the Greek city-states of his time rarely exceeded 10,000 people, all the 'citizens' of which voted with black and white stones on the questions of the day in open forum.

Aristotle's complaint was that it was only the men and not women or slaves who were allowed this privilege and slavery, of course, can hardly be equated with democracy.

In most of the world today we do not have anything like real democracy. We have, in fact, Westminster type *parliamentary democracy,* a very brief history of which is (Mackenzie, 1950):

Pre 1066 (Saxon times). The barons and King met each year at Easter, Whitsun and Christmas.

1258 (in the reign of Henry III). A meeting of the barons of England at Oxford was the origin of the *House of Lords.*

1264. Simon de Montfort, on the King's behalf, organized a meeting of two knights from each county.

1265. Two citizens from each county were included in the latter meeting, constituting the origin of the *House of Commons.*

In the reign of Elizabeth I the puritans became the first party and were the opposition to the crown.

In the reign of Charles I the cavaliers and roundheads emerged as two opposing political forces.

1681. The origin of the names *Whig* and *Tory.*

This system has evolved in England, Australia and New Zealand into the two main parties being a conservative party, which supports the capitalist ruling class, and a Labour Party which traditionally supported the workers or modern-day slaves.

The Conservative Party is said to be *right wing* and the Labour Party *left wing*, a fine example of the power of emotive language.

Now, however, big business has considerable influence on both parties and the policies of the Labour Party are often more conservative than those of its opposition conservative party.

The result is a revolving door parody of democracy in which stooges become our leaders for relatively brief periods but their policies are greatly influenced by the business sector and the economic imperialism of traditional allies in war, in Australia these being the US and UK.

In this parody the 'fat cats' of the public service wield more influence in policy-making than do average members of parliament (Self, 1977).

Capitalism

While so-called democracy prevails in most of the world, the reality is that, with the world's markets becoming increasingly global, transnational companies and thence unrestrained capitalism provides the power and influence that runs the politics of most countries.

In the 1930s John Maynard Keynes proposed that a multiplier effect existed such that small increases in government spending in the community have a much greater effect upon the productivity of the nation. This is the *fiscal* approach and was widely adopted by many countries in the West for about 50 years.

Milton Friedman and other economists favour the free market or *monetarist* economic philosophy. This stems from the 17th century and is based on the equation (Wonnacott & Wonnacott, 1979):

MV (aggregate demand) = PQ (aggregate supply)　　　(11.1)

where M = the amount of money in circulation (per year)
　　V is its velocity of circulation (in transactions per year)
　　P = the price of goods in circulation
　　Q = the quantity of goods in circulation (per year)

Here V is the only relatively stable quantity and is based on the fact that, when you buy a product, the money you pay for it might be passed on quite soon as wages for somebody in the company you bought the product from. Then that person spends their wages on food and other necessities, and so on. Typically V takes a value of around 4 in modern economies.

This little or no government monetarist approach has led to more rampant capitalism than ever before. As a result an 'establishment' that effectively rules capitalist countries is formed (Blondel, 1963).

This establishment deplores the mildest hint of socialism and thence government ownership of industry, or even influence over industry. *They* tell government to reduce company taxes further and to cut back on government spending to do it and governments continue to heed them.

Effectively running military-industrial countries like the UK and US as they do, the barons of capitalism have ensured that their governments fight the evil threat of socialism, for example leading to the British secret service providing considerable covert support to the White Russian army resisting the 1917 revolution. When that failed they began counter terrorist activities against the new Russia such as Lieutenant Agar's sinking of the Red Fleet cruiser Oleg in Kronstadt Harbour in 1919 (Brook-Shepherd, 1998).

Some evidence of such policies was given by the first president of the National Civic Federation in the USA when he wrote in 1909: "Our enemies are the socialists and other labor people and the anarchists among the capitalists."

In the 1970s David Rockefeller funded the Trilateral Commission which in 1975 funded a meeting of multinational corporate executives to consider the "excess of democracy" afflicting advanced capitalist countries and to "rationalize the US economy through capitalist dominated planning and in conjunction with other leading capitalist nations to reassert US authority on a world scale" (Crough et al., 1980).

Modern neo-colonialism

Former colonies of rich nations remain heavily linked to the First World in dependent relationship often termed 'neo-colonialism' (Bell & Hall, 1991). Reasons for this dependency include:

➢ International trade and investment policies usually favour the rich nations which, for example, often set tariffs to protect their own agricultural industries.

➢ Multinational companies are sometimes more powerful than Third World countries and establish factories using cheap labour, using the threat of withdrawal from the country to keep wages very low.

➢ The practice of lending large sums of money to poor countries has left them with unpayable debt burdens which have undermined their economic growth.

➢ Western investment policies, educational programs and aid usually benefit the elite and modern sectors of Third World economies, distorting development patterns and reducing economic diversity.

➢ Western advertising of products such as tobacco and bottle milk formula has distorted consumption patterns in some poor countries and also caused long-term health problems.

➢ The high cost of Western arms cripples strife-torn countries in such places as Africa.

➢ The high cost of Western pharmaceutical products, for example for treating AIDS, adds another crippling burden to the fragile economies of poor countries in Africa.

Not surprisingly the former USSR was actively trying to encourage socialist governments in some poor countries in northern Africa in the 1970s and 1980s. The political situation in some of these countries remains unstable at the present time.

Socialism

It is important at the outset to note that *socialism* refers to the 'means of production' being owned by the state whereas *communism* refers to the means of production being owned by the people. The two terms are often confused but in a complex and highly technological modern society it is doubtful that communism is practical. It is doubtful, for example, that the very large companies required in some industries, many of these now transnational ones, can be owned and run by the 'people', taking people to mean those in a particular community.

What is clear, however, is that the 1848 Marx-Engels manifesto was anti-capitalist and this was the real spirit of the 1917 Russian revolution, a spirit which many believed would eventually spread globally. This revolution created a socialist state with a long term view towards forming a communist society.

Marxists argue that the capitalist *class* accumulates increasingly more capital or a 'surplus value' in fact created by the workers. The working class, therefore, are left to accumulate misery or, as Marx put it (Marx, 1933):

In proportion as capital accumulates, the lot of the labourer be his payment high or low, must grow worse.

Critics of this view will point out that in practice state ownership leads to totalitarian government which makes the people worse off, rather than better.

Marxists will also argue that in capitalism monopolies or oligopolies eventually develop, in turn influencing the political system so that something akin to totalitarianism can result.

In defence against this view critics of Marxism will argue that it is better to reform the capitalist system, not replace it, for example by introducing antimonopoly laws.

Theoretical arguments aside, revolutions have always occurred when there are high levels of unemployment and poverty.

Capitalism, however, relies upon a substantial pool of unemployed to keep the price of labour down (Sweezy, 1946). As a result, some studies found little reduction in poverty in the USA in the years 1947-1960 (Townsend, 1970) whereas socialism has reduced poverty and famine in China dramatically (Maxwell et al., 1977).

The USSR System

Though the USSR has been more or less dismantled, some aspects of its system remain whilst socialist systems operate elsewhere in the world. Moreover, the communist party in Russia, for example, still has a good deal of support. Hence some discussion of the USSR system as it was is still worthwhile, principal features of that system being:

In the USSR policy was based on five year plans. Critics would argue that this was too inflexible and did not allow for adjustments. But business plans might typically be five year ones and allow for adjustments, so this argument is invalid.

Without a free market coordination was difficult. Supposing we wished to increase steel production, for example, then we needed extra plant to make it and in turn extra steel to make the plant, but where could we get if from? In other words it is difficult to be self sufficient as a single entity despite a perhaps massive size.

Again the argument is invalid, there being nothing to stop a country like Russia from having two steel organizations, typical of the common duopoly situations in the USA.

Circa 1970 investment in the USSR ran at about 30% of GNP (about the same figure as Japan at the time and twice that for the USA), this funded by a 30% general sales tax (GST). This high level of investment was aimed at building industry but resulted in excessive restrictions in consumption and chronic shortages in goods.

Such a rate of expansion, however, was never going to be permanent and therefore must have been a positive developmental stage, a period of shortages for the general public being far less of a problem than the sacrifices involved in war, economic or otherwise.

In the USSR system there was effectively no such thing as unemployment as everyone could be given a job, however unproductive.

Russia has now established a free market economy but still has an authoritarian government whose style is reminiscent of that of the USSR and which has much more control over the economy and business than in the West.

What of the future?

Not long ago some economics texts asked the question about socialism and capitalism: "Are the systems converging?"

About the USSR, at least, it is now safe to say that its system has changed and some aspects of socialism, such as centralization of power, have been much reduced. Before the USSR was dismantled, however, there had long been changes such as a greater tendency to pay highly skilled workers more, less interventionist government and slow opening up to outside (and hence not state) capital.

About the future in the USSR, or China, for example, it therefore seems safe to say that there has been a move in the direction of capitalism (and democracy, but this is not necessarily synonymous with any particular economic system).

What can we say about the USA and like countries?

Clearly there is some disenchantment with the two-party system that may begin to crystallize somewhere. In Australia, for example, minor parties and several independents currently hold the balance of power in the upper house or senate which is required to approve legislation from the lower house.

In the USA, on the other hand, it is not impossible to imagine a (rich, if not very rich!) independent being elected president.

Some mention should now be made of the Arab and other Muslim countries that have attracted much attention of late. These, taken collectively, may have an increasing voice and influence in world affairs.

Finally, what can we say about China? What influence will such a potentially powerful country have in the future? Presumably it will increasingly join the global economy and consequently move a little to the right politically.

Proposals for change

Some authors suggest that inequality in capitalist societies should be reduced by reducing the inheritability of wealth, in other words by increasing death duties (Broom et al., 1980).

This is an unpopular proposal to both the rich and the middle class. As a result the Australian state of Queensland abolished death duties many years ago and other states only apply them to large fortunes.

Others have suggested a policy of equalizing outcomes, an approach that might penalize effort as well as inheritance (Jencks et al., 1975). A more original proposal was made by Peter Jay (1981), a former economics editor of *The Times*:

- - that the enterprises which create the wealth, the firms, the corporations, should belong to, be owned by, should have their directors exclusively appointed by and their net assets and their residual earnings should belong to, and exclusively to, the people who work at them.

Jay suggested that it is an accident of history, not a law of economics, that the entrepreneur has tended to be the person who supplied the risk capital. He proposed that in modern economies worker-owned companies should be able to raise debt finance from banks and equity finance from shareholders in the usual way.

Capitalists are happy to have their workers become shareholders, of course, because shareholders do not have to be paid dividends in bad times whereas banks always require interest to be paid on loans.

Jay's proposal goes a lot further and might eliminate the absurd salaries, share and rights bonuses, and retirement packages we see today. Indeed, it would only seem fair that *all* workers for a corporation should receive share issues as a nontaxable part of their income.

A criterion that the modern welfare economist employs in deciding whether a given change is 'efficient' was developed by Vilfredo Pareto (Buchanan & Tullock, 1962). This relies on the ethical postulate that the 'welfare' of a group of individuals is said to be increased if:

[1] Every individual in the group is better off, or if

[2] At least one member of the group is better off, without any member of the group being made worse off.

This is illustrated for the case of just two individuals X and Y in Figure 5.1 where the axes measure 'welfare' or 'utility' of the individuals and any point on the line $X_m Y_m$ is a Pareto-optimal state. Any movement from such a point to another point on or outside the curve must reduce the utility of one of the individuals.

If we assume some initial position A, then moving to any point on the curve between B and C is clearly Pareto-efficient because both parties are better off. Moving to point D, on the other hand, is not Pareto-efficient because Y will be worse off.

Here it should be noted that a person is deemed better off when they move from one position to another freely of their own choice, that is, 'better off' is subjectively evaluated. A common example might be people who reduce their working hours and salary in order to improve their overall quality of life.

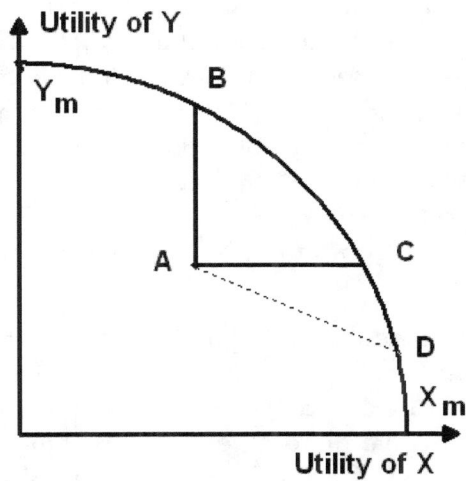

Figure 5.1. Illustration of Pareto-optimal states.

There are clearly many changes that can be made to either of the capitalist and socialist extremes that might result in a compromise that might improve the overall position of people. That monarchies no longer play an active role in government in the world is an example that significant change is indeed possible.

The first author's father

The first author's father worked in Rutherford's team in Cambridge University's Cavendish Laboratories when they split the atom in 1931). Subsequently, having got wind of such developments, the KGB ran meetings at Cambridge and Oxford which, ostensibly on the basis of decrying the prospects of war with Germany, influenced students and staff like Kim Philby, Donald MacLean, Guy Burgess and Anthony Blunt to become lifelong socialists and double agents for Russia within the British secret service.[1]

---

[1] In fact, Philby later said that he had been recruited first and had recommended the other 3 of the 'Cambridge Four' (Knightly, 1988).

CBO too was a socialist, being a long-time member and one-time president of the Australia-Soviet Friendship Society, an organization kept under close scrutiny by ASIO and its allies.

On consumerism he held that something was not a bargain at any price if you didn't need it, and also that the more gadgets you owned the more trouble and expense you will have maintaining them. He never smoked and drank very little, at one time introducing the family to the range of Baitz liquers after Friday dinners, the company having been started by a Russian immigrant.

Ourselves, we believe in *real democracy*, more of a middle ground between socialism and capitalism such as occurs in China, economically at least, with spectacular success.

This would involve governments still owning at least some of the banks and most, if not all, of the essential utilities because, undoubtedly much of the current economic malaise in many of the Western economies today is because Governments have sold off these cash cows to avoid growing debt and help pay for often bad and expensive election promises.

Now they have nothing left to sell. As it is, in Australia, at least, bank and mining company profits are obscenely great whereas Government ownership of some of the banks and resources gives more competition and control in the sector. In contrast, China is able to exert far more control over its interest and exchange rates and thence its economy, and the results speak for themselves.

Conclusion

In Westminster the Tories vs. Whigs farce has changed to Tories vs New Labour, with the Liberals on the fringe somewhat.

A former Australian finance minister wrote in his 2011 book *Dumbing Down Democracy* that politicians now consider appearances far more important than outcomes, lamenting that the resulting "sideshow syndrome" was eroding informed democracy as the basis of decision-making.

Thus we conclude that the politico-economic systems of both the 'east' and the 'west' will continue to change slowly.

Whilst current trends are towards freer capitalist markets it is certain that this trend may be slightly reversed at some point.

The communist party in Russia might currently have less than 50% of the vote but that might not last. Thus Russia could still be counted as roughly 7 on the 'commie scale' at present, with India perhaps about 5.

China, run by its Communist Party in the National Hall of Congress, but having adopted a combination of socialist and capitalist practices, is perhaps 8 on the 'commie scale'.

Some countries in South America and much of Africa, on the other hand, are in a state of economic collapse, as usual, and God only knows what 'colour' their politics is. In some cases not simply 'red' to some extent, but often the politics of chaos.

China, currently in the middle stages of a 1960s style Japanese economic build up, will play an increasing role in the world economy. So too will Russia and India.

Indeed, Russia and China, of course, have a common socialist past and retain cooperation in some areas. For example, in July 2016 it was announced that they would hold joint naval exercises in the South China Sea in September, this at a time of international tensions over China's disputed territorial claims in the area.

China, of course, is not immune from corruption. Some claim, for example, that corruption by government officials is rife, some having siphoned off large amounts of money to remote banks, eventually investing the laundered money in the US and elsewhere.

One of the Chinese companies involved in this activity, Longtop Financial had Deloitte as their auditor for six years but, after recent forensic investigations, Deloitte felt forced to quit.

China, however, is now the biggest holder of US debt, so that the aforementioned corruption (according to Deloitte) may, in fact, be part of how that came about, perhaps with some degree of official encouragement from the Chinese government at large.

A reader's letter in *The Age* newspaper on Friday 29 July, 2016, sums up another key issue:

Congratulations to - - on realizing that selling off state assets leaves us, the public, out of pocket. Let's hope the scales will now fall from the eyes of other masters in relation to tax evasion dressed up as tax avoidance.

Regardless of the politics of a country, however, politicians will always mislead the brainwashed public. Edward Suchman gave useful definitions of some of the tactics used to cover-up failures in policy (Davis, 1974):

[1] *Eye-wash:* deliberately selecting for evaluation only those aspects that 'look good' on the surface.

[2] *White-wash:* avoid any objective evaluation.

[3] *Submarine:* 'torpedo' the program.

[4] *Posture:* use evaluation as a 'gesture' only.

[5] *Postponement:* delay needed action by pretending to seek the 'facts'.

So what can you do about it?

Most of us realize just how cynical the so-called democratic process in the world today is and we don't care.

One thing you can do, however, is become a member of the local branch of the political party of your preference. At the meetings of this you will be able to express an opinion that will be heard by at least one politician, as well as the other members of the branch.

Perhaps you might even end up starting your own party, or at least thinking about running for election yourself!

Then it might pay to remember a tactic for getting on with people mentioned in John Dean's book *Blind Ambition*.

Dean was President Nixon's Attorney General and the youngest ever to occupy that post. He wrote that in the White House at that time they used the term *stroking* to describe how one can 'butter up' (with perhaps artificial compliments, praise, niceness etcetera) a person who one wanted to persuade in some way. Worth considering!

PART 2
PRESENT PROBLEMS

Chapter 6

EDUCATION

Whereas a rattle is a suitable occupation for infant children, education serves as a rattle for young people when older.
Aristotle, Politics bk 8 (1340 BC).

Indeed one of the ultimate advantages of an education is simply coming to an end of it.
B.F. Skinner, The Technology of Teaching (1968).

A brief history of education

In Western Civilization our recorded history of education centres on the Greek and Roman civilizations. In the last stages of the classical Roman education system the Trivium (grammar, rhetoric, logic) and Quadrivium (music, astronomy, geometry, arithmetic) evolved and these were the basis of the medieval arts course in Europe centuries later (Niblett, 1969).

Elsewhere, before the medieval period academic pursuits were largely limited to clerical education in monasteries.

By the 12th century a few cathedral schools were established and these began to study law, but mainly clerical law.

Gradually small schools were established in most towns where basic education in reading and writing was given for a few years. Few families could afford to pay for such education, however, and much of the population was semiliterate at best.

The thirteenth century saw the development of the first Universities, in Paris and Oxford, and the 14th and 15th centuries saw many new Universities established in Europe. In these training was based on the three stages of membership of the craft-guilds: apprenticeship, journeymanship and mastership.

The ancient Trivium and Quadrivium, however, were still the framework of the arts course that all had to take before moving on to the higher courses of Theology, Medicine and Law.

A preliminary examination was required for entry to the first apprenticeship stage, one of study, at the end of which the student was examined for the bachelorship. The bachelor was then still under instruction but assigned certain courses of lectures. Then finally he was examined for his mastership, a licence to teach.

In the 14th century the Inns of Court were established in England to meet a growing demand for teaching common law

In 1368 the master-surgeons formed a guild and in 1540 the Company of Barber-Surgeons was set up with a monopoly of practice and teaching.

In both law and medicine, therefore, professions were raised in status and competence by initiatives of their members that were more responsive to the needs of society than academic institutions.

During the renaissance, as in biblical times, apprenticeship remained the main method of training.

The 17th century saw interest in science increase and new colleges began training in technologies such as mineralogy and glassblowing. By the end of the century most scientific work in England took place in laboratories in London, not in Cambridge and Oxford.

The 18th century saw many new academies established which spread higher education to a middle class of trade and industry.

In the 19th and 20th centuries the school curriculum grew to place more emphasis on science to educate students for an increasingly technological world.

Today, however, students in most Western countries spend at least 12 years at school and this is excessive. The early years of school are, as much as anything, simply conditioning for the routine for working life.

To add insult to this injury tertiary education courses have been introduced for a myriad of areas for which they were not required in the past.

Worse still, countless absurd postgraduate courses such as Sexology and Puppetry have been introduced, reducing the education system to long drawn out farce.

Preschool education

The brains of infants develop very rapidly (Mohr et al., 2017). It is very important to take advantage of the resulting capacity for early learning to provide infants with a stimulating environment which should include a 'personal learning centre' (PLC) that includes educational pictures and toys.

By the second year they should be involved in small learning groups supervised by a specialist teacher so that they can begin real learning (Packard, 1978). In the third year they should begin kindergarten for at least a couple of days a week and these learning efforts should continue. By now they have a modest vocabulary and are capable of *cognitive learning* which processes and stores *abstract* information.

At this stage deliberate effort should be made at 'IQ building', noting that IQ tests include questions testing verbal, spatial and numerical ability. If a child has a problem with numbers, for example, early detection and correction of this will prevent far greater problems later.

Then, given a head start,[1] they should commence school at age four, rather than the usual five in most countries.

Learning curves

Suppose the degree to which a person or group has learnt something or been conditioned is given by the probability $p = 0$ to 1, and p depends on n, the number of repetitions of the learning process.

If we assume that the learning process is hyperbolic so that the degree of learning gradually increases towards 100% or the asymptote $p = a$ with $a = 1$, then this is represented by the hyperbola of Figure 6.1(a), the equation for which is $p = an/(b + n)$

---

[1] 'It's never too early to start teaching our kids', *The Weekend Australian,* Aug. 13-14, 2011.

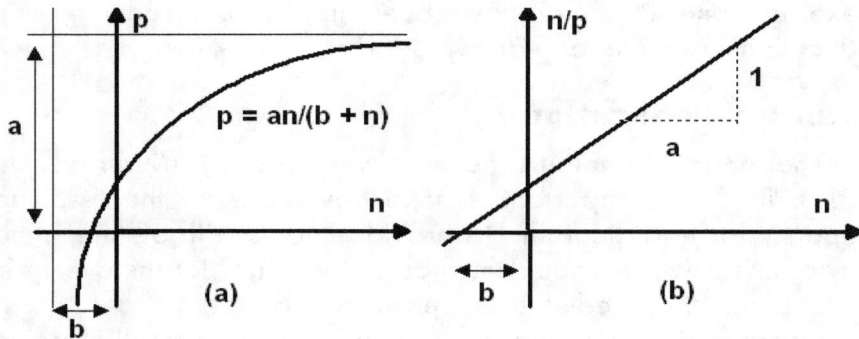

Figure 6.1. Mohr Plot for learning.

This equation can easily be rearranged to give

$n/p = (b + n)/a$

so that if we plot n/p against n the straight line of Figure 6.1(b) is obtained and the magnitude of the intercept with the n axis = b whilst, of more interest, the inverse slope of the line equals the horizontal asymptote a of the hyperbola.

In experimental situations this plot is useful in testing whether results are indeed hyperbolic and, if so, estimating the 'ceiling' value towards which some variable is converging.

Applied to the memory of a single person we set $a = 1$ and a typical result might be $b = 3$, $n = 3$, giving $p = 0.5$, or 50% memory retention after three repetitions. Here p is either:

(a) How well an item is learnt. People's names might be a good example of this. Ourselves, we often think one needs about three repetitions of such things to remember them.

(b) How much of a 'block' of information is learnt. An example might be a list of names where, because of *interference,* words at the beginning (the *primacy effect*) and end (the *recency effect*) are remembered best.

For a slower learner, on the other hand, b might double to 6 so we need $n = 6$ to get $p = 0.5$ or 50% learning.

Applied to conditioning of the populace by advertising, p is the proportion of the population affected and larger values of the asymptote b which flatten the curve might occur when there are two or more competing advertisers in the market. In politics this highlights the advantage of dictatorship.

In education it perhaps highlights the importance of avoiding conflicting messages so that it is often best to learn one subject at a time.

Thinking

In education the four elements of thinking should be used carefully:

[1] **Images.** We often use *visual imagery* in thinking. For example, we often find it easier to describe the shape of something by sketching it or a physical operation by demonstrating it.

[2] **Symbols.** Language involves the spoken and written use of symbols. These symbols can be words, mathematical formulae, pictures (including diagrams, maps and graphs) or gestures that represent either *objects, operations, relationships* and *qualities.*

[3] **Concepts.** Concepts can be defined as categories that represent a class of objects, events or qualities wherein each item has a number of common features. A simple example are birds which 'mentally' are a concept and these have common properties such as two legs, wings, flying and the ability to fly and lay eggs.

Such categorization is important for both efficient learning and memory storage and efficient recall and thence thinking.

Learning of concepts is made easier by *transfer* when they are similar to already familiar concepts.

When driving, for example, when you see a set of traffic lights (a concept) you note which colour is 'on' and quickly decide (a thinking process) what action to take.

[4] Rules. Rules involve connections between features of a concept and between different concepts.

In the example of traffic lights we should know the rules and have only to choose 'yes' or 'no' as to whether we follow the appropriate rule.

The rule for traffic lights might be represented as

(green = go) OR (amber = slow down) OR (red = stop)

and the rule for driving might be written

(accelerator = go) OR (no accelerator = slow) OR (brake = stop)

so to stop at a red light we have to connect the two rules, a process probably carried out in short term memory.

Creative thinking

Creative thinking to obtain new ideas often involves *divergent thinking* (Morgan et al., 1979) and typically occurs in three stages:

(a) Preparation: define the problem and resources needed.

(b) Incubation: acquire information and think or dwell on the problem.

(c) Assembly: combine information to form the solution.

In a much too drawn out education system endless classes with a lecture format should occasionally be replaced by sessions with a seminar format. Sometimes these could involve *brainstorming* to solve a problem, for example devising an effective advertising campaign for a product.

Group brainstorming has been found effective because:

[1] People tend to have twice as many ideas in the group situation because of the more stimulating environment, 'cross fertilization' of ideas and arousal of competitive spirit.

[2] Alternation of individual and group thinking improves results.

[3] As more ideas are produced they tend to improve.

[4] Second sessions a few days later improve results because of the 'incubation' process so important in creative thinking.

[5] The group uses *critical thinking* to evaluate the ideas.

Shortening the school program

No better example of *Parkinson's Law* exists than in education. Parkinson's Law is simply (Parkinson, 1980):

Work expands so as to fill the time available for its completion.

Leonardo da Vinci and Michelangelo were apprenticed at age 14 and Francis Bacon went to Cambridge University at age 12 and left at age 14.

The development of modern science from the 16th and 17th centuries is, perhaps, one of the reasons for the considerable growth in the number of years required at school.

Nevertheless, our system of 12 years at school is far too drawn out and should be reduced to 10 years for the 'average' student, this involving six years at primary school and four at secondary school.

Here the curriculum for the last four secondary years could remain much as now so that reduction to 10 years would be achieved by condensation of the first eight years of the 12 year system to six.

This might simply involve

(a) Making preschool education compulsory and thus removing the need for at least the first year at school.

(b) Acceleration of the learning of the three R's in the first few years and elimination of most unnecessary material.

The result should be better educated and brighter children who will be better prepared for life and the faster pace of tertiary courses.

Less fragmentation

Classes at both school and University are usually scheduled in a somewhat haphazard fashion so that hours of subjects A, B and C appear as A, B, C, A, B, C and so on. This results in a 'parade of clowns' effect that does more to confuse students than anything else.

The first author has always found it better to, for example, give two lectures consecutively, rather than at almost random times in the week a day or more apart.

This has the advantages of:

[1] It saves students and/or staff a considerable amount of inconvenience.

[2] It results in better learning because more *proactive interference* and less *retroactive interference* occurs (Morgan et al., 1979).

[3] A break of about 10 or 15 minutes is allowed in the middle and this provides a good opportunity for questions and discussion.

[4] The result is a more mature and friendly seminar approach and more motivated, inquiring and effective students.

Similarly, in the first years of school it might be better to tackle the 12 times tables, for example, by devoting a few weeks to it, rather than spreading it over years.

Then if the learning task is returned to a week or two later it should be found that *latent learning* has occurred and good progress has been made.

Indeed, it might be a good idea in later school years to fit classes into four days to allow students a fifth week day to do homework. If unnecessary activities were removed as far as possible then, for example, just half an hour more of formal classes per day might allow all the required class work to be fitted into four days.

Application of this less fragmentary approach is possible at University when students might have four or five subjects with one day of the week dedicated to each, rather than having them randomly spread throughout the week in bits and pieces.

University courses

There has been excessive proliferation in new University courses. My father, also an academic, used to joke about there being degrees in bee keeping in the USA. At the more reputable Universities there this may not, in fact, be the case. In Australia, however, this has come to pass with degrees where none were needed before, examples being journalism, marketing, nursing and viticulture.

There has also been a plethora of new postgraduate certificates and diplomas and Masters Degrees. Some of these, such as courses in Sexology, Puppetry or Citizenship studies are either lightweight, absurd or both.

Material that is really essential should have been included in undergraduate courses.

Some so-called postgraduate courses, on the other hand, introduce an entirely new vocational area. If these are all that is required in these areas then these courses should be offered as relatively short undergraduate certificate or diploma courses.

That we have masters "courses" at all is questionable. Mastership in Universities took its meaning from the Master status conferred by the craft-guilds of 500 or more years ago and was given after a relatively short period of teaching experience. Consequently, Cambridge and Oxford award Masters Degrees on completion of undergraduate courses.

Why then do 'latter day' Universities enslave their students for a couple of further years in usually redundant, if not frivolous Masters Degrees?

The answer undoubtedly comes in two parts:

(a) The education bureaucrats are ignorant.

(b) Simply money. The longer the education process, the more "products" and the more money to be made.

Research degrees may also be questionable. As just noted, Masters degrees as separate and additional courses are redundant. As for PhDs, historically these were awarded for further self-study, usually by academics. This involves no teaching so it is absurd that graduates are enrolled as "students" and then used as slave labour at the whim of supervisors for often impractical, if not useless, research topics.

TAFE

TAFE, an acronym for Technical and Further Education that originated in the UK, is an important alternative to University for school leavers. Here students are trained for the *real* occupations in the basic industries essential to human life, that is, food, clothing and shelter.

In contrast, and increasingly so, University courses are, strictly speaking, unnecessary. In other words we can usually live without a doctor or lawyer, house builders can usually do without an architect or engineer if need be. People used to run businesses without business degrees and we certainly don't need degrees in Sexology and Puppetry.

Many TAFE courses are part-time ones for apprentices. Unfortunately, many apprenticeships are unreasonably long and bordering on exploitation of a cheap labour source. An example are hairdressing apprenticeships which we believe take up to 6 years in Australia, certainly too long when most us would think a couple of weeks training would suffice.

Another looming problem is the slow introduction of diploma and degree courses in business to TAFE institutes when absurd numbers of people already do these in the Universities. Even MBA courses, let alone undergraduate business courses, are lightweight material that could and should be taught at school.

Problems in education

There are many problems in the education sector today, including:

[1] Children being incarcerated in long-day-care centres which, cruelly, do little more than expensive babysitting almost from birth. This is an inhuman practice that reduces children to toys that amuse parents after work, a sick situation that must do more harm than good.

[2] As the discussion of brain development in infants in Chapter Two points out, the early years are a critical time that should not be lost. Weiss and Mann (1978), for example, refer to a project in Milwaukee that found that children given more attention by the mother or a specially trained teacher, showed markedly higher IQ.

This is no doubt the reason that only children tend to have higher IQ and that, in families with more than one child, the eldest child has a slightly higher IQ on average (Vernon, 1960). The youngest child in larger families, on the other hand, does not do too badly compared to those 'sandwiched' in the middle and perhaps most deprived of attention.

[3] As noted earlier, 12 years at school is too long and 10 years would be a more sensible norm.

[4] There is far too much rote learning at school.

[5] Poor teacher training. Sykes (1995) reports widespread disillusionment with modern teacher training, much of which is a hotchpotch of psychology, sociology and history that cannot develop real expertise in any of these areas.

He cites several examples of recent doctorates in education being granted for dissertations with such titles as:

"The use of goal setting and positive self-modeling to enhance self-efficiency and performance for the basketball free-throw shot" for a PhD at the University of Maryland.

After such largely useless studies, Sykes laments, 'educrats' move into educational administration and oversee a decline in standards over the whole spectrum of education comparable to that evidenced by their largely irrelevant doctoral studies.

[6] Declining academic standards. A survey of 24,000 students in twelve countries by the Educational Testing Service in Princeton found that, compared to 40% of US students scoring at the 500 level in a standard test, the results were 78% for Korea, 73% for Quebec and 69% for British Columbia (Sykes, 1995). A similar decline in standards has occurred in Australia.

[7] In the USA outcome based education (OBE) has gone a long way towards disallowing fail grades, instead allowing students to retake tests until they pass. The idea of this is to avoid attaching negative labels to students, and much effort is also made to avoid attaching positive labels to the brightest students as well.

[8] Similarly, OBE eschews 'tracking' to permit accelerated learning for gifted students, despite conclusive evidence of its positive results, in this way ensuring that the overall standard of education is lowered further.

[9] In the USA new 'soft' approaches to teaching and grading reading and maths have led to a dramatic decline in literacy and numeracy skills.

[10] Drugs for school-age children. The overlong school education system should bore anyone with half a brain. To make matters worse increasing numbers of 'unruly' children are diagnosed with such doubtful disorders as Attention Deficit Hyperactivity Disorder (ADHD) and prescribed drugs such as Ritalin to sedate them.

In the USA and Australia in turn, increasingly large numbers of children suffer this fate. Reports of up to 15% or more children in some areas being on such drugs have not brought action to curb this disturbing trend as yet, but visions of a future society in which both parents and children have to be drugged to cope are unacceptable.

[11] Overgrown educational bureaucracy. In the US in 1960 one third of education employees were not classroom teachers. By 1991 46.7% were non-teaching staff and the teaching staff's share of the total payroll had shrunk from 54% to 41%. Much the same has occurred in England and Australia both in school and tertiary education.

[12] Growing up faster. Today's young, thanks to better nutrition grow faster than in the past. Da Vinci observed that children were half their ultimate height at age three. Now that figure is about 55%. Along with that, in part because of the ubiquitous media today, in many ways they mature faster than ever before.

Many children by their mid-teens, therefore, are becoming bored with school and drop out. Robertson (1981), for example, reported that 100,000 assaults against teachers occur in US schools each year. Doubtless this is one of several factors that contribute to the increasing discipline problem in schools.

[13] There are far too many assignments, tests etc. at school and University. When the first author was an undergraduate and teaching in Universities in Australasia there were 8 subjects in second year engineering, yet in Engineering Maths students were given sheets full of problems each week.

It should be all about showing *how* to do things and giving *answers*, not asking endless questions. At Auckland University these maths problem sheets often involved 2 or 3 different areas lectured by different people, an absurd situation. Including the secretary who typed them, up to four morons helped fill their week redoing these sheets each year, a fine example of Parkinson's Law for both the staff and students.

Needless to say:
(a) The staff were simply a pathetic, mindless bunch of no-hopers who had never, and never will, achieve anything.
(b) The students were somewhat demoralized. Eight Uni. subjects in a year is too much, let alone being asked to spend up to several hours on the worse than useless homework for just one of them.

[14] Many University courses overlap with school. At Auckland University, for example, top school leavers were exempted from the first year of the course. Q: Why on earth, therefore, was that year needed at all? A: To employ a few more dumb academics. Excessive growth in tertiary courses.

77

[15] The ridiculous University courses like those in sexology were mentioned earlier in the chapter. MBAs etc. are not much better and are now so common that with an MBA one might now only be able to gain employment as a salesperson, if that.

[16] Once upon a time correspondence courses were poorly regarded. We are such slaves to fashion, and thence brainwashing, that the morons in Universities are happy to run courses by *distance education* over the Internet.

[17] There is insufficient emphasis on developing inquiring minds capable of finding answers to their own questions, rather than zombies so used to endless rote learning and tests that they have become too tired and bored to care about anything but going through the motions of life as perpetual consumers and slaves to big businesses that produce and sell mass marketed consumer products.

Conclusions

IQ in the UK diminished by 1.5% between 1920 and 1950 (Vernon, 1960) and two decades ago it was claimed that the average American IQ was diminishing (Fancer, 1985), some claiming that it is now dropping by about 1 point per generation. Judging by the international survey results quoted earlier this has, indeed, happened and the country is deep into reverse evolution.

Australia is probably the most Americanized country in the world and our education system, particularly in the Universities, has certainly become farcical. There it is no longer a matter of education but one of highly paid 'educrats' who have never done anything significant overseeing invention of increasingly ludicrous courses to advertise to increase the size of the University.

From birth to death it is all corporate stuff at the day care centre, school and University and, increasingly, those being brainwashed pay for the privilege.

With the invention of more silly courses and nearly everyone having an MBA students are expected to study longer and longer.

During the first author's undergraduate student days a lecturer explained that, owing to the *time value of money*, we would not in our lifetimes make as much money as a plumber who had started work at 15, even if we were paid substantially more. Plumbers make far more money now than they did way back then!

If your parents spent a lot of money on a private school education the comparison is even worse. Unless they were rich they should have spent just a little of that money to give you the edge at a government school. The rest they should have invested at a good interest rate to buy you a shop in which to start up a lucrative business.

Then you might not need to go to University to study Accountancy, Architecture, Engineering, Dentistry, Law, or Medicine, businesses in which it really is best if you start up your own practice and that may be in a shop front office anyway!

As for postgraduate study, this is a form of slave labour. The first author recalls a physicist saying *"You're past your best at 26."* True of nearly all bludging academics who regurgitate from some text book they don't understand and sit on their backsides while graduate students do their research for them.

Recently, however, the Vice-Chancellor of Monash University said, in arguing as usual for greater University funding, that "University research is important for our democracy", and there may be a little truth in that in Australia, at least (ABC News Radio, 5 AM, 3/3/19).

[6] Education

Chapter 7

GLOBAL DISASTER

> *The human race will be the cancer of the planet.*
> Sir Julian Huxley, British biologist (1887 - 1975), attributed.
>
> *There were no more than twenty-six days in which there was no war somewhere in the world. On any given day there is an average of twelve wars going on somewhere in the world.*
> Anthony Sampson, *The Arms Bazaar* (1978),
> referring to the results of a study of the years 1945 - 1978.

Overpopulation

In the first author's view the world's (human) population is about twice the level that can be sustainable with any reasonable standard of living for all. The prodigious effects of unchecked population increase can easily be demonstrated by simple calculations:

> *In 1956 Professor W.A. Lewis calculated that if the world population were to double every 25 years (a rate of increase currently observable in some parts of Africa and Asia), it would reach 173,500 thousand million by the year 2330, at which time there would be standing room only, since this is the number of square yards on the land surface of the earth.*
> John Carey, *The Faber Book of Science* (1995),
> 'The Menace of Population.'

Such calculations are easily made using Equation 12.4 in which putting $k = 0.028$ a little more than doubles population in 25 years. Currently k is more like 0.014, giving doubling in just under 50 years and this rate will give standing room only in about 735 years from now.

Cipolla (1974) shows that a graph of human population growth from the beginning of the Agricultural Revolution (12,000 BC) has a gently sloping line until the Industrial Revolution (1750 AD), at which point it 'takes off' vertically upwards to 2,485 million in 1950 AD.

He notes that a biologist likened this enormous human population explosion to that of a microbe population in a body suddenly afflicted with an infectious disease!

One reason for this great spurt in human population are advances in medical science such as the discovery of bacteria by Pasteur and Koch, the first use of antiseptics by Lister, and Fleming's discovery of penicillin.

Cipolla points out that what we need to aim for now is an improvement in the quality of the human species, not growth in its quantity. As he laments, however, our continuing predilection for war has the opposite result:

> *Instructing a savage in advanced techniques*
> *does not change him into a civilized person;*
> *it just makes him an efficient savage.*

Had the richer nations not indulged in the insanity of the Cold War NBC arms race after WWII the massive amounts of money wasted on stockpiling WMDs could have been spent on educating and improving the quality of life for the starving millions in the poorest parts of the world.

That, in turn, would have done a great deal to slow the alarming population growth.

Why? Because if you fill a house with, for example, a TV and a PC for each member of a family of four (if we want ZPG), there tends to be sufficient activity going on without the need to add further children or other distractions.

Pollution

Pollution is a much greater problem than most of us realize, for example (Wagner, 1978):

➢ The harmful effects of asbestos are now well known but still surface from time to time. Asbestos, however, is a good example of how long it takes for us to become aware of problem pollutants.

➢ Sulphur dioxide smogs caused by domestic and industrial coal burning were once common in the UK and other countries, sometimes causing heavy casualties and fatalities. Coal is still widely used for electrical power production in, for example, until recently in the Australian state of Victoria which has large reserves of brown coal, so that such usage is likely to be resumed.

➢ Mercury compounds are used by more than 80 industries and are found in such products as plastics, electronics, and fungicides for agriculture. As a result disturbing levels of mercury in fish and birds eggs have been found.

➢ Lead was once added to paints and petrol and is still used in the ink used for the glossy colour pages of magazines. Observations in the Arctic, the Antarctic and world oceans indicate that lead is increasing in the environment.

➢ In the 1980s studies showed that children living close to city freeways had lower IQ.

➢ Cadmium is used in twice the quantities of mercury. Like lead and mercury it accumulates in the body. A limiting level of cadmium in food suggested by some experts would be exceeded by most oysters harvested in the US. Smokers accumulate significant levels of cadmium.

➢ Beryllium is used in the phosphor of fluorescent lights. It is highly toxic and has caused deaths of factory workers.

➢ The harmful global effects of DDT became evident over 20 years ago but remain an example of how *biocides* can cause serious environmental problems. DDT is one of a number of organochlorides, another being the polychlorinated biphenyls (PCBs) which cause suffocation and have also emerged as an environmental problem.

PCBs are also used in manufacturing electrical capacitors, insulating fluids, carbonless copy paper and many other products.

➢ Organophosphates are used as biocides and interfere with the action of nerves, quickly resulting in convulsions, paralysis and death. Their use is now limited in most countries.

➢ Shortly after WWII herbicides called auxins which involve plant hormones were developed. The most famous of these was Agent Orange which caused massive defoliation in Vietnam but also stillbirths and deformities in children in Indochina.

➢ Antibiotics control various poultry and stock diseases but some people are allergic to them. The greater danger, however, is that of bacteria developing resistance to them, and this has already happened to the point that bacteria have evolved that are resistant to all man-made antibiotics.

➢ Hormones are given to animals to fatten them up. One of these, diethylstilbesterol (DES), has been found to cause cancer in humans.

➢ Vinyl chloride is used to make 'plastic' bottles and packaging. In the US the exposure limit for workers in 7500 plants using the substance in manufacturing was set at 1 ppm. Levels of 2 ppm have been found in the air above landfills in the US.

➢ Bis-chloromethyl ether (BCE) is widely used in the textile, chemical, and paper/wood industries and has been found to cause cancer in animals exposed to concentrations of BCE of as little as 0.1 ppm.

➢ Pollution by carcinogenic chlorinated hydrocarbons is caused by petrochemical industry wastes and by the use of chlorine to 'purify' some water supplies.

➢ Overexposure to some food additives such as antioxidants, acids, and emulsifiers can cause minor health problems.

➢ Food dyes used to make cherries red, oranges orange and butter yellow are a risk. Many dyes have been found to be carcinogenic.

There is much propaganda and misinformation too about nuclear power. According to the Club of Rome's report on man's environmental and resource depletion problems, projected annual release of nuclear wastes from the cooling towers of nuclear power plants in the US in the year 2000 was a massive 30 million Curies (Meadows et al., 1974). A Curie is the radioactive equivalent of one gram of radium and is such a large amount that environmental concentrations are usually measured in microcuries.

In other words, the long-term safety of nuclear power is very doubtful.

Depletion of the ozone layer as a result of burning oil and coal around the world has been responsible for significant global warming already.

Pollution problems are, of course, greatly exacerbated by our spiraling population, as well as by poorer parts of the world being modernized.

Resource depletion

The world's finite resources are being depleted at an alarming rate, for example:

➢ Thanks to largely unnecessarily widespread use of the car as a heavily marketed status symbol we have almost exhausted reserves of oil in only some 100 years.

➢ We have also largely used up coal and natural gas reserves.

➢ Several other minerals such as chromium are now in short supply and many others, such as gold, mercury, tin and zinc will be in short supply in the foreseeable future (Meadows et al., 1974).

➢ Up to two-thirds of the Australia's original tree cover has been removed and the situation is worse in some other countries (Bell & Hall, 1991).

➢ Up to 75% of Australia's rain forest has been lost to logging and other human activities (Bell & Hall, 1991).

➢ Fish stocks in several parts of the world have been seriously depleted.

➢ In Australia some 78 plant species have become extinct and many are threatened (Bell & Hall, 1999).

➢ In Australia 16 species of mammal are now extinct with 106 of the remaining 204 being threatened.

➢ The environmentalist David Suzuki predicts that in 200 years up to 80% of all animal and plant species will be extinct.

➢ Around 20% of all land is desert and each year some 6 million hectares of land is lost to desert.

The bottom line is that the human species has reached plague proportions and we are, so to speak, eating ourselves out of house and home and vandalizing that home in the process.

Privatization and globalization

For the last few decades the establishments of leading capitalist countries have been privatizing public utilities and globalizing the world's economy.

A long-term problem of this is that, many governments having crowed about having reduced government debt by selling off transport, water, power and gas industries, are faced with the serious future problem of never being able to reduce debt in this way again.

Under increasing pressure from the private sector, however, governments have consistently reduced company tax, having roughly halved it in Australia in the last three decades.

This means that more and more taxes, for example a GST in Australia about a decade ago, must be introduced to keep the budget manageable. The result is a continuing decline in *real* living standards for the people while the overpaid CEOs of big business laugh all the way to the bank.

A result of this lowering of real family income is that more and more women with young children have work and thus confine their children in long-day-care from the earliest of ages, an inhumane situation. In these children are treated rather like lab rats with in a large observation box with a tiny playground outside. In other words, bringing up preschool children like lab rats or monkeys is becoming the norm and thence a big business.

After this children are forced to spend 12 years at school which, as discussed in Chapter 6, is far too long.

Why so long? Because repeating the same old stuff from a book day after day is a cushy job and the teachers, like the medical profession, are pretty good at keeping up their numbers and their business.

Having finished school more and more children are obliged to pay ever higher fees to attend once nonexistent and unnecessary University courses that have literally reached the situation of having degrees in such things as bee-keeping, once an idea advanced as a joke about American Universities.

Then, chances are, they will find that, after working a couple of years for a multinational company, it will close and move its operations to another country where labour is cheaper.

Modern slavery

In Australia the 40 hour week was introduced almost a century ago and this is still commemorated by a public holiday called *Labour Day*. Now, however, people enslaved by increasingly greedy big businesses have to work longer and longer hours in ever poorer conditions.

There is less and less job security and greater use of casual labour without holiday or any other entitlements.

More and more people commute huge distances on clogged freeways, for which they pay a toll, to then work in soul destroying tower blocks like human filing cabinets in which the open office layout introduced by the Japanese is favoured.

The purpose of this is to make sure supervisors can see everybody to make sure nobody takes more than a few seconds off the job.

Every effort must be made to improve the bottom line at all costs yet, if we were really concerned with efficiency, wouldn't we want to consider just how much value for money do highly paid people in higher management provide? Some of them make in the order of $500 a minute for sitting around a big table and making decisions that are, as often as not, poor ones. On the gigantic salaries of many CEOs, however, they can retire comfortably with a 'golden parachute', after a few years, even if the company crashes.

We can all understand the concept of a minimum wage, so why not a maximum one? Plato thought the ratio of these should not be more than about 5. A century ago some thought it should not be more than 20. Now it reaches a ratio of around 500 quite often.

In addition, surely it is more important that *people* are able to make a decent profit and save some of their earnings. Business, on the other hand, need not make huge profits. What counts from the community point of view is that local workplaces survive and continue to provide employment in the area at decent wages. Whether the business is profitable enough to expand to other areas and perhaps nationally, or even internationally, should not be quite as important.

Most absurd, however, is regression to Dickensian working conditions when the world is grossly overpopulated. Unemployment is unavoidable unless we create service industry jobs in which people are busy in such meaningless activities as shuffling paper.

Like Packard (1963), we recommend introduction of a four day week. This could involve 36 hours, rather than 40, only a 10% reduction. If in a family both husband and wife worked 8 days a week between them surely that should be sufficient, bearing in mind that not long ago women did not work at all but stayed home to look after home and family.

Packard also suggests that there should be less emphasis on more efficiency and a little more on quality of life.

As Keynes put it:

> *The moral problem of our age is concerned with the love of money.*
> John Maynard Keynes, *Essays in Persuasion* (1925).

From overpaid CEOs who enslave thousands to those of us brainwashed into spending our hard-earned money on often frivolous junk this statement certainly appears to be true.

Sociological devolution

In the Western world sociological devolution is taking place at an alarming rate. In the megacities built around grouped towers that are a shrine to global capitalism inner suburban areas of many cities have spiraling crime rates.

Much of these cities is covered in graffiti produced by bored youth, many of them addicted to drugs and living without hope.

Divorce rates are around 50% so that most children have direct or indirect contact with shattered families.

Unemployed men over 40 live without hope of ever getting a job again. Many have been retrenched by factories seeking to improve their bottom line with greater efficiency or by moving to a location where their operations will be cheaper.

In schools, the church, and homes, bullying and sexual abuse is rampant to the point that newspapers have articles about bullying in schools every week and public libraries often have at least a couple of dozen books on bullying on their shelves.

In the megacities house prices have escalated absurdly so that the young have little hope of getting into the house market.

In the US it is said that 1 in 6 children live in poverty. In the UK a BBC radio report on 29 April 2005 said that the gap between rich and poor in the UK had increased to what it was in Victorian times. As a result people living in such places as Glasgow had a life expectancy 11 years less than that of better-off people living in places like Dorset.

A little divination

So what is the future likely to hold for us? In another 50 years the human population, already being at least twice that which is sustainable, will have continued the 'almost vertical rise' compared to that before the industrial revolution and doubled again.

By that time:

➤ We will have run out of the earth's reserves of oil, coal, natural gas, chromium, mercury, gold, tin, zinc, aluminium etc.

➤ Stored waste from nuclear power plants will have rendered large areas of the world uninhabitable. Pollution of the air and waterways by nuclear power plants will be massive.

➤ Up to 99% of the world's original tree cover will have gone.

➤ All the world's rain forests will have long gone.

➤ Half of the arable land remaining will have been reduced to desert. As a result food and water will be in short supply almost everywhere.

➤ Around 80% of the species of animals, birds and other wildlife in the world will have become extinct or nearly so.

➤ The world's oceans will be so heavily polluted that most marine life will be extinct and safely edible fish stocks will be few and far between.

➢ The ozone layer will have become do depleted that humans in most parts of the world will have to dress like Arabs to prevent sunburn and melanoma. Blindness will be epidemic.

➢ Many bacteria will be resistant to antibiotics and human mortality rates will begin to revert to those before the time of Pasteur and Lister.

➢ Epidemics of new strains of influenza will appear and kill hundreds of millions of people.

➢ Viruses like Ebola and Marburg will have evolved to wipe out half the populations in countries in Africa and elsewhere and affected countries will have to be quarantined.

➢ Other viruses like Asian Bird Flu will have jumped to humans and will be decimating populations.

➢ Religious conflicts such as those between Islamic sects and Islam, Christianity and Hinduism will have killed millions of people.

➢ Political unrest and revolution as a result of unemployment and poverty will have occurred in many countries, including the US which is likely to have major southern states devolve from the union.

➢ Nuclear wars will have occurred in one or more regions of the world, for example between China and its allies and the British-American alliance (Clark, 1967). These will have rendered large parts of the world uninhabitable.

➢ Biochemical warfare with hybrid smallpox-Marburg type viruses will have been used extensively, killing billions.

➢ Since suicide bombings are now routine it is very likely that before long terrorists will infect themselves with deadly viruses such as smallpox and Marburg and promptly fly to their target countries while the disease they carry is still in the incubation period. The results are certain to be far more frightening than anything the human race has even dreamt of in its worst nightmares.

What will be left when the last three events occur?

As the first author has written in the book *2045* (Mohr, 2014a), small pockets of survivors in remote parts of the world will return to life like that after the Agricultural Revolution.

Then, however, such permanent damage will have been done to the earth that their long-term survival is unlikely.

For example:

(a) There will no longer be enough plant life to provide oxygen at previous levels and ozone levels will be so depleted that growing plants for food will be difficult.

(b) Newly evolved deadly viruses, or viruses spread by biological warfare might be carried by birds or insects such as mosquitoes to the last remaining arable regions inhabited by these survivors and wipe them out.

Global warming

Recent findings suggest that global warming is proceeding far more quickly than expected.

According to the UN's Intergovernmental Panel on Climate Change (IPCC) the earth's temperature increased by up to 0.9°C during the 20th century.

Colorado's National Centre for Atmospheric Research predicted a further rise of about 1°C by 2030 and the IPCC up to a whopping 5.8°C by 2100 and there are more pessimistic estimates.

These estimates fit closely (with $R^2 = 0.999$) to the exponential curve

$$T = 0.134 \exp(0.0197\, t) \tag{7.1}$$

where T = temperature and t = years since 1900, giving the result shown in Figure 7.1.

This clearly shows how our population 'took off' after the industrial revolution and how global warming has now done likewise as a result of both the greater population and the increasing spread of industrialization.

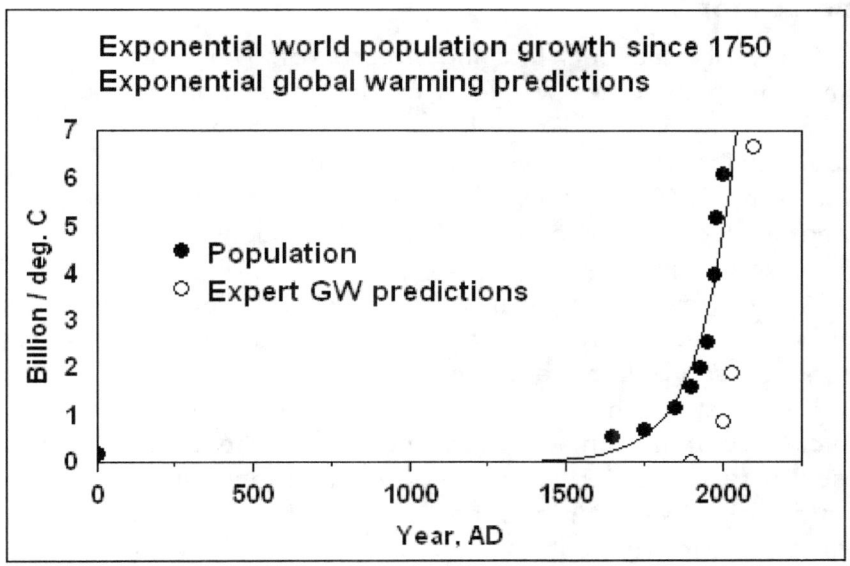

Figure 7.1. Predictions of global warming.

If GW is indeed taking off exponentially then within a few thousand years the planet will become a lifeless dust bowl. Worse still, in all probability much, if not all, the GW to date is irreversible and, even worse still, it may be that the planet is already stuck in a 'one-way street' of rapidly accelerating GW no matter what we do.

In any case, it is perfectly obvious to all but the most purblind that governments and big biz are, as usual, just spouting bullshit on the issue and making token efforts, if that. This, after all, is normal politics, that is, for any problem give glib assurances that something is or will be done and set up some new committee to prognosticate interminably at high rates of pay over the matter and, eventually, do little or nothing beyond make some facile recommendations.

Conclusion

Many of us expect that the stresses of overpopulation and diminishing resources will lead to steady economic decline, in turn resulting in disputes, political unrest and instability, and as usual, human conflict in many parts of the world.

In other words, as usual we will behave just like lab rats when housed beyond a certain population density, we will start killing each other.

We, however, will be in an even worse situation, suffering not only increased overcrowding but also a worsening physical, economic and political environment.

The first author shows in his book *The Doomsday Calculation* that man will be extinct before the year 3000 as a result of resource depletion, loss of arable land, starvation, war and disease. Even with half the rate of global warming shown in Figure 7.1 our population will have halved by the year 3000.

A good example of how this might come about is the very new Zika virus that originated in South America and became particularly prevalent in Brazil. On 31st July, 2016, Australia's ABC News 24 radio station reported that four cases of Zika virus had been reported in Florida, and that these were the first cases of "local transmission" reported in the USA, it being thought that the transmission had been from Miami.

The bottom line is that the human race has been collectively stupid to behave like second or third rate animals and breed like vermin and ravage our planet so badly, and David Wallace Wells' recent book *The Uninhabitable Earth* predicts that the incidence of war will double, global warming will increase, and that eventually all life forms will be impacted (PBS News Hour, 1/3/2019).

Chapter 8

BIG BUSINESS

> *Corporation. An ingenious device for obtaining
> individual profit without individual responsibility.*
> Ambrose Bierce, *The Devil's Dictionary* (1881-1906).
>
> *Honour sinks where commerce long prevails.*
> Oliver Goldsmith, *The Traveler.*
>
> *International business may conduct its operations with scraps of
> paper, but the ink it uses is human blood.*
> Eric Ambler, *A Coffin for Dimitrios*, ch. 5 (1939).

Mohr's law of money

The fundamental principle of capitalism is the exponential growth law:

$$d(\$)/d(t) = \text{const.} \times a \ (=\text{activity}) \quad \text{where } a = \text{const.} \times \$ \qquad (8.1)$$

Here the rate at which money is made is proportional to the rate of business activity, this in turn proportional to the amount of money available to fund this activity.

Combining the two constants above as $k = c_1 c_2$ we have:

$$d(\$)/d(t) = k\$ \text{ where } k \text{ is the } \textit{growth factor.} \qquad (8.2)$$

This is *separable* so that it can be integrated in the form:

$$\text{Integral } [\ d(\$)/\$ \ ] = \text{Integral } [\ k \, d(t) \ ] \qquad (8.3)$$

giving, with the inclusion of the initial values, the following exponential growth law:

$$\log_e \$ - \log_e \$_0 = k(t - t_0), \text{ or } \$/\$_0 = \exp[k(t - t_0)] \qquad (8.4)$$

If, for example, the growth rate is 10% per year, that is $k = 0.1$, then over 10 years we obtain the growth ratio $/$_0 = 2.7$, so that we have nearly *tripled* our money. Not bad at all!

The same law governs population growth (using a symbol such as x for population in place of $), for example if every 25 years 0.5 more children are born than people die we have $k = 0.02$, and this will give a 22% increase in population every 10 years, or 2.7 times in 50 years.

Noting that old adage about suckers:

There's one born every minute.

this population growth could also be factored into the calculation of Equation (8.4), further increasing the profits.

Finally, note that the foregoing calculation considers business *growth*, not interest rates. In most cases the business is financed by both debt (bank loans) and equity (share issues) and interest and dividend payments need to be subtracted from the growth ratio result. If the cost of capital, that is the weighted average of the interest rate and the dividend rate is 10%, the same as the growth rate, then we will have had to pay out this 10% ten times so the profit = (growth ratio - 1) = (2.7 - 1) = 1.7.

Still quite good as we have here borrowed *all* the money for the business and repaid none of it. If we now repay all the debt we are still left with a tidy 0.7 profit.

The finance and insurance industries

The crux of how the banking system works is as follows.

The reserve bank holds the *statutory reserve deposits* (SRDs) of the trading banks, a set ratio called the *reserve ratio* (R) of their total deposits.

If, for example, $R = 0.2$ and $M1$ is deposited by a customer in a bank. The bank can now lend $M0.8$ to another customer who passes this as payment for property etc. to a customer of another bank. This second bank can now lend 80% of this amount and so on, so that a series of demand deposits results:

δD = original deposit + 80& of latter + 80% of latter - - - -

$$= 1 + (1 - R) + (1 - R)^2 + - - - - \quad = 1/[1 - (1 - R)] = 5 \qquad (8.5)$$

so that $M5 of demand deposits are created as a result of the original $M1 deposit, an effect called the *multiplier effect.*

If you are the only bank in town, of course, then all the business flowing from this one deposit is yours! In other words, the banking business is easy money compared to real work.

Indeed, around 1200 AD the church reviled people who charged interest on money and by the 17th century the Jews were despised by some people in Europe because of their association with banking and money lending. Indeed, this may have been Hitler's gripe with them. Another theory is that he had caught syphilis from a Jewish prostitute but that seems less likely.

The insurance industry is another nice one to be in. Again something like a multiplier effect occurs so that you need only have enough funds to cover a small fraction of the number of insurance policies you issue.

On a smaller scale, of course, is the pawnshop, a pretty ruthless and sad business if there ever was one, and interest rates of the order of 10% per month are the norm.

Some say that second hand shops, and thus pawnshops, thrive in times of depression (Batra, 1988). Like all too many other businesses the pawn business has gone multinational with companies like Cash Converters. This is obviously because now rampant capitalism has created a large underclass in most of the world. In England, for example, the lower class have a life expectancy 11 years less than the well-off, a figure that would be causing riots if it applied to a racial group.

Very big business: arms and drugs

The arms race is the world's biggest business (Sampson, 1977; Pringle & Spigelman, 1981) and a ruthless one too, resulting in huge areas of the world being littered in land mines that kill and main innocent people years after they were laid.

Ancient man, presumably, made spears for hunting and then started using them in tribal warfare, perhaps a bit like using the kitchen knife as a weapon today.

A poster published in *New Internationalist* many years ago pointed out that world expenditure on arms every two weeks was then sufficient to provide "adequate food, water, education, health and housing for everyone in the world" (Bell & Hall, 1991).

Perhaps the figure 'two weeks' no longer applies but even if it were now four weeks that is still scandalous.

At a wild guess, the world's population is at least twice what is sustainable in the long term with a reasonable standard of living for all, 'reasonable' implying a fairly substantial use of resources by everyone.

Had the immense amounts of money wasted on the cold war between the USSR and the US and its allies been plowed into educating and thence reducing population growth in the poorest countries on earth then the outlook for the human race might not be so bleak as it undoubtedly is at present.

Worse still, continuing massive arms sales around the world can only lead to further conflict on a global scale. Good for business if you are in the arms business! Bad perhaps if you are not.

This is a situation that must be addressed, for example by immediately banning both the use *and* possession of nuclear and biochemical weapons.

Obviously land mines should be banned as well.

Perhaps a little optimistic, one might as well go a little further and ban any kind of bombs, cannons, and perhaps even guns as well.

That the arms industry is so massive is a symptom of sick societies infecting a sick world. Another is the huge illegal drugs industry which is often said by the news media to be the world's second biggest industry.

In this evil business the wholesale markup is 500 or even 1000 percent, the huge profits being laundered, a process involving 3 stages:

1. Immersing: replacing cash with bank accounts, traveler's cheques and other negotiable instruments or valuable objects.

2. Layering or 'heavy soaping': creating a 'paper trail' often involving foreign banks, for example Banco Ambrosini which had branches in the Bahamas, Luxembourg, and Nicaragua but not in London or Wall St.

3. Repatriation and integration or 'spin drying' (Blundell, 1982).

If we included alcohol then certainly the drug business would be the world's biggest. If one then included the businesses that involve alcohol such as hotels, and thence the tourist industry, hotels, pubs, clubs, brothels and restaurants, and heaven knows what else, then it is easy to see that Western economies would collapse if booze were banned. Just loosing the excise on booze would put a big hole in national budgets.

The tobacco business, of course, used to be one of the greatest users of advertising and the booze business still is. Here the pyramid effect of social learning also plays a major role in getting children hooked for life and, of course, the best businesses are those which persuade and brainwash us into becoming lifelong consumers of their products.

Junk food

The junk food business is now, of course, a massive international one and every day staggering numbers of people around the world eat junk.

Then there are almost countless other junk food businesses such as KFC, Wendy's (= Hungry Jack's in Australia), Subway, Pizza Hut and countless Chinese take-away and old-fashioned fish and chips shops.

These all seem to involve the psychology of eating something unhealthy every day, as well as 'proper' healthy food.

To add insult to injury, fat-laden hamburgers, pizzas and chips are washed down with Coke and other sugary soft drinks.

Of course, junk food is marketed heavily to brainwash children with the general concept, not just the particular brand, and there is always a junk food shop around the corner to tempt children on their way to and from school.

To this unhealthy consumption we can add heavy-in-fat chocolates, sugar loaded sweets, and several types of salty snacks fried in unhealthy oil. These products too are marketed heavily to brainwash children directly or through the pyramid effect of social learning.

We can also add countless other unhealthy items in the supermarkets such as frozen pizzas and pies, high-in-fat biscuits, and soft drinks.

Entertainment, booze, sports, gambling and sex

The movie business is still big and TV, videotape and DVD perhaps make it bigger than ever. Similarly, the music business remains big thanks to the CD and, latterly, MP3 players.

Nowhere more than in these businesses are children brainwashed into acting like characters they identify with, in order words acting stupidly, aggressively and irresponsibly.

At 'rave' parties for young people primeval music seems to go hand-in-hand with drugs and booze. All good for business!

Sport, of course, has become big business too. The once tribal affair of young men occasionally playing games with stones and spears has turned into a global business in which an almost endless variety of sports and games are played.

Not long ago the various types of football were played between local teams on Saturday afternoons. Now they are played on two or three days a week both in the afternoons and evenings and televised to millions.

Motor car racing is a big business well supported by motor manufacturing companies in most countries and the Formula 1 championship series is a billion dollar business event contested in almost 20 countries and televised globally. Motorcycle racing is also a big business.

Golf and tennis are now massive sports with their main championships also televised globally.

The world soccer championships vie with the Olympic games for the title of the biggest sporting event in the world, both involving massive amounts of money.

Not only are many sports big business, they are also associated with massive amounts of advertising and the most highly paid sports stars, who already earn millions, earn even more from appearing in advertisements.

In addition, the sports equipment industry is also massive.

Gambling is now one of the world's biggest businesses. Gambling associated with horse racing is fairly big business but the casino and poker machine industries are truly massive international businesses.

As Skinner boxes do to rats, poker machines seem to hypnotize some people, with the result that they become problem gamblers some of whom ruin their lives by getting into debt way beyond their means.

Remarkably too, it is often more women than men, and often older people, that we see playing the pokies morning, noon or night. Presumably younger men are more interested in booze, watching sport on the TV or playing pool, darts etc.

The sex industry is now big business with legalized up-market brothels being a far cry from the seedy back street affairs of the past.

Sex shops abound in major cities, selling pornographic magazines and videos, and strange sexual equipment.

Ads for phone-talk or dating with sexy ladies and men appear on TV and newspapers and many of these are doubtless simply fronts for prostitution.

Many of these are for homosexuals who in our permissive, decadent and decaying society might eventually outnumber heterosexuals in some cities such as San Francisco.

Closely associated with entertainment, booze, and sex, the tourism industry is also massive. This literally props up many industries such as the airlines, as well as the economies of several countries.

Technology based industry

With the industrial revolution came the need to sell products such as:

[1] Transport: cars, boats and airplanes.

[2] Clothing: new fabrics, some with such features as 'permanent press.'

[3] Food: tinned and frozen food and countless new food products created in laboratories such as packet soups.

[4] White goods: refrigerators and washing machines.

[5] Home appliances such as motor mowers, vacuum cleaners, toasters, blenders etc.

[6] Radio and TV.

[7] Recorded music and movies.

[8] PCs, computer software and computer games.

[9] The burgeoning phone industry, including the Internet.

[10] The wine cask has helped expand the wine industry and the 'widget' (a small plastic ball) has helped give beers like Guinness their traditional head when poured from a can.

Perhaps there was no better product innovator in the 20th century than Clive Sinclair. He began making miniature amplifiers in the 1960s, then radio kits, then a 2 inch flat screen TV. In the early 1970s Sinclair's company made pocket calculators with many functions. These were small and much cheaper than competing models and a further development was the Wrist Calculator, a technical disaster but modest commercial success.

Then Sinclair moved into the fledgling microcomputer market and in 1978 produced the MK14, a computer kit with only 256 bytes of RAM that sold for around £40 only but needed a £34 VDU (video display unit) to interface with UHF TV sets and a £10 tape unit to store programs.

This was followed in 1980 by the ZX80. This was based on the MK14 but had 1 kb of RAM, came assembled for £100 and used a truncated version of ANSI Minimal BASIC. Additional 1 kb memory chips cost £16 each, however, so that to compete with its nearest competitor the Acorn Atom the total cost ran to around £300 (Adamson & Kennedy, 1986).

In 1981 Sinclair's company followed with the ZX81 which had 4 kb of ROM to store the operating system and some BASIC. With a 16 kb RAM pack included it sold for £120. The ZX81 was a great success and was one of the first microcomputers to spread the market beyond hobbyists to children and schools. Sales were 500,000 worldwide in 1982.

The ZX Spectrum followed in 1982, a colour computer amenable to simple computer games which played a key role in the massive expansion of the microcomputer market. It was followed by the Sinclair QL or 'Quantum Leap' microcomputer in 1984.

By the mid 1980s, however, IBM, ICL, Olivetti, Hitachi and many other competitors had moved into the PC market with machines with at least 640 kb RAM. Sinclair's QL microcomputer cost £400 but with monitor and printer included this rose to almost £1,000. Originally designed to have 32 kb ROM another 16 kb had to be 'tacked on' to hold the QDOS operating system and the QL's SuperBASIC.

The QL was beset with hardware and software bugs from the outset and was outsold by its cheaper predecessor the Spectrum. This was in part because the QL had failed to meet the requirements of business users whereas the Spectrum retained a games market amongst children.

At the same time Sinclair was losing money on his electric tricycle, the C5. All too typically of the impatient Clive Sinclair, this was a hastily conceived affair with a polypropylene body which measured about 6 feet long by 2.5 feet high and wide and was driven by a modified washing machine motor made in Italy. The worst bungle was that it had only lead-acid batteries to keep the price low but longer lasting nickel-cadmium batteries should have been used to give the C5 longer range.

The ugly C5 was priced at only £400 whereas one of its only competitors, the Dutch Whisper cost around £4,000 but at least looked like a conventional car. Seen by many as more of a toy than a practical vehicle the C5 was a commercial disaster.

At the start of the 20th century 35% of the vehicles sold were electric and at the time of the launch of the C5 in 1985 there were 30,000 electric vehicles in commercial use in the UK, 90% of these 'milk floats'.

As with most of his inventions Sinclair had aimed 'too small' and too cheap and he ran into financial difficulties. He was bailed out in 1985 by the publishing magnate Robert Maxwell but in 1986 was forced to sell his PC business to Amstrad. Nevertheless, he had played a major part in the PC revolution.

Value-adding

One thing that Bill Gates could have taught Clive Sinclair is value-adding. Originally the operating system and some form of BASIC came free with your PC. Bill Gates changed all that!

Now you can buy a perfectly good new PC for as little as about $A500 if you look around and, if you are lucky, that might include a basic 'home' version of the Windows OS. But if you want latest full versions of Windows and Visual Basic that will set you back around $A2000. If you want a business version than runs on several PCs Microsoft Office will set you back circa $A1000.

This has been achieved by an immense amount of value-adding, bells and whistles covering the skeleton of a basic product that would otherwise cost a great deal less. One of these is MS Internet Explorer which, despite complaint and litigation from opposing software companies, is pushed at you to make you more likely to use MS as an Internet provider, yet another example of how big business tries to lead us by the nose and very often succeeds.

The modern motor car is a superb example of value-adding, the bells and whistles including four-wheel drive, CD players, electric windows, TV, and heaven knows what else. Very few have dual circuit braking systems, standard on Volvos long ago, which should be mandatory!

For subliminal stupidity, though, you can't go past including TVs on the front of huge stainless steel refrigerators that cost thousands. Never mind that you'll throw this expensive hulk out when the motor, which is probably worth about $20, packs up! You really have to be brainwashed to buy one of these, even if you do have too much money.

Planned obsolescence

In a mid 1950s article in the *Journal of Retailing* marketing consultant Victor Lebow suggested that (Packard, 1963):

Our enormously productive economy ... demands that we make consumption our way of life, that we convert the buying and use of goods into rituals, that we seek our spiritual satisfaction, our ego satisfactions, in consumption ... We need things consumed, burned up, worn out, replaced, and discarded at an ever increasing rate.

It seems that, as always, the government agreed with big business because in mid-1960 reports from the US administration advocated that faster tax write-offs of business equipment should be permitted to allow for business equipment becoming obsolete earlier (Packard, 1963).

As the second quotation introducing the present chapter suggests, the car industry is perhaps the classic example of planned obsolescence. Cars could be made to last you for life but that would not be good for business.

Tyres are an example of this. A 1959 article in the *Journal of the Society of Automotive Engineers* (USA) stated that Consumer Union had found that over a three-year period the tread-wear life of a range of tyres had declined by 18% (Packard, 1963).

More recently the plastic lids on many washing machines or the plastic doors on the freezer compartments of many refrigerators were a fine example of planned obsolescence.

Another occurs in the cheaper brands of sound equipment put out by multinational companies. In these you will find that some important feature such as the controls for such things as the tape drives will change every year or so. With this experimentation comes a virtual guarantee of something going wrong before 'too long'.

Privatization and globalization

An ongoing process in the West has been privatization of government run public utilities such as public transport and electricity, gas and water supply. Along with this the practice of outsourcing road building, recruitment and other activities has long been on the increase. These businesses are a licence to print money because they are essential services so that they *can't* go out of business. When the private company gets into trouble they are invariably bailed out by the government.

The multinational companies that persuade countries to sell off their assets invariably sack a good proportion of the work force as soon as possible so that the government has to foot the bill for yet more people on the dole.

The negative effects of globalization are felt nowhere more than in the clothes industry were brands such as Nike set up factories in Mexico, China and other poorer regions of the world to make use of their cheap labour that will work under conditions that would not be tolerated elsewhere.

Indeed, everywhere you look privatization and globalization are having negative effects and taking us back to Dickensian conditions and lifestyles.

In Australia one government organization once controlled all our phones and our mail. The now massive phone industry is now entirely privatized, resulting in decreased government revenue so that new taxes such as a GST were needed.

As things stand there is little left for the government to sell except its soul, if it has one that is, which much, if not most, of the public doubts.

Such sales have retired a good deal of government debt but, with almost no tariff protection remaining for local industry, foreign debt has begun to climb yet again. But in the future there will be nothing left to sell and we shall regress amongst the nations to what might be termed a 'second world' status, if we have not reached that point already that is.

No matter how bad things really get, however, don't hold your breath waiting for the government to admit it rather than brainwash you with the usual 'econobabble' and empty lies.

Input-Output Analysis (IOA)

One of the major purposes of the Numerical Methods (NM) chapter was to introduce matrix techniques necessary for input-output analysis. This technique was developed by Wassily Leontief at Harvard in 1931 and his study of the US economy with it gained a Nobel Prize and later Laurence Klein applied IOA to the world economy, also receiving a Nobel Prize.

At a basic level IOA analyses the interdependence of various industries. Consider, for example, three companies X, Y and Z that sell/buy products/materials to/from each other, the value of these transactions over some regular period being shown in Table 8.1.

Table 8.1. Input-output analysis data.

| | Purchases | | | | Total |
	X	Y	Z	External	Output ($)
Sales					
X	-	60	40	100	200
Y	40	-	100	260	400
Z	50	100	-	50	200
Labour	110	240	60	-	410
Total input	200	400	200	410	1,210

This table also includes labour costs for the period, as well as *external* sales (other than to the other two companies). Then company Y, for example, sells $40 of goods to X and $100 to Z, the remaining $260 of its total output ($400) being sold externally.

To produce this output Y purchases $60 in goods from X and $100 from Z, also spending $240 on labour costs.

Then from Table 8.1 we can easily calculate *input coefficients* by dividing the three X,Y,Z columns by their totals, giving the results shown in Table 8.2.

Table 8.2. Input coefficients

	X	Y	Z
X	-	0.15	0.2
Y	0.2	-	0.5
Z	0.25	0.25	-
Labour	0.55	0.6	0.3

Then for company Y, for example, Table 8.2 shows that for each $1 of output produced 15 cents is spent on purchases from X, 25 cents on purchases from Z and 60 cents is spent on labour costs.

Then using the coefficients of Table 8.2 we can write the outputs x,y,z for companies X, Y,Z as

(ME18a) $\quad x = 0.15y + 0.20z + 100$

(ME18b) $\quad y = 0.20x + 0.50z + 260$

(ME18c) $\quad z = 0.25x + 0.25y + 50$

Now suppose we wish to determine the effect of increasing the external sales of X to $120 (from $100). Then we change the last number in Eqn ME18a and rearrange the equations to give:

(ME19) $\quad \begin{bmatrix} 1 & -0.15 & -0.20 \\ -0.20 & 1 & -0.50 \\ -0.25 & -0.25 & 1 \end{bmatrix} \begin{Bmatrix} x \\ y \\ x \end{Bmatrix} = \begin{Bmatrix} 120 \\ 260 \\ 50 \end{Bmatrix}$

and solving these equations using a routine such as that given in Sec. NM4 of *The Scientific MBA* (Mohr, 2017) we obtain

$$x = \$223, \ y = \$408, \ z = \$208$$

From these results we are then, for example, able to calculate the increased labour costs resulting for each company as:

X: 223 x 0.55 = 122.7   (increase of $12.7)
Y: 408 x 0.60 = 244.8   (increase of $4.8)
Z: 208 x 0.30 = 62.4   (increase of $2.4)

Here a 'flow through' effect to other companies is immediately apparent (a more superficial approach would predict the increase in labour cost for X as increase in external output (20) multiplied by 0.55 = $11 and effects on other companies would be neglected).

Input-output analysis is an important technique, one which illustrates how just 3 companies can interact financially, with their costs divided between purchases of products from the other two companies, and their labour costs.

The workers

In the wake of the Industrial Revolution there came an increase in capitalism and thence globalization of many industries.

The results have included a massive increase in white collar workers at the expense manual workers (Blondel, 1963), including farm workers. This has decimated rural communities which, arguably, constituted man's natural way of life.

It cannot be deemed natural, on the other hand, for man to live or work in what a Scottish Union leader termed "an architectural representation of a filing cabinet."

In these tall buildings workers for 'heartless' multinational companies or ever greedier national ones work longer and longer hours in ever worsening conditions (Packard, 1961):

Even the layout of the large office is coming more and more to resemble that of the factory, with straight-line flow of work and in some cases assembly belts
for moving paper work from one point to another.
Each worker does a fragment of the complex operations.

Increasing use is made of casual labour without holiday or any other halfway humane entitlements. In Australia the age at which women can get the old-age pension has increased from 60 to 65 and the pension age will increase to 67 for everybody in a few years.

These days even women with very young children are expected to work when once they didn't yet the liars in government or the purblind economists will assure you that we never had it so good. Nothing could be further from the truth with house prices absurd in capital cities, ever worse working conditions, children sent to long-day-care almost from birth, and ever decreasing standards in schools and everywhere else in the community.

In the USA things are so bad that one in six children live in poverty. In the UK, as noted earlier in this chapter, the poor have an average life expectancy 11 years less than the rich, a shocking figure that would cause riots and revolution in countries where people are less heavily brainwashed.

Retirement age

A few years ago a Liberal Party government, being 'conservative' or on the side of big business, increased the mandatory retirement age for eligibility to pensions etc., from 65 to 67.

Cyril Northcote Parkinson, of *Parkinson's Law* fame,[1] proposed that:

"Ages of compulsory retirement are fixed at points varying from 55 to 75, all being arbitrary and unscientific. Whatever age has been decreed by accident and custom can be defended by the same argument. Where the retirement age is fixed at 65 the defenders of this system will always have found, by experience, that the mental powers and energy show signs of flagging at the age of 62. This would be a most useful conclusion to have reached had not a different phenomenon been observed in organizations where the age of retirement has been fixed at 60.

---

[1] *Work expands to fill the time available for its completion.*

"There, we are told, people are found to lose their grip, in some degree, at the age of 57. As against that, men whose retiring age is 55 are known to be past their best at 52. It would seem that, in short, that efficiency declines at age of R minus 3, irrespective of the age at which R has been fixed" (Parkinson, 1958).

According to the *Oxford Book of Work* (Thomas, 1999):

"Compulsory retirement is a relatively modern invention. In 1900 nearly two thirds of men over sixty-five in Britain were still in full employment. - - -. Many continued working until they died. Only in the twentieth century has the development of state and private pension schemes made customary the practice of mandatory retirement at a fixed numerical age.

This abrupt transition from full-time work to enforced idleness has created as many problems as it has solved."

There is some truth in both these views, but we believe that compulsory and recommended retirement ages should, of course, depend upon the type of work. People who 'talk' for a living, such as politicians, upper level managers, teachers, lecturers, and journalists, for example, should be able to work, on average, OK up to age 65. Beyond that, though most would not admit it, their abilities and IQ will have declined significantly, as illustrated by our proposal of *real IQ* declining with age and perhaps illness, the rate of decrease being decreased substantially by continued learning or 'mental exercise' (Mohr et al. 2017; GA, RS & PE Mohr, 2018b).

As for workers in heavy industry, and particularly for jobs such as those of roof tilers, 'ditch diggers' etc. which are both laborious and somewhat dangerous, retirement age (at least from such occupations) should be more like 55, and perhaps less in exceptional cases such as active military service.

White collar crime

White collar crime has always been rife. In recent years we have only seen the tip of a great iceberg come to light in the media.

Routinely companies:

[1] Sack workers and refuse to pay them pension and other entitlements.

[2] Lie about their profitability and trade when insolvent.

[3] Fiddle their taxes using such artifices as massive and premature asset write-offs.

[4] Pay executives increasingly inflated salaries and bonuses as well as giving them huge stock parcels and options annually and upon retirement after only a few years. In contrast, shareholders are often struggling retirees make minimal return on their investment after inflation is taken into account.

On the latter point it might be noted that Plato felt that the top people in a society should be paid no more than five times as much as those earning least. Several decades ago some people felt that ratio should not exceed 20. Now ratios of about 500 are almost commonplace.

Everyday examples of white collar crime include bank employees embezzling money, lawyers absconding with trust accounts and doctors fiddling their books with entries for treatments never carried out, for example one doctor who would issue government 'patient service' forms to friends at parties to fill out (Hall, 1979).

Examples of jailed corporate crooks in Australia in recent times include (*The Weekend Australian,* April 16-17, 2005):

➢ The CEO of a real estate company who bribed a politician.

➢ The leader of a women's group stole $A4 million from it.

➢ A merchant bank CEO who obstructed investigation into its failure.

➢ The CEO of an investment company who committed fraud.

➢ The CEO of a retail chain misappropriated company funds.

➢ The CEO of a corporate empire "stripped" it of $A1.2 billion.

➢ A leading stockbroker convicted for insider trading.

The part IBM played in recording the details of Jews later sent to the Nazi death camps is well known. In 1998 a consortium of Swiss banks settled out of court to the tune of $US1.25 billion for transferring the accounts of thousands of Holocaust survivors to the Nazis around the beginning of WWII (Aarons & Loftus, 1999; Black, 2001).

The future

Recently, the first author heard some fool who is global head of a leading US advertising agency talking about a book *Lovemarks* he had just had published. He advocated marketing products so that people would come to identify with and 'love' them and had lectured such rubbish in Cambridge, Stanford and like-minded Universities.

At the moment the USA, much of it already having been bought up by petrodollars since the 1970s oil price hikes by OPEC (Smith, 1981), and since then by Japan, China etc., is gain on the verge of financial crisis and has had to yet again increase its limit on foreign debt. This is exactly what Osama Bin Laden pledged that he would help bring about.

A few years ago the Chinese hi-tech company Lonovo took over IBM's PC business and China's second largest TV set maker has just merged with a French company to form the world's largest TV maker of TV sets.

The South Korean white goods company LG makes one in every three microwave ovens in the world and now has almost half of the US market for small refrigerators.

This is selling sand to the Arabs stuff which bodes ill for the already troubled US economy. It forebodes an even greater role for Asia in the world market.

The Chinese, however, ignored pleas to take over the bankrupt MG-Rover car business in the UK, seemingly good business tactics!

No doubt parts of Africa will follow the Chinese lead and industrialize using cheap labour to get an early edge in the global marketplace. By the time that happens resource depletion in an already grossly overpopulated world will become even more frightening.

Do they brainwash the citizens of China? Surely the situation cannot be as bad as in the "force-fed society" of the USA (Packard, 1963). Surely not as many as one in six children in China live in poverty, as in the supposedly richest country in the world, the USA. Surely the average life expectancy of the poor is not 11 years less than that of the well-off, as it is in the UK.

Surely too the Chinese are unlikely to become as decadent as the West any time soon and, one hopes, they do not have the appetite for war that has punctuated the history of England and later its now staunch ally the US.

Still, given time, no doubt the Chinese will become as corrupt and incompetent as we are in the West.

For example, obsession with growth has led to the building of whole cities of empty high-rise apartment blocks that few can afford, suggesting China's growth will slow and plateau ere long, in part because wages will gradually increase, reducing its competitive advantage in manufacturing.

As for Australia, as far back as 2007, Tim Colebatch, economics editor for the Melbourne 'Age' newspaper said that the average household could no longer afford the average home, suggesting that tax breaks such as 'negative gearing' which helped subsidize property investors be phased out.

This then, is another example of how things are stacked in favour of big biz so that the rich get richer and the poor get poorer, a process on the verge of having gone too far for the community at large to tolerate in some countries such as the USA and, to a lesser extent, Australia.

Australian author David Williamson summed up the behaviour of highly overpaid CEOs nicely with:

"Once you're on top the last thing on your mind is the long-term survival of your firm and the care of its employees. The thing to do is slash and burn and get the share price up temporarily by cost-cutting measures made at considerable human cost, then getting the resulting bonuses you've built into your already huge package, before the firm you've gutted falls to pieces. By that time you'll have a golden handshake and be off to another corporate trough."

[8] Big Business

Chapter 9

HIERARCHICAL ORGANIZATIONS

> *I'm the boss. I'm allowed to yell.*
> Ivan Boesky, q. in *Den of* Thieves, James B Stewart, 1991.
>
> *In every one of those little stucco boxes there's some poor bastard*
> *who's never free except when he's fast asleep*
> *and dreaming that he's got the boss down the bottom*
> *of a well and is bunging lumps of coal at him.*
> George Orwell, *Coming Up For Air,* part 1, ch. 2 (1939).

The origins of hierarchy

Historically, almost all armies have been hierarchical organizations, even in the newest and most democratic nations.

Armies that were not hierarchical suffered a similar fate to that of the ancient Britons under Boadicea, their great female warrior leader.

According to Hilmer and Donaldson (1996):

The tightly disciplined Roman legions under their hierarchical command structure faced the vastly larger British horde. The British were fighting on their home ground for the independence of their island. They were enthusiastic but lacked hierarchy and organization. In the ensuing rout, most British casualties were sustained through Britons being crushed to death in their confusion. The only way to successfully defeat an aggressive invader who is organized hierarchically is to organize one's own defense forces into a hierarchy for clear command and control.

The smallest organizations require only two levels, one or two leaders, and the rest of the group, examples being ancient tribes with a tribal leader and a witch doctor, and families with two parents managing their children.

The need for hierarchies is most evident, of course, in large organizations so that political parties have a few levels in their hierarchical structure, whilst large multinational businesses may have several levels of hierarchy.

Corporate structure

Corporate structure is the hierarchical structure and communication channels giving rise to the chain of command and response in a company or organization.

Most companies have a functional structure, larger companies having a divisional structure, with a functional structure for each division, as in the example of Figure 9.1.

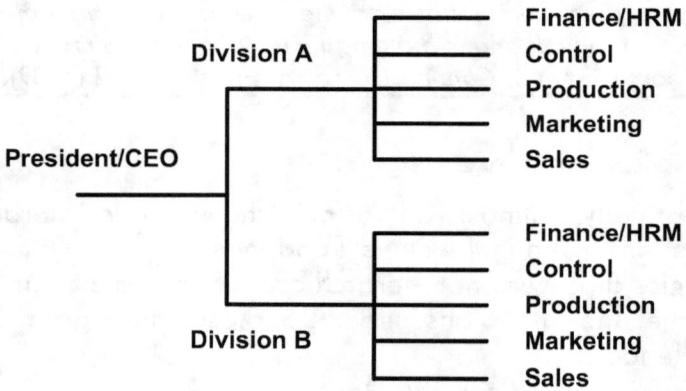

Figure 9.1. Divisional corporate structure.

The Peter Principle

Dr Laurence Peter drew on his experiences in the education sector to try and explain why we always seem to have lousy leaders (Peter & Hull, 1969). The result was his *Peter Principle:*

In a hierarchy every employee tends to rise to his own level of incompetence.

In other words, *the sour cream rises.*

A corollary is: *In time every post tends to be occupied by an employee who is incompetent to carry out his duties.*

In his often tongue-in-cheek book Peter gives a few excellent historical examples of his celebrated principle, including:

(a) Socrates was a brilliant philosopher but a lousy defence attorney.

(b) Hitler was a brilliant politician but a lousy general.

Mohr's Law of Hierarchies

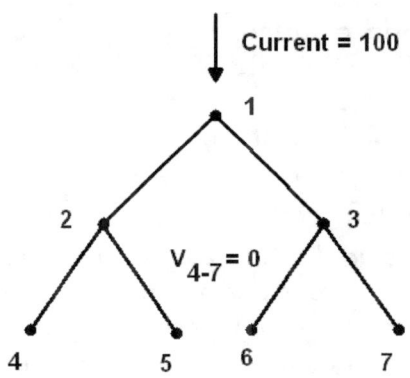

Figure 9.2. Hierarchical network.

This can illustrated by the small (hierarchical) DC network shown in Figure 9.2 which can be modeled as a DC network using a simple Finite Element Method program (Mohr, 1992, 2012a, 2018b).

At node 1 we have the pyramid building and lunatic 'boss' and a current 'load' of 100 is input. This is done by specifying the voltage at node 1 as 100, this being equivalent to adding a 'load' to the network.

Then zero datum voltage is specified at nodes 4-7 and unit resistance is given to all 6 elements so that the results from the program are:

Voltage 75 at node 1.
Voltage 25 at nodes 2 and 3.
Zero voltage at nodes 4 to 7.
Currents 50 in the top two elements and 25 in the rest.

This illustrates what the 'econobabble' of economists and politicians calls 'the trickledown effect', that is, the boss of this very small hierarchy has 3 times the voltage (or power, money and status) of his subordinates (the front line managers) one rung below. The workers at the bottom have no status at all.

If we add a further bottom row of 8 nodes in Figure 9.2 then now the 'voltage hierarchy' is 87.5, 37.5, 12.5, 0 so that the boss now does 7 times as well as the 'front line managers' on the row above the bottom row.

Then if we add a further fifth row of 16 nodes the voltage hierarchy is 93.75, 43.75, 18.75, 6.25, 0 and the boss does 15 times as well as the front line managers and infinitely better than the workers at the bottom!

The latter 'voltage hierarchy' is the fundamental principle of modern management, leading to Mohr's Law of Hierarchies:

In hierarchical organizations the amount of real material-producing work people do is inversely proportional to their rank or level in the organization.
The amount of compensation they receive, however, is proportional to their level, sometimes to an exponential degree.

For such people their earnings might be expressed as an exponential function: $\$ = C \exp(kR)$

where $\$$ = salary, R = rank, and C and k are constants.

This, of course, is not fair at all.

In ancient times philosophers felt that nobody should be paid more than about 10 or 20 times as much as anybody else, and even that is a great difference, of course, but it might be justified in the case of an elected national leader who must be able to present a strong, powerful image and might have only a relatively short term in office.

In the case of big business, however, things have got out of hand and remuneration of CEOs is often tens of millions, on top of which they get huge share issues as annual bonuses, huge 'golden handshakes' when they retire, and gigantic 'golden parachutes' then the company collapses.

To add insult to the injury of poverty, the worker-slaves endure 'top-down one-way' (TDOW) communication as they did all through their long years at school, in other words, they are treated like shit.

This is grossly unjust as the poor peasants who work on farms, in factories or on building sites produce what is essential to human life, that is, food, clothing, housing etc.

So those posters often seen in the USSR decades ago which pictured the workers as heroic perhaps made some sense. Then, of course, the hammer and sickle on their flag was also symbolic of the importance of the workers.

So the bottom line is that we have to create fairer societies which have real or *direct democracy* and leaders who 'check their ego at the door'. In these, greed, hunger, famine, war and other evils will not be tolerated by the people.

Power corrupts

As figure 9.2 illustrates, the higher up you are in a hierarchy the more 'power' you have, which might be stated symbolically as:

$$P = C R^n$$

where P = power, R = rank, and C and n are constants.

Assuming the value of n is 2 then when one is twice as high in the hierarchy one has four times as much power.

Then, as we all know, power corrupts, one of the major factors in mankind's endless history of conflict.

As noted in the previous section, salaries may increase exponentially in hierarchical organizations and this result can be related to Mohr's Law of Capitalism which is the exponential growth law of money ($) with time (T):

$$d(\$)/d(T) = c_1(\text{activity}) \quad \text{where} \quad \text{activity} = c_2 \$$$

Here the rate at which money is made is proportional to the rate of business activity, this in turn proportional to the amount of money available to fund this activity.

Combining the two constants above as $k = c_1 c_2$ we have

$d(\$)/d(T) = k\$$ where k is the *growth factor*.

where $\$$ = money made.

This last equation is *separable* which means that it can be integrated in the form

Integral [$d(\$)/\$$] = Integral [$k\,d(T)$]

giving, with the inclusion of the initial values, the exponential growth law $\$/\$_0 = \exp[k(T - T_0]$

If, for example, the growth factor is 10% per year, that is k = 0.1, then over 10 years we obtain the growth ratio $\$/\$_0 = 2.7$, so that we have nearly *tripled* our money.

The only real beneficiaries, however, are those higher in the hierarchy. The workers at the bottom who do all the *real work* (sitting and raving at sometimes boozy board meetings is not hard work) can't usually save any money and thus are slaves to all intents and purposes.

This is an intolerable situation and the CEOs who earn 'megabucks' are, of course, corrupt, and such corruption has always sown the seeds of discontent that have always, sooner or later, ended up as revolutions.

Thus socialism tends to be ruled by a single dictator, but capitalism by a multiplicity of petty dictators:

> *Capitalism tends to produce a multiplicity of petty dictators each in command of his own little business kingdom. State Socialism tends to produce a single, centralized totalitarian dictatorship, wielding absolute authority . . . through a hierarchy of bureaucratic agents.*
> Aldous Huxley, *Ends and Means* (1937).

Politicians too are often corrupt, of course, often being found to take bribes from big business.

Monarchs and dictators, of course, have nearly always been the greediest of all. Not only do they help themselves to plenty of money and live in grand palaces, but throughout history their hunger for power and thence territorial gain has led to one war after another.

Conflicts in society

Societies have a hierarchical structure, of course, English society, for example, still being regarded as having an upper class (the rich), a middle class, and a lower class of the poorest people.

Throughout history the oppressed people in the lower classes have often become discontented and revolted, an example in ancient times being the revolt of the slaves led by Spartacus, examples in more recent times being the Russian and Cuban revolutions.

On a smaller scale, in modern so-called democratic societies unions are often in dispute with companies and sometimes governments over grievances over pay and conditions, occasionally this leading to conflict. In extreme cases, indeed, national strikes sometimes occur, often resulting in the army being called out to quell the violence that often occurs during these.

In society there are many other organizations with special causes, for examples The Green and Gay movements, and such organizations often organize large demonstrations that sometimes result in conflict with police called to attend them.

Terrorist organizations

When external parties initiate conflict with cities or nations, of course, things happen on a grand scale.

Sometimes, indeed, the initial conflict may be on a very small scale yet result in a massive response, the assassination of Archduke Ferdinand of Austria being one of the causes of World War 1.

Terrorism, of course, has always been a weapon of revolutionaries, WordWeb 6 defining terrorism as:

The calculated use of violence (or the threat of violence) against civilians in order to attain goals that are political or religious or ideological in nature; this is done through intimidation or coercion or instilling fear.

Modern examples spring readily to mind, particularly the decades of conflict in Ireland between Protestants and Catholics, and the IRA's (established in 1919) decades of paramilitary operations aimed at ending British influence in Northern Ireland.

Currently, however, Muslim terrorism affects many countries still, the al-Qa'ida organization being the best known Muslim terrorist group.

In such groups hidden leaders like Osama Bin Laden operated through a hierarchical structure beginning with a couple of trusted 'lieutenants' (Kawahiri and Zawahiri in al-Qa'ida in the 1990s) and ranging through to those in command of training camps and those selected to lead particular teams for larger scale attacks such as the 9/11 attacks in the USA.

Here, as always, the second quotation that heads this chapter rings true, Bin Laden being in hiding in Afghanistan when the 9/11 operation was carried out, and George Bush being far away in Washington when he responded by taking over Iraq.

How hierarchies operate

Hierarchies operate through a chain of command, leaders meeting with a chosen few top-level executives responsible for overseeing the various operations of the organization. In the case of government, for example, there are ministers for defence, treasury, education, health, and so forth.

In each of these areas there is a permanent and hierarchical bureaucratic department with several levels of seniority ranging from head of the organization and department heads to front-line managers who manage teams of workers.

Through the whole chain of command there is an implicit level of intimidation and fear that usually makes sure that everybody does as they are told. At the front line, however, things often get ridiculous, for example the traditional screaming of army sergeants at their miserable subordinates.

Bullying is said to be a "learned behavior", and the army is a good example of a place where it is taught.

It is through such bullying and intimidation, of course, that soldiers are brainwashed into following orders without question or delay, essentially becoming expendable slaves to satisfy the whims of their leaders. Don't worry about 'executive stress,' therefore, worry about 'slave-stress.'

Indeed, our many sports with a relationship to conflict, for example absurd rugby with its 'charge at the enemy' no matter what the risk of injury, or archery and rifle shooting, all relate to our historical predilection for conflict.

Throughout hierarchies there is, of course, ambition to rise, often leading to a good deal of competitive behaviour, much of it often downright dishonest and unfair. In politics, for example, plenty of 'backstabbing' goes on day in and day out.

This corresponds quite closely, perhaps, with the alpha-male behaviour seen in several animal species, notably our close relatives, gorillas. The result is, of course, that those who end up as leaders may well be the most rotten people in the organization and, indeed, historically in both government and business this has always proved to be the case to some extent at least. That is, leaders are always greedy and bossy to some extent at least, but often they are exceptionally so.

Within hierarchical organizations there is also conflict, particularly over the 'rat race' involved in rising in the hierarchy.

Indeed, often ambitious, driven people are psychopathic, the pathology of their condition involving lying, cheating, aggressiveness, and bullying to get to the top.

Given power, it seems, they become psychotic with dreams of greater wealth and power and thus superiority. Alexander the Great, for example, began to think that he must be divine.

The problem is that, being people who have proved themselves good at the 'rat race', they tend to be the worst leaders, exactly in accordance with the Peter Principle.

Not only that, power not only corrupts, it makes people vain, self-centred, neurotic, obsessive, and, basically, mad. Here we must hasten to note Mohr's 10th Law, that is, that things such as madness must be judged on a scale of 1 to 10, not merely as a true-or-false judgment.

Furthermore, we like to make the important distinction between *bad mad* (depression etc.) and *sad mad* (Mohr, 2018b; Mohr, 2018c; Mohr, 2018d; Mohr et al., 2018b), and all too often political leaders have been bad mad, for example Nero and Hitler.

In 1980, Canadian clinical psychologist Dr Robert Hare, who worked in prisons, released the first version of the Hare checklist for identifying psychopaths, and several further versions followed.

As shown in Table 9.1, it divides 20 personality traits into four groups: interpersonal, affective, lifestyle, and antisocial, these measuring traits including charm, propensity to lie, lack of remorse, and need for stimulation.

After an interview each trait is scored as 0 (not present), 1 (present but not dominant), or 2 (dominant), so that the maximum possible score is 40.

Average people score from 3 to 6, non-psychopathic criminals score from 16 to 22, whilst in the UK and US respectively, scores of >25 and >30 are taken as a positive diagnosis of psychopathy (Gillespie, 2017).

Their total score of 12 seemed too low, as both seemed at least somewhat psychopathic, suggesting that Table 9.1 might apply more to hardened criminals for which item 17 relates to a form of 'treatment', namely continued imprisonment, presumably because of little or no sign of rehabilitation or remorse. Similarly, items 16 and 19 relate to past history.

Thus criteria for judging a bad boss should include:

➤ Bossiness.

➤ Assertiveness.

➤ Dishonesty and lying.

➤ Selfishness and greed.

➤ Vanity.

➤ Bullying.

Diagnosing psychopaths

Table 9.1. The Hare checklist for psychopaths.

	TRAIT	SCORE
	Facet 1: Interpersonal	
1	Glibness or superficial charm	1
2	Grandiose sense of self-worth	1
3	Pathological lying	2
4	Cunning or manipulative	1
	Facet 2: Affective	
5	Lack of remorse or guilt	1
6	Emotionally shallow	1
7	Callous or lack of empathy	1
8	Failure to accept responsibility for their own actions	1
	Facet 3: Lifestyle	
9	Need for stimulation (easily bored)	1
10	Parasitic lifestyle	1
11	Lack of realistic, long-term goals	0
12	Impulsivity	1
13	Irresponsibility	0
	Facet 4: Antisocial	
14	Poor behavioural controls	0
15	Early behavioural problems	0
16	Juvenile delinquency	0
17	History of conditional prison release being revoked	0
18	Criminal versatility	0
	Other traits:	
19	Many short-term marital relationships	0
20	Promiscuous sexual behaviour	0
TOTAL SCORE		**12**

In Table 9.1 the first author has scored 2 bad bosses he once had, both of whom were too young and inexperienced for being HOD, and played a major role in destroying his promising University career when he was less than 40.

Dealing with psychopaths

Gillespie (2017) suggests that organizations which are run using 'Management by Objectives' (MBO) are conducive to psychopathic bosses:

"The only way for a psychopath to succeed in a structure based on MBO would be to fall in with the objectives of his team and his superiors. Anything else would mark him out for removal from the organization."

Alternatively, Gillespie suggests that persons deemed to be psychopaths can be got rid of by getting them 'fired', but this, of course, is very difficult to bring about when the only person in the part of the organization in question able to do firing is a psychopathic boss, as is often the case.

When you do go above his or her head seeking to get them fired they counterattack, usually resulting in the person or persons complaining being disciplined or fired.

Most workers, therefore, simply have to endure bad and mad bosses and a 2016 study of Australian workplaces with "toxic leaders" concluded that the following strategies were unwise (Gillespie, 2017):

➢ Confronting the leader.

➢ Avoiding, ignoring or bypassing the boss.

➢ Whistleblowing.

➢ Worrying to excess about the boss.

➢ Continued anger and frustration.

➢ Focusing on work to try and forget about the boss.

➢ Taking sick leave (giving only short-term relief).

Instead, Gillespie says one should behave as a polite and compliant employee and do whatever one is told, no matter how much one dislikes it.

Then to survive in this way one should also:

➤ Think about a future, better job.

➤ Make sure your fellow workers don't 'tell' on each other.

➤ Check the accuracy of what the boss says.

➤ Don't show any anger and frustration.

➤ Build a support network.

➤ Document every bad thing the boss does, noting the time, date and names of any witnesses.

In this way one can survive for the medium term, at least, and perhaps build a case against the bad boss that might result in him being disciplined, demoted or shifted sideways, or even fired.

The bottom line, of course, is that there is a lesson to be learnt by any reader from this, that is, if having problems with a bad boss, give plenty of thought and get as much help as needed to deal with the problem and, hopefully, resolve it somehow, whether that help is simply support from one or two other staff members, or help from people above the bad boss in the hierarchy, and, if need be, lawyers.

Conclusion

Hierarchies are difficult to deal with over the long term.

When one is young, and not long out of the education system, they are simply a learning experience at first. Over time, however, grudges over being treated badly, and impatience over lack of promotion, grow and grow to the point at which getting another job may seem the only hope of improving one's life and career prospects.

If one has a psychopathic 'bastard boss', however, it may be impossible to get a halfway supportive reference from them, without which getting a decent job, or any job at all in line with your abilities, qualifications and experience, may prove difficult.

Some of the concepts and suggestions made in the foregoing chapter may be of some help, however, to workers with bad bass problems.

Primarily, of course, one needs at least one or two helpers within the organization in question. A problem here is that the workers at the same level in the hierarchy are also competing for the same promotion that you are. Thus, if you are in a group of, say, 10 seeking promotion to 'Senior xyz', then one might establish a mutually supportive relationship with just one of them, hoping that you will both be the next two workers promoted.

With the recent rise of the ME TO movement, bullying in the workplace has, like sexual abuse in the Catholic Church, become a prominent issue.

In dealing with a bad boss it helps to:

➢ Identify any psychopathic behaviours of the boss.
➢ Try to speak carefully to the boss about the problems, perhaps with a friend or colleague to back you up.
➢ Get as much as possible from the bad boss in writing.
➢ Consider recording bad behaviour somehow.
➢ Ask advice from friends and family about any problems.
➢ Go above the bad boss in the hierarchy about problems.
➢ Speak to counselors and perhaps lawyers about problems.
➢ Consider using a simple 'person scaling' survey of fellow workers to get a 'rating' of the bad boss which might then be given to people higher in the hierarchy.

The bottom line, however, is that when one suffers bullying, threats etc. from bad bosses, one should make careful records of such behaviour and seek help in dealing with the issue, being careful to behave at a professional and courteous manner at all times, hoping not to exacerbate the situation, but to resolve it as well as possible, and to the benefit of all parties.

Chapter 10

WAR AND TERRORISM

> *The broad mass of a nation . . . will more easily fall victim*
> *to a big lie than a small one.*
> Adolph Hitler, *Mein Kampf* (1933), ch. 10.
>
> *All wars are planned by old men*
> *in council rooms apart.*
> Grantland Rice, *Two Sides of War* (1955).

Warmongers

When Adolph Hitler came to power in Germany in 1933, the book *Why War?* by Albert Einstein and Sigmund Freud, the world's two most famous living Jews, was thrown on the Berlin book bonfire along with Einstein's other books. Four of Freud's five sisters were to die in the death camps by the end of World War II (Cornwell, 2003).

> *In Germany they came first for the Communists,*
> *and I didn't speak up because I wasn't a Communist.*
> *Then they came for the Jews,*
> *and I didn't speak up because I wasn't a Jew.*
> *Then they came for the trade unionists,*
> *and I didn't speak up because I wasn't a trade unionist.*
> *Then they came for the Catholics,*
> *and I didn't speak up because I was a Protestant.*
> *Then they came for me*
> *and by that time no one was left to speak up.*
> Martin Niemoeller, attributed.

That Hitler was a bit cranky was witnessed on one occasion by the famous pioneer of thoracic surgery Ferdinand Saerbruch. He had been summoned by Hitler so that he could be sent to attend to the Turkish Minister for Foreign Affairs who was seriously ill (Sauerbruch, 1953).

Having earlier been warned about Hitler's temper, Sauerbruch was taken to a large room to wait for Hitler who arrived preceded by an enormous dog which bounded towards Sauerbruch.

Used to dogs, Sauerbruch stood stock still and spoke soothingly to the dog. Hitler threw a colossal tantrum on account of the dog's lack of aggression which lasted several minutes and threatened to have Sauerbruch arrested but Sauerbruch, as he had done with the dog, managed to calm Hitler down.

There are those, admittedly few, who viewed Winston Spencer Churchill too as something of a warmonger. Educated for the military at Sandhurst, there is no doubt that Churchill enjoyed a fight whether in the army or in parliament (Churchill, 1959).

A consummate writer, Churchill could easily craft a speech to persuade a nation at the worst of times:

> *The sufferings of a people or class may be intolerable,*
> *but before they will take up arms and risk their lives*
> *some unselfish and impersonal spirit must animate them.*
> *In countries where there is education and mental activity or*
> *refinement, this high motive is found in the pride of glorious*
> *traditions or in a keen sympathy with surrounding misery.*
> Churchill WS, *Churchill In His Own Words,*
> Capricorn Books, New York (1966)

The latter part of this statement, however, is in accord with the verse by Kipling given in Chapter Five and referring to the 'White Man's burden' to colonize heathen nations and lift them to civilized standards. As we noted there, this was also good for business and the European colonizers also plundered the nations they took over (Cowie at al., 1994).

Perhaps the key words in this statement are *glorious traditions* for indeed there can be no nation in history with a longer and bloodier history of war, one which they may have inherited from the occupying Romans almost two thousand years ago, and also the Normans nearly a thousand years ago.

Military training

Nowhere is brainwashing used more extensively than in military training. The constant marching to the screaming of sergeants is conditioning the troops for total obedience so that, when the time comes, they will unhesitatingly leap into action without thinking of the risks to themselves.

Perhaps the most extreme example of brainwashing, however, is that of children selected and brainwashed by the CIA to act as agents (Hersha et al., 2001).

Electric shock and drugs were used to condition them to carry out orders. In one training drill a small group of children were strapped to wired chairs and subjected to electric shocks which they could avoid if they pressed a button that would administer shocks to the other members of the group instead.

Though only in their early teens, the girls were trained to use sex as a weapon. The tactic they were taught was to go to bed with a man and slip some poison into his drink during the evening.

Military intelligence

Nations have had military spies and information or intelligence gatherers since Roman times, if not before. The 'spook' business is not as glamorous as in the movies and can be sordid and messy (Doyle, 2000).

A case in point would be the 'Cambridge four' of Philby, Blunt, Maclean and Burgess recruited by the KGB in the early 1930s. No doubt they helped Stalin win World War II hands down (Philby R et al., 2000).[1]

---

[1] Philby's information emboldened Stalin prior to the crucial Yalta conference. He also helped thwart a number of covert CIA-SIS Cold War operations against the USSR, for example that in Albania in 1949.

Stalin was also helped by a group of Soviet Jews code named MAX which fed the Germans the lie that, around the time of the battle of Stalingrad, the Russians were weakening. Nothing could be further from the truth and the Russians dropped powdered Tularemia bacillus on the unsuspecting Panzer divisions in Stalingrad, an act that may have been the decisive turning point in the war (Alibek, 1999).

One of the greatest intelligence blunders of all time was the FBI in the USA ignoring several intercepted signals during 1941 that suggested the Japanese might attack Pearl Harbour (Hughes-Wilson, 1999).

Still recovering from the Great Depression which nearly destroyed the Union, the USA had no 'overseas' intelligence organization at that time.

In more recent times the Weapons of Mass destruction fiasco leading up to the Iraq invasion of 2003 was, perhaps, not so much an error but an excellent example of brainwashing the public into accepting the necessity for yet another war. This was done with repetitive showing in the media of a picture of Sadam Hussein holding a rifle.

The same sort of negative imagery is used in the TV documentaries and print articles about Hitler that still appear every week or so. 'War begets war' it is said and the authors are of the view that such propaganda is brainwashing to keep us willing to accept the possibility of war against anyone our government chooses to declare an enemy and denigrate heavily prior to war. We, the brainwashed public, will associate the new villain shown with Hitler and agree that he must be dealt with.

On military intelligence, however, there is no doubt that the allies were well aware of Hitler's treatment of the Jews both before and early in WWII. Much more could have been done to liberate people from the death camps but it would have been sound military policy to let Hitler continue to devote resources to decimating his own population.

The brutal realities of war

War has always been a brutal affair. The Romans crucified captured enemy soldiers in droves. Mass graves have been discovered after many wars and the Nazi Holocaust of WWII was the most spectacular instance of genocide in human history, though Stalin's purges may have killed just as many people, if not more.

During the religious based conflict in the former Yugoslavia a journalist visited a death camp in Bosnia and wrote (Silber & Little, 1996):

The men are at various stages of human decay and affliction, the bones of their elbows and wrists protrude like pieces of jagged stone from the pencil thin stalks to which their arms have been reduced.

There is nothing quite like the sight of the prisoner desperate to talk and to convey some terrible truth that is so near yet so far, but who dares not. Their stares burn, they speak only with their terrified silence and eyes inflamed with the articulation of stark, undiluted, desolate fear-without-hope.

In 1987 the first author had the misfortune to meet Shaun Carew at the 'Espy', a famous hotel in Melbourne's St Kilda suburb. Proudly Celtic, he served in the British Army's campaign against the red peril in Malaysia circa 1951, remembering 2 sentries on guard duty having to sit backs to either side of a tree in fear of communist guerrillas. He had a terrible temper easily ignited by anyone saying the wrong thing and some attributed this to a steel plate in his head, a result of war service. In one bad mood, for example, he tried to rebreak a kneecap the first author had broken tripping and then cartwheeling 20+ feet down a two-story flight of airport stairs and landing heavily on one knee.

War and big business

War is an essential part of capitalism and can only be abolished by changing the present social system. This is the task which history has assigned to all those who suffer most by war.
George Padmore, *Africa and World Peace* (1937).

135

Table 10.1. US & Soviet Nuclear Armaments (Bethe, 1991).

	US	USSR
Delivery vehicles		
ICBMs (intercontinental ballistic missiles)	1,050	1,400
SLBMs (submarine launched missiles)	630	950
Bombers	350	140
Total	2,030	2,490
Warheads		
ICBMS	2,150-2,250	5,500-6,400
SLBMs	4,750	1,750-1,900
Bombers	2,500-3,500	280-550
Total	9,400-10,500	7,530-8,850
Equivalent megatons		
ICBMs	1,300	5,900
SLBMs	800	1,200
Bombers	3,500	900
Total	5,600	8,000

War and big business go hand in hand. The arms trade is the world's largest (Sampson, 1977; Pringle & Spigelman, 1981) and, as a result, large tracts of land in several parts of the world remain littered with land mines which continue to maim innocent people.

The arms race of the cold war was certainly one of the best examples of Keynes' view that war was like digging a hole and pouring money into it. The staggering number of nuclear missiles (see Table 10.1) accumulated by the USSR and USA, along with of large stockpiles of biological weapons, was one of the greatest acts of insanity in history.

Note that, in Table 10.1, 2 megatons = 1.59 equivalent megatons. The latter is the best measure of the area that can be destroyed, whereas megaton is the best measure of fallout.

Had that money been spent helping educate and thence control population growth in the poorest parts of the world the outlook for the human race would not be as bleak as it is.

That humans devote so much time to accumulating weapons of war is great insanity and those responsible should be brought to justice and, of course, we need to make nuclear and biochemical weapons illegal.

For the companies that manufacture arms war is good for business, of course, including modern cold war or 'rocket rattling'.

The punched card system of recording data was invented in Germany by Herman Hollerith in the late 19th century. By the 1930s, however, IBM controlled about 90% of the world's market in punch cards and sorters.

At that time the CEO of IBM was the unscrupulous Thomas Watson who happily agreed to take on the task of accumulating data on all the Jews in Germany (Black, 2001). For the purpose he gathered together a number of IBM subsidiaries in Germany under the name Dehomag and in 1933 one-half million census takers went door to door gathering information to fill out questionnaires on each household in the country. The information included the religion of the head of the household and whether the person was in a mixed marriage.

IBM continued to work for Hitler throughout WWII, as did a few other US companies such as Du Pont who provided chemicals used to gas Jews.

Terrorism

The term global terrorism is the catch cry of many leaders around the world to the point that it is becoming very boring. Terrorism is the weapon of the revolutionary, of course, whereby small groups of people can disrupt governments with far larger armies at their disposal.

Religious based terrorism was discussed in the preceding chapter and this is ethnic conflict, more often than not between sects within the same country or region thereof.

The purpose of terrorism with a religious pretext is not always clear. The grievance of the Palestinians at having lost most of the land that was called British Palestine in the 1930s is readily understandable.

In Northern Ireland the situation is much less clear. The media make only the obvious clear, as always, in this instance that the conflict is between the Protestants and Catholics. They do not reveal the reason, namely that the originally Catholic north of Ireland was annexed by the British about two centuries ago. The Catholics, therefore, simply wanted removal of British control of the country which was, until relatively recently, administered from London. The Protestants, some of whom had migrated to Northern Ireland as part of the British occupation, were naturally seen as the enemy and therefore made a target of ongoing terrorism (Hollingsworth & Fielding, 1999).

The French revolution disposed of the monarchy and had a socialist basis. So did the 1917 Russian revolution. The revolutions in China in 1947 and Cuba in 1959 also had a socialist aim.

As Fidel Castro put it:
Revolution is not a bed of roses,
it is a struggle to death between the future and the past.

Castro was of such concern to the US that no less than 30 attempts were made on his life during the 1960s.

The Russian Revolution, on the other hand, had the powers that be in the UK and US even more concerned and the British secret service provided considerable covert support to the White Russian army resisting the revolution. When that failed they began counter terrorist activities against the new Russia, for example Lieutenant Agar's sinking of the Red Fleet cruiser Oleg in Kronstadt Harbour in 1919 (Brook-Shepherd, 1998).

It seems certain, therefore, that Hitler's socialist Nazi party would also have been a matter of concern to the UK and US governments. One cannot help wonder, therefore, whether England found Hitler's invasion of Poland an excellent excuse to go to war with them. After all, much more time could have been allowed to try and seek a diplomatic solution.

It is true, however, that Hitler had publicly declared considerable territorial ambitions years earlier and, perhaps, the anti-socialist motive was just a part of England's willingness to war with Germany.

As with the question of why the allies did nothing about the concentration camps, we may never know the answer.

As the US politician and reformer Hiram Johnson put it in a speech to the US Senate in 1917:

The first casualty of war is the truth.

This is especially true of terrorism where just a few malcontents can foment hatred and prejudice. Whether they claim to be fighting for a supposedly religious cause, or for a political ideal such as socialism, one cannot always be sure that their real motive is not simply power, to which end they inveigle others to do their dirty work for them.

Biological warfare

Biological warfare dates back to Roman times when dead soldiers were thrown into the water supplies of cities under attack.

In modern times the Russians dropped tularemia on the unsuspecting German Panzer divisions freezing on the outskirts of Stalingrad during WWII, bringing them to a virtual standstill for some time (Alibek, 2000).

Before that the Japanese used biological weapons on the Chinese during the 1930s. During air raids they dropped porcelain canisters of fleas infected with plague and other primitive biological weapons and killed thousands of Chinese in rural areas of Manchuria (Alibek, 2000).

Iraq had a modest BW research program and in the late 1980s Sadam Hussein used primitive BW material such as mustard gas on the Kurds in Northern Iraq. In the Middle East, Israel and other Arab counties such as Syria are also thought to have engaged in BW weapons research.

In 1995 the religious cult Aum Shinrikyo released sarin nerve gas in the Tokyo subway (Lifton, 1999), killing 12 people and injuring 5,500.

Table 10.2. Soviet BW facilities (Alibek, 2000).

Location	Nature of facility
Almaty	BW research [reserve for times of war]
Aralsk	testing grounds
Berdsk	BW research and production [reserve]
Golitsino	BW research
Irkutsk	BW research
Kirisi	unspecified
Kirov	BW research and production
Koltsovo	BW research
Kubinka	unspecified
Kurgan	[reserve]
Leningrad	BW research
Lyubuchany	BW research
Minsk	BW research
Moscow	10 BW research, 5 unspecified
Nukus	testing grounds
Obolensk	BW research
Omutninsk	BW research and production [reserve]
Otar	BW research, testing grounds
Panza	war mobilization
Pokrov	BW production [reserve]
Rebirth Island	testing grounds
Reutov	storage
Saratov	unspecified
Sergiyeb Posad	BW research and production
Shikhany	testing grounds
Stalingrad	BW research
Stepnogorsk	BW production [reserve]
Stritzhi	BW research and production
Sverdlovsk	BW research and production
Tashkent	BW research
Vilnius	unspecified
Vladimir	BW research
Vladivostok	BW research
Yoshkar-Ola	unspecified
Zima	storage

The USSR had an enormous BW research program with many research centres and storage facilities (see Table 10.2).

Table 10.3. Soviet & US peak BW agent production levels in metric tons per year (Miller et al., 2001).

Agent	USA	Soviet U
staphylococcal enterotoxin B	1.9	0
tularemia	1.6	1,500
Q fever	1.1	0
anthrax	0.9	4,500
Venezuelan equine encephalitis	0.8	150
botulinum	0.2	0
bubonic plague	0	1,500
smallpox	0	100
glanders	0	2,000
Marburg	0	250

After WWII the US also implemented a large BW research program, though not nearly as extensive as that of the USSR (see Tables10.3 and 10.4). This US program was based mainly at one facility, Fort Detrick in Maryland.

Table 10.4. Other BW agents studied in Russia (Alibek, 2000).

Argentinian haemorraghic fever (Jinin)
Bolivian haemorraghic fever (Machupo)
brucellosis
dengue fever
Ebola virus
epidemic typhus
Lassa fever
Russian spring-summer encephalitis

In this frightening arsenal the haemorraghic filoviruses Ebola and Marburg are amongst the most frightening because they are highly contagious and turn all the body's organs to liquid.

At the main Russian BW research facility Vektor a scientist named Ustinov accidentally infected himself with Marburg virus. In the 15 days it took him to die a new more virulent strain developed in his bloodstream.

The Russians called this new strain Marburg Variant U and weaponized it for delivery by SS16 and SS17 rockets.

On the 6th of April 2005 *The Australian Newspaper* reported that a new outbreak of Marburg virus in Luanda, the capital of Angola, had killed 169 people. A day or two later the toll had risen to over 200 dead.

To date, however, there have been no large scale BW attacks but in December 1943 news arrived in London that Germany intended to use a pilotless plane or rocket called the V-1 to deliver biological weapons. US intelligence learnt that they intended to use botulinum and the US had already developed an antidote to botulinum. By the summer of 1944 they had manufactured 4,000 gallons of this antidote, enough to immunize 700,000 troops (Regis, 1999).

In the spring of 1944 a worried Winston Churchill asked the US to provide him with 500,000 anthrax bombs. Churchill wrote in a memorandum, *"We should regard it as a first installment."*

The Americans set up for production, aiming to produce a further 500,000 anthrax bombs for their own use. Fortunately, the task was never completed owing to the first successful atomic bomb test in July 1945 and then its use on Hiroshima in August, ending the war a month later.

That Germany, the US and UK were preparing for massive BW warfare towards the end of WWII, therefore, suggests that there is a serious risk of future BW warfare on a large scale.

The Clinton government in the US received numerous intelligence reports during the 1990s that it was "highly likely" that a terrorist group would threaten or launch a BW attack on the US within "the next few years" (Miller et al., 2001).

Well into the future, therefore, nuclear *and* biochemical warfare (NBC) will remain a threat.

Infrastructure warfare

Information warfare (IW) is another threat to which the US is particularly vulnerable and it seems likely that some of the most sophisticated 'viruses' that have been let loose on the Internet might have been produced by terrorist organizations such as al Qa'ida who have vowed to bankrupt the US.

If such organizations can disrupt the banking systems or the stock exchanges of their major opponents such as the US and UK then serious damage could be done (Adams, 1998; Alexander, 1999).

IW is, of course, only a particular form of *infrastructure warfare* and poisoning water supplies, disrupting power and oil supplies, destroying bridges and hijacking aircraft are just a few of the many alternatives open to terrorists.

September 11, of course, was a spectacular example of such warfare. That numerous anthrax letters were posted around the country, resulting in the closure for long periods of public buildings, was perhaps another. Here there was no great aim to cause loss of life but, more important perhaps, to cause panic and disruption.

Another example of 'media spin', akin to brainwashing over time, the anthrax attacks were written off as having originated locally and being of little consequence. That seems unlikely indeed and it is only a matter of time before further attacks of this kind occur.

The USA

*As long as there are sovereign nations
possessing great power, war is inevitable.*
Albert Einstein, 'Einstein on the Atomic Bomb',
Atlantic Monthly, Nov. 1945.

Nowadays the USA is often referred to as the world's only superpower. Since 1917 it has stood alongside the British in resisting socialism and protecting capitalism.

That fight began with their failed counter revolutionary activities against Russia in 1917 and continued against Hitler's socialist Nazi party in WWII. It resumed in Korea and Malaya in the early 1950s and continued in Vietnam.

Over the last 50 years covert activities have overturned numerous governments deemed undesirable in the name of democracy.

Most recently Sadam Hussein, sometimes referred to as a Marxist and a fan of Stalin, has been overthrown.

In all this the propaganda about democracy is churned out ad nauseam almost daily:

> *It is politics which begets war. Politics represents the intelligence, war merely its instrument, not the other way around. The only possible course in war is to subordinate the military viewpoint to the political.*
> Karl Marie von Clausewitz, *The War* (1883).

As we shall discuss in this book, we have only Westminster style parliamentary democracy in much of the West, not true democracy as Aristotle defined it. In the US, which is now almost a shrine to capitalism, the Republican party is run by a group of rich families including the Kennedys, Rockefellers and Bushs. Both they and the Democrats, on the other hand, rely so much on funding from big business that they can hardly be called impartial or representative of the common people.

Increasingly, thanks to a global marketplace increasingly dominated by transnational companies, this is the case in other so-called democracies as politicians are persuaded, if not bribed, to sell public assets and utilities which private operators are not prepared to invest in to expand them to meet growing demands. On the contrary, they are more interested in pruning their costs to increase their bottom line.

At present the US economy is in dire straits, in part because the greed of companies like Nike in using cheap Chinese labour in situ has seeded the growth of what looks likely to become the world's largest economy in a decade or two.

Yet China still has a socialist government, India is somewhat that way inclined, and Russia is still run in a somewhat totalitarian way. In this environment it looks likely that the US will have increasing difficulty selling its democracy message, let alone enforcing it. As Kissinger put it (1999):

Blessed by history and a benign environment, we are tempted to view our power as a dispensation and to use it to impose our preferences. Such an attitude runs the risk of being viewed as hegemonic by the rest of the world and will gradually be opposed by it. Excessive reliance on power and excessive insistence on our virtue may wind up corroding the very values in the name of which our policy is being conducted.

Like many other species, man is a territorial animal. It is only thanks to the agricultural revolution that we began to live in larger groups. Indeed, until relatively recently in history Australian aborigines and Bushmen of southern Africa were hunter-gatherers and their diet was not much dissimilar to that of chimpanzees (Weiss & Mann, 1978).

Stalin won WWII and took as much territory as Hitler had coveted. The Korean War has been called an unfinished one. The Vietnam War was comprehensively lost by the Americans. China has said it will be patient about Taiwan but expects to reclaim it eventually (Kissinger, 1999).

The enemy within

We must in one voice, cry out that we will not tolerate their stinking, murdering, lying, corrupt government.
Louis Beam, speech at the 'Rocky Mountain Rendezvous' (1992), a meeting of several far-right groups.

I suspect Americans will begin engaging in terrorism on a scale the world has never known.
William Pearce, author of *The Turner Diaries* (1978) and leader of the National Alliance, a US neo-Nazi group.

Another problem that might face the US in the future are several sectarian and religious militia groups such as the Klu Klux Klan, Aryan Nation, Posse Comitatus, The Order, and The Texas Militia (Dees, 1996; Jones & Israel, 1998; Snow, 1999).

145

The 1995 Oklahoma City bombing, in which 168 people were killed, was the most spectacular act of terrorism on US soil before the September 11 attacks. The FBI charged Timothy McVeigh and Terry Nichols with the bombing but only McVeigh was convicted. McVeigh's chief defence counselor, however, found that McVeigh and Nichols had had contacts with Aryan Nation, other people with neo-Nazi sympathies and, most interesting of all, Nicholls had been to the Philippines several times were he had been in contact with a Ramzi Yousef who in turn had had contact with Al Qa'ida and Osama Bin Laden (Jones & Israel, 1998).

Not only must the US expect further attacks from external organizations like Al Qa'ida, there is also the very real possibility of further attacks organized by one or more of its many militia groups. If these attacks were made with even small nuclear weapons or, worse still, halfway sophisticated BW agents, then yet more cracks will appear in a country already morally and economically bankrupt.

The bottom line, perhaps, is that if the West once feared and painted the USSR as some frightening kind of monster (doubtless they thought likewise of the US), then the US as the 'world's only superpower' will be seen as an enemy by many other countries and creeds who will over time wear the US down, just as the USSR was worn down not long ago.

It seems likely that the disenchanted groups within the US will play a part in that process. In addition, corrupt executives on excessive salaries will play their part in that process of decay. It would be going too far to predict a revolution in the US, but not to foresee that its days as the pre-eminent world power that it once was are numbered.

Indeed, with the US in serious economic trouble yet again, in mid 2011 it was suggested that the American dollar should be replaced as the major global currency by a basket of currencies such as the US dollar, the Yuan, the Deutschmark and the Yen.

Conclusion

An article in the August 20-21, 2011, edition of *The Weekend Australia* sums it up quite well:

"The number of worldwide terrorism attacks rose to 11,604 last year [2010], up by more than 5 per cent from the 10,969 in 2009" and "terrorism last year claimed 49,901 victims, who were killed, injured or kidnapped."

"In Afghanistan, terrorist attacks rose by 55.6 per cent last year to 3307, compared with 2125 in 2009. In Iraq, attacks rose to 2688 from 2458 the report said."

"Counter-terrorist and defence officials said al-Qa'ida remains an increasing threat to Western interests.

At present, however, much of the world is afflicted by Islamic terrorism, countries throughout the Middle East and much of Africa being terrorized by dozens of mostly Islamic terrorist organizations. Some of these, for example Islamic State (IS), now control large areas of several countries, resulting in mass migrations on a hitherto unprecedented scale. Indeed, some writers, including the present authors, now refer to this situation as *World War 3* (Mohr, Fear & Sinclair, 2015).

In this book it is suggested that the creation of the state of Israel in the UN-mandated British Protectorate of 'Palestine' in 1948 was one of the key 'seeds' of WW3. The 'seed' for the creation of that new state came with the Balfour Declaration of the 2nd of November, 1917. According to Chambers Dictionary of World History (1993) this was:

A short communication from the British Foreign Secretary, A.J. Balfour, to Lord Rothschild, expressing the British government's disposition towards a Jewish national home in Palestine.

The central portion reads: *"His Majesty's Government views with favour the establishment in Palestine of a national home for the Jewish people ... it being clearly understood that nothing shall be done which may prejudice the civil and religious rights of existing non-Jewish communities."*

Britain having received the Mandate for Palestine in 1920, the vagueness of the Balfour Declaration was clarified in 1923; Jewish immigration was to be encouraged; an appropriate Jewish body formed to that end; the rights of non-Jews were to be protected; and English, Hebrew and Arabic were to be given equal status. However, the ensuing two decades showed Britain to be either unwilling or unable to deliver its promise to the Jews, especially in view of increasing Arab hostility to Jewish immigration.

As for the issue of democracy, though the 'Cold War' is supposed to have ended circa 1990, political conflict continues between the US, in particular, and socialist states such as China and North Korea, and also Russia, which we still regard as somewhat socialist with ex-KGB man Putin having been leader for many years now.

For example, with there being current political conflict in Venezuela because of acute economic problems, the US has backed the opposition leader in his claim of being the 'new president', whilst Russia, China and Cuba back the current socialist president Maduro.

Finally, an extreme example of political BS, recently the leader of the Taliban said that:

Everyone in Afghanistan wants to live under Shariah Law.

Interviews with a few people on the street suggested that this was not the case (Deutsche Welle English News, SBS TV, 7/3/19).

The Russians having failed to defeat them, and now the Americans also, we fear that the Taliban will eventually control most, if not all, of Afghanistan, so whilst territory overtaken by ISIS has now been reclaimed in recent years, WW3 still continues.

PART 3
THE PSYCHOLOGY OF PERSUASION & CONFLICT

Chapter 11

CONDITIONING, MEMORY AND BRAINWASHING

The real persuaders are our appetites, our fears and above all our vanity. The skillful propagandist stirs and coaches these internal persuaders. Eric Hoffer, *The Passionate State of Mind* (1955).

"For your own good" is a persuasive argument that will eventually make a man agree to his own destruction.
Janet Frame, *Faces in the Water* (1961).

Introduction

The preceding chapter dealt briefly with modeling which plays a crucial part in the early learning of infants. Mention was also made of how we also instinctively use *conditioning*, for example repetitive presentation of items associated with simple skills to be learnt, often followed by praise when satisfactory progress is made.

Conditioning is a fundamental learning process but it also has applications in psychotherapy, for example behaviour modification using *aversion therapy,* and thence more sinister ones in 'brainwashing' prisoners of war or crime suspects to obtain information from them or to make them 'switch sides'.

In the modern era, however, it is more relevant to everyday life than ever as conditioning is used to some extent in advertising to repetitively expose people to a brand name. They quickly develop recognition of the brand and, before long, some degree of acceptance, if not approval.

Much of the excessively long and drawn out education process is also conditioning for obedience and routine. Military training, of course, is one of the more extreme examples of conditioning.

Some understanding of the mechanics of conditioning is therefore well worthwhile in an age when we are confronted with it almost at every turn.

Classical conditioning

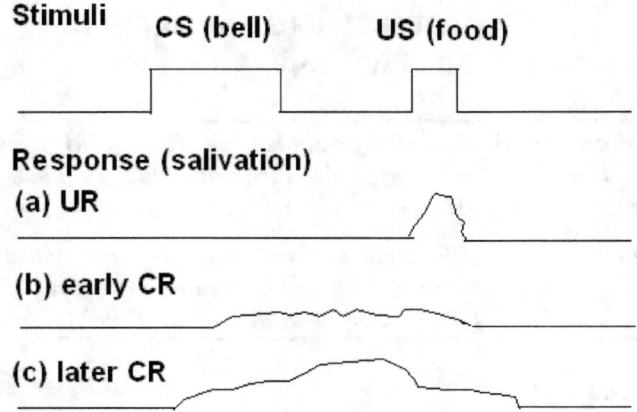

Figure 11.1. Pavlov's classical conditioning experiment:
(a) Bell precedes food presentation.
(b) Bell the only stimulus.
(c) US resumed temporarily - then only CS giving result shown.

Classical conditioning, or learning by association, was first demonstrated by Ivan Pavlov's celebrated experiments with dogs in the 1890s.

In these he noted that a caged dog's mouth salivated when it saw food on a pan swung within its reach. Here the food is the *uncontrolled stimulus* (US) and salivation is the dog's *uncontrolled reaction* (UR)

Next, a bell was rung shortly before presentation of the food and the dog's saliva collected in a cup to measure the amount. Here the bell is the *controlled stimulus* (CS).

It was found that the after a few repetitions of the paired stimuli of bell and food the dog would begin to salivate with the ringing of the bell alone, this being the *controlled reaction* (CR).

Similar results can be obtained with almost any stimulus that consistently evokes a reflex response such as electrical shock.

For example, a dog or a human given a mild shock to a leg will quickly withdraw the leg.

If the electrode giving the shocks is attached to the leg, on the other hand, flexion of the leg will occur in response to shock, the US. Then when a prior conditioned or 'neutral' stimulus is given as warning conditioned response is developed and remains after the US is removed.

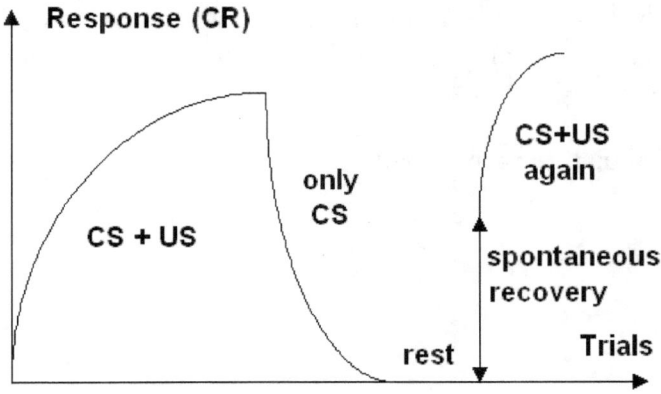

Figure 11.2. Conditioning, extinction and recovery.

After many trials the results can be graphed as a *learning curve.* Typically this takes the form shown in Figure 11.2 where the curve gradually flattens as the number of trials increases.

Here the US and CS remain paired. If the US is removed, however, *extinction* occurs and the response (the CR) decreases. Then, if the US is again added after the CS, the response recovers, the initial amount of response being called the *spontaneous recovery.*

Advertising often uses classical conditioning by repeatedly associating a product with positive ideas and images, thereby encouraging people to have positive feelings towards the product itself.

151

Operant conditioning

Operant conditioning, or learning by consequences, is characterized by the use of *reinforcement* which encourages a response in which the subject *operates* in some way, rather than just exhibiting a passive reflex response as in classical conditioning.

The classical experiments in operant conditioning were conducted in the 1940s by Skinner, a Harvard psychologist. In these he placed a rat in a box in which there was a lever that delivered food to it when pressed.

Initially the lever was operated from outside and soon the rat learnt the association between seeing the lever move and the appearance of food.

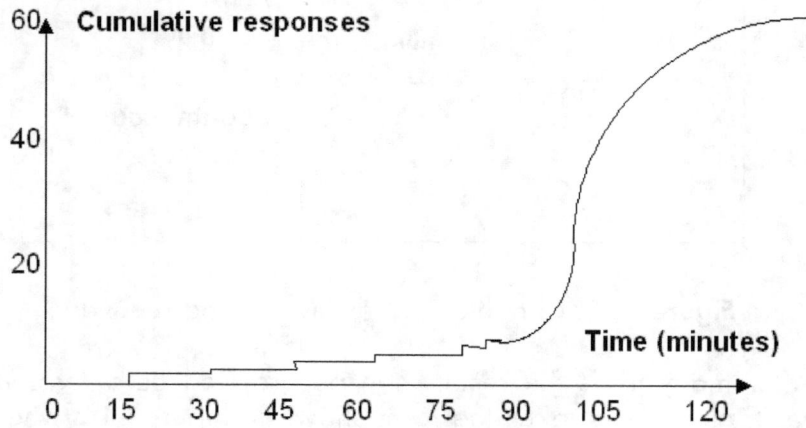

Figure 11.3. Operant conditioning responses by rat in Skinner Box. First response at 15 minutes, second at 30, third at 45, but after 75 minutes the rate of response becomes high.

After a while it operated the lever itself to obtain food and continued to do so with increasing frequency as it became more familiar with the routine, as shown in Figure 11.3.

In the result of Figure 11.3 the rat in the 'Skinner Box', as it came to be called, took 15 minutes to successfully operate the feed lever.

152

Four more intervals of about 15 minutes occurred before following operations when, the rat having fully learnt the procedure, the rate of operation accelerated markedly.

We instinctively use operant conditioning in bringing up children, the reinforcement to encourage desired actions being smiles and vocal approval.

Note that the timing of reinforcement is important. In a Skinner box, for example, the greater the time delay between the rat pressing the lever and the delivery of the food the longer it will take the rat to associate the two events and thus learn the feeding operation.

As with classical conditioning, *extinction* occurs when reinforcement ceases. This 'unlearning' process may be stronger still when *negative reinforcement*, typically some form of punishment in the educational context, is used.

Conditioned physical responses may be accompanied by emotional feelings or responses and many of our feelings are developed by conditioning.

In the case of classical conditioning *conditioned emotional responses* (CERs) may develop. Indeed, our feelings about many people and other things in our lives develop in this kind of way.

Advertising is also a case in point where an ad reminds us of a familiar product, evoking feelings of recognition and approval whilst the implications for education are all too obvious.

Generalization and discrimination

When alternative conditioned or 'signal' stimuli are used in classical conditioning the subject may learn to *discriminate* between them and respond more strongly to one than the other.

In Pavlov's classical experiments, for example, he found that dogs also responded to a buzzer as a CS instead of a bell, but less strongly.

This is called *generalization* and the more similar the alternative CS the better the response. Sometimes, however, the conditioned responses occur when a new but similar CS is used that has never been paired with the US previously.

In this way a child can develop a fear of dogs after being bitten by a black dog. It may then generalize that fear into a phobia about other harmless black objects.

When two stimuli are used but pairing of the US or 'reward' is not maintained with the second stimulus the subject develops *discrimination* and begins to learn to ignore the second stimulus.

Behaviour shaping

In operant conditioning *shaping* can be used to speed up the process. In Skinner's rat experiment, for example, shaping might begin by remote operation of the 'food lever' only when the rat gets close to it, gradually decreasing the distance of the rat from the lever before the lever is operated.

Then the lever is only operated when the rat touches the lever. Next the lever is only operated when the rat attempts to depress it.

Thus behaviour shaping involves reinforcing *successive approximations* to the desired behaviour pattern.

In this way conditioning can be accelerated and quite complex patterns of behaviour can be taught, a familiar example being circus bears that have been taught to ride bicycles in this way (Lindzey, Hall, & Thompson, 1978).

Packard (1978) reported that up to 20% of teachers in the eastern USA were systematically using behaviour modification techniques that involved systematic use of rewards and punishments in their classrooms.

Two teachers in Montana went too far by extending the 'Skinner box' idea to a four-foot high box for miscreant students. It had no lighting and no ventilation other than two small holes for observation. The relatives of a retarded child that had been locked in this box complained and the teachers were sacked.

A better example of 'behavior-shaping' was tested by University of Kansas researchers. They had the teacher divide the class into two teams, and the team which incurred fewer violations of several rules for good class behaviour was given various rewards. The researchers reported good results.

Objections to such applications of behaviour shaping are that they focused on restricting behaviours such as talking in class whereas advocates of 'open' classrooms encourage a freer learning environment.

The advent of the PC in schools, however, has brought a highly mechanized learning process, some aspects of which progressive educators are pleased with.

With the use of appropriate teaching software, PCs become a 'teaching machine' with which students can learn at their own pace and receive instant reinforcement for correct answers.

Reinforcement schedules

To this point we have assumed reinforcement, when used, was applied on a continuous basis, that is, after each response.

In operant conditioning reinforcement can also be made according to some fixed schedule. Examples include:

[1] The *fixed-ratio schedule* gives reinforcement after a certain number of responses.

[2] The *fixed-interval schedule* where reinforcement is given after a fixed interval of time, regardless of how many responses are made.

[3] In *variable-ratio* schedules reinforcement might come, for example, after three, then six responses, then three again. Similarly *variable-interval schedules* vary the time intervals between reinforcement.

Another obvious alternative is *random interval reinforcement,* that is, choosing an average interval and multiplying it by a random number between 0 and 1 produced by successive applications of a random number generator such as the RND( ) function of BASIC and other computer programming languages.

As might be expected, extinction is slower after cessation of scheduled reinforcements. This is the situation in human life where, for example, parents can only occasionally reward or punish a child's behaviour.

The result is that we may continue doing things we were shaped to do early in life long after reinforcement has ceased.

Primary and secondary reinforcement

A primary reinforcer, or unconditioned reinforcer, is effective for an untrained subject, for example food as a positive reinforcer or electric shock as a negative reinforcer.

A secondary reinforcer, or conditioned reinforcer, must be learnt by being paired with a primary reinforcer.

In a Skinner box, for example, a gong could be sounded every time the primary reinforcement of food was obtained. As in classical conditioning, the subject would associate the gong with the food and soon it would become an effective secondary reinforcer.

A better example occurs in child rearing where parents typically reward children for good behaviour with food treats or presents as primary reinforcers, accompanied by praise as secondary reinforcement. Ultimately the secondary reinforcement of praise may become the most frequently used and important form of reinforcement.

Contiguity of reinforcement, that is the time interval, is also important. The smaller the interval in time between the two reinforcements to be associated, the sooner the secondary reinforcement is learnt.

Understanding the workings of the brain

The role of chemicals

An example of the power of conditioning is cited by Packard (1978). This came about from experiments with flatworms whose brains have only about 400 cells. The worms were conditioned to "scrunch up" when seeing a light go on when this was followed by electrical shocks. It was found that when the worms were cut in half, or even several pieces, the pieces regenerated brains that remembered the conditioning.

Similar results were then obtained with various species of vertebrates.

Even more startling was the 'memory transferability' achieved by making soup of the brains of rats conditioned to shun darkness and feeding it to hamsters. The injected hamsters soon began to shun darkness!

This led before too long to the suggestion that students should eat their professors!

Later Georges Ungar and coworkers detected a peptide compound ¶ in the brain of a conditioned rat that caused it to avoid darkness.

[¶ Peptides link chains of up to thousands of amino acid molecules to form *polypeptides*. Proteins are naturally occurring polypeptides].

They pooled the brains of 4000 rats to obtain a sample of this compound large enough for analysis and synthesis of the compound (Ungar et al., 1972).

Subsequently Ungar's group reported discovering several other brain peptides that seemed to transfer learning from one animal to another (Jonas, 1974).

The role of electricity

That electrical stimuli in the brain play an important part, however, was demonstrated graphically by Jose Delgado by rigging a bull for radio-triggered mild electrical stimulation of a part of its brain (Delgado, 1971). He then stood in front of the animal. When it charged the tiny electrode in its brain was triggered and the bull stopped. After triggering the stimulation several times the bull was so pacified that it allowed witnesses of the experiment into the ring without charging them.

In humans electrodes implanted in the brain have been found to cause recall of long forgotten memories.

It has been found that the speed of conduction of impulses or *action potentials* in nerves is approximately proportional to the square root of the fibre diameter, a result familiar in cable theory (Schmidt-Nielsen, 1979). In myelin coated axons, however, the conduction speed is approximately proportional to the fibre diameter.

The 'strength' of memories

Memory storage is sometimes so effective and indelible that sometimes we can't forget things we would like to such as bad habits.

Sometimes *motivated forgetting* suppresses memories of traumatic experiences but this generally occurs subconsciously and we are not able to control the repression process at will.

One clue is that when we do consciously forget certain things we quickly dismiss them from our thoughts as soon as they enter them. When happier thoughts cross our minds, on the other hand, they may linger a little longer and almost involve a euphoria comparable to that which might be induced by small doses of tranquilizers like alcohol.

In other words we use processes like elaborative rehearsal to 'tag' memories with appropriate emphasis as important, good, bad and so on.

It is also clear that we have different 'layers' of memory so that past memories are in 'background memory' and take from seconds to days to recall.

Presumably items in foreground memory are chemically tagged and, over time, the pathways and neurons that store them become depleted in these markers.

Supporting this view, research in Sweden found changes in RNA in rat's brains compared to those of a control group after they had been given a learning task.

Such work clearly demonstrates that, just as DNA stores genetic coding, macromolecules of RNA play an important role in memory processes.

Effect of experience

The environment enrichment experiments with rats of Krech's group at Berkeley found that rats given an 'enriched' environment developed larger brains (Packard, 1978). These were perhaps the first physical evidence that the brain is modified by experience.

Memory structure

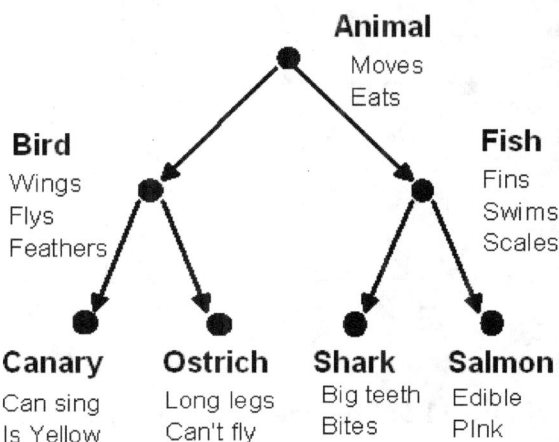

Figure 11.4. Hierarchical organization of the mental lexicon.

Figure 11.4 shows a proposed structure in which the brain stores information about animals as categories and sub-categories with properties attached to each 'node' in the structure (Collins et al., 1969).

Some experimental results do not fit this model, for example Ripps et al. (1973) found that people were quicker to agree to the truth of the statement: *A cat is an animal* than they were to the truth of the statement: *A cat is a mammal.* They argued that MAMMAL should be closer to CAT than ANIMAL in the hierarchy.

More important, however, is that the word ANIMAL is much more frequently used than the word MAMMAL and frequency of reference to a memory certainly does enhance the speed of recall.

The present authors would also argue that the brain almost certainly must store memories in a *precedence network* based on the order in which learning occurs.

In such a network a memory search that succeeds in finding a 'connection' or *common* property shared by a 'new' item in short term memory and an item in long-term memory might then store the data on the new item in the same physical area.

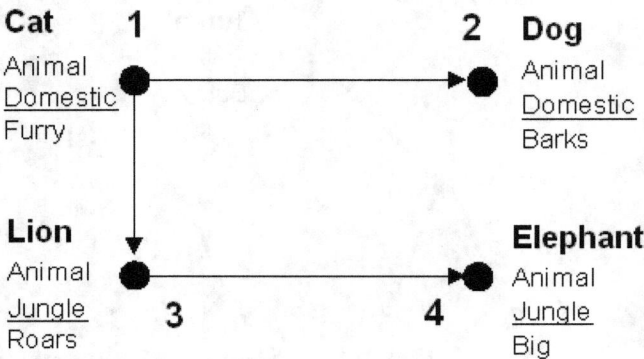

Figure 11.5. Precedence memory network.

For example, the first animals that most children encounter are domesticated cats or dogs so that they will begin forming the memory structure shown in Figure 11.5.

Here four memories have the *common property* 'animal' and cat is the first animal encountered by an infant and thence the first memory stored (at node 1, perhaps one or more brain cells). The second memory is dog, the third lion, and so on. Then cat and dog are associated by the property *domestic* (in the child's language perhaps 'house' or 'home') whilst lion and elephant are associated by the common property *jungle*.

Such memories have a considerable visual 'content' and the ease of recall of a memory will depend its 'strength' which will depend on such factors as the degree of elaboration with which it was committed to long-term memory and the frequency and recency with which the memory has been revisited.

Network models of the brain

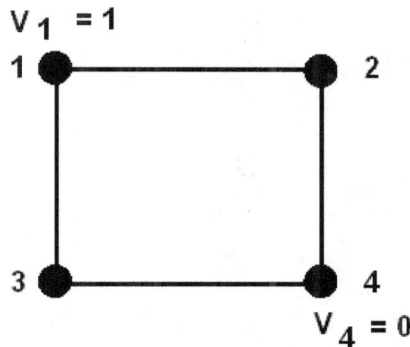

Figure 11.6. FEM model of simple DC network
Resistances 12, 13, 24, 34 all = 1.
Potential at node 1 is 1 and at node 4 it is 0.

In the brain long axons extend from neurons and their terminals connect to the short dendrites of other neurons.

Such networks can be modeled using the *Finite Element Method* (FEM). As a very simple example Figure 11.6 shows a direct current (DC) network with four resistance *elements* connecting four *nodes* (corresponding to a group of neurons storing a memory item) and this corresponds to the simple *precedence memory model* of Figure 11.5.

The numerical FEM model for this 'structure' is obtained by summing matrices for each element formed by using Ohm's Law to write the current flow in each element *ij* as:

$$Q_{ij} = (V_i - V_j)/R_{ij}$$

where V_i and V_j are the voltages at nodes *i* and *j* at each end, and R_{ij} is the *resistance* of the element.

Then writing the two equations for current flow at each end of the element as a matrix we obtain

$$\left\{ \begin{array}{c} Q_{ij} \\ -Q_{ij} \end{array} \right\} = (1/R_{ij}) \left[\begin{array}{cc} 1 & -1 \\ -1 & 1 \end{array} \right] \left\{ \begin{array}{c} V_i \\ V_j \end{array} \right\}$$

161

Doing this for each element and writing the entries from their *element matrices* in a *system matrix* in positions corresponding to the node numbers for each element we obtain the system equations:

$$\{Q\} = \begin{Bmatrix} Q_1 \\ Q_2 \\ Q_3 \\ Q_4 \end{Bmatrix} = \begin{bmatrix} G_{12}+G_{13} & -G_{12} & -G_{13} & 0 \\ -G_{12} & G_{12}+G_{24} & 0 & -G_{24} \\ -G_{13} & 0 & G_{13}+G_{34} & -G_{34} \\ 0 & -G_{24} & -G_{34} & G_{24}+G_{34} \end{bmatrix} \begin{Bmatrix} V_1 \\ V_2 \\ V_3 \\ V_4 \end{Bmatrix}$$

where $G_{12} = 1/R_{12}$ is the reciprocal of the resistance or *conductance* of element 12.

This *assembly* process for the system matrix is easily done by a computer program and the matrix problem can be solved using a short matrix solution routine (Mohr, 1992).

First, either input or output currents must be specified at some nodes to 'force' current flows. Alternatively, voltages are specified for at least two nodes, one of these being a 'datum' potential which is often zero.

This is done in the present example, in the program calculating equivalent current 'loads' by multiplying the columns in the system matrix for 'specified voltage nodes' by the voltage specified at them and adding the result to the load matrix { Q } or array V( ) in the program.

Then the problem is solved to determine the nodal voltages or potentials and the element currents are calculated using

$$Q_{ij} = (V_i - V_j)/R_{ij}$$

A short QBASIC[1] program that assembles and solves this problem is given below.

---

[1] QBASIC was included with DOS 5 and has been used in recent books on PCs. With a first line 'Show' added the same code lines can be used in VB if attached to a form but now a separate (text) file is needed to read the data.

For this program the key notation is:

NN(,)	matrix storing the element node numbers
R( )	matrix storing the element resistances
C(,)	the system matrix
V( )	the nodal voltages
NP	number of nodes
NE	number of elements
NS	number of nodes with specified voltage
a$, b$	format specifier strings
X, S	temporary numbers

```
DIM NN(20, 2), R(20), C(20, 20), V(20)                      1
a$ = "###": b$ = "######.###"                               2
READ NP, NE, NS                                             3
FOR K = 1 TO NE                                             4
READ I, J, R: NN(K, 1) = I: NN(K, 2) = J: R(K) = R          5
C(I, I) = C(I, I) + 1 / R: C(I, J) = C(I, J) - 1 / R        6
C(J, I) = C(J, I) - 1 / R: C(J, J) = C(J, J) + 1 / R        7
NEXT                                                        8
FOR K = 1 TO NS: READ N, S                                  9
FOR I = 1 TO NP                                             10
C(N, I) = 0: V(I) = V(I) - S * C(I, N)                      11
C(I, N) = 0: NEXT I                                         12
V(N) = S: C(N, N) = 1: NEXT                                 13
FOR I = 1 TO NP: X = C(I, I): V(I) = V(I) / X               14
FOR J = I + 1 TO NP: C(I, J) = C(I, J) / X: NEXT            15
FOR K = 1 TO NP: IF K = I THEN GOTO NEXK                    16
X = C(K, I): V(K) = V(K) - X * V(I)                         17
FOR J = I + 1 TO NP                                         18
C(K, J) = C(K, J) - X * C(I, J): NEXT J                     19
NEXK: NEXT K: NEXT I                                        20
PRINT " Node   Voltage"                                     21
FOR I = 1 TO NP                                             22
PRINT USING a$; I; : PRINT USING b$; V(I): NEXT I           23
PRINT " Element  Current"                                   24
FOR K = 1 TO NE: I = NN(K, 1): J = NN(K, 2)                 25
Q = -(V(J) - V(I)) / R                                      26
PRINT USING a$; I; J; : PRINT USING b$; Q: NEXT            27
DATA 4,4,2                                                  28
DATA 1,2,1, 1,3,1, 2,4,1, 3,4,1                             29
DATA 1,1, 4,0                                               30
```

The program reads the data in lines 3, 5 and 9, 'deploying' the element matrices into the system matrix in lines 6 and 7 and modifying the RHS 'load' vector V( ) for the specified voltages in line 11.

Then only lines 14 to 20 are required to solve the problem using Gauss-Jordan reduction, a standard method of inverting matrices, also applying this to the load vector V( ) to obtain the solution directly (Przemieniecki, 1968).

Here X is first used to store the *pivot* for 'row division' operations (line 14) and then used to store the 'row multiplier' (line 17) for the row subtraction operations (line 19) and doing these on the RHS vector V( ) (line 17) as well yields the solution.

Note that the RHS line numbers are not part of the program.

The data appended to the program (lines 28 - 30) is for the problem of Figure11.6 for which the solution is $V_2 = V_3 = 0.5$ and currents = 0.5 for each element.

The foregoing program also proves useful for modeling hierarchical networks such as that of Figure 9.2.

FEM network models also lend themselves to 'structural' models of memory such as that of Figures 11.4 and 11.5.

That the resulting numerical model is a matrix suggests that some form of database model might also be used to model memory storage in the brain, not a particularly startling idea!

Another possibility is to combine the two model types so that each node in Figure 11.6 is a database of some category like those in Figure 11.4 and the links between the nodes are the *joins* between common *fields* in these databases.

As there are about 10^{12} neurons in the human brain, however, we can only hope to model its memory processes on a small scale.

Long-term potentiation

The resistance of each element in Figure 11.6 can be compared to the *frequency* of use of a path in the brain's network and the voltage at each node can be compared to the *strength* of a memory 'image' or information 'bundle' stored in a neuron.

In practice a signal between two neurons is an electrical impulse passed along the axon of the first to the dendrites of the second via a synaptic junction. At this junction neurotransmitter chemicals pass the signal across a 'synaptic gap.' Evidently these chemicals react with RNA or peptide macromolecules in the neurons that play a role in memory *coding*.

In the case of classical conditioning, therefore, with frequent 'dosing' in this way the storage of a memory is made more permanent, an effect called *long-term potentiation* (Vander et al., 1994). Therefore, a more realistic FEM model of a neural network might include a capacitance property for nodes so that the charge stored at these could model the strength and/or recency of a memory.

Brainwashing

The term 'brainwashing' derives from a Chinese word and BW was first used by the Chinese military on Americans captured in the Korean War in trying to convert them to communist ideology using 'The Three D's' method:

[1] **Debilitation**: 'Softening up' by sleep and food deprivation.

[2] **Dread**: Rough treatment and threats of torture or death.

[3] **Dependency**: The subject realizes that they are dependent upon the brainwashers for survival and is treated as converted and allowed to mix with other converts who complete the persuasion process.

The American Heritage Dictionary of English defines brainwashing as:

1. *Intensive, forcible indoctrination, usually political or religious, aimed at destroying a person's basic convictions and attitudes and replacing them with an alternative set of fixed beliefs.*

2. *The application of a concentrated means of persuasion, such as an advertising campaign or repeated suggestion, in order to develop a specific belief or motivation.*

In line with the second definition, most people now believe that a great deal of brainwashing is done via the mass media. In the present work, therefore, the term *brainwashing* is generalized to include implanting ideas where none existed before, not just changing a person's ideas. This is important in view of the predilection of advertisers to target children of all ages when they are open-minded, if not naive, and thus willing to try new things.

In this context advertising needs only to succeed in a small percentage of the target age group and *social learning*, a form of imitative learning, will occur and ensure that other members of the target group follow the lead of those first persuaded by the advertising.

The results are nothing short of spectacular, of course, as young children are persuaded en masse what to wear, how to act, and to smoke, drink Coke, buy mobile phones, etc.

This, indeed, is *conditioning* on a grand scale.

Conclusion

Conditioning techniques are used in many stages and areas of life, including religion and politics, and also advertising which is discussed in Chapter 13, and are often used to an extent that does, indeed, justify the use of the term *brainwashing*.

Chapter 12

THE MASS MEDIA

> *The idea that the media is there to educate us, or to inform us,*
> *is ridiculous because that's about tenth or eleventh on their list.*
> *The first purpose of the media is to sell us shit.*
> Abbie Hoffman, speech at U South Carolina (September 16, 1987).
>
> *The whole world is becoming humanoid - creatures that look human*
> *but aren't. - - The whole world's people are becoming*
> *mass produced, programmed, numbered and . . .*
> Peter Finch as Howard Beale in the movie *Network* (MGM, 1976).

The print media

The *Acta Diurna* of the Romans contained daily official reports, and the Chinese claim to have had a similar journal of much greater antiquity (Egerton Eastwick, 1896).

The earliest regular newspaper is thought to have been the *Notizie Scritte* published in Venice around the middle of the 16th century. The paper could be seen at various places in the city for the price of a small coin, the *gazeta,* from which came the term Gazette.

Around the end of the 16th century casual publications of various professions, parties and other special interest groups had limited circulation in England. In 1622 the one-page *Certaine News of the Present Week* was first printed and followed by many other one-page weeklies.

Later, two-page newspapers circulated twice a week appeared, eventually being printed daily. In 1785 a newspaper renamed *The Times* three years later was established and by 1829 it was eight pages. During the Crimean war the first war-correspondent letters appeared and the circulation rose to over 50,000. The era of the modern newspaper had begun.

Today's major newspapers are larger than ever and many have large weekend supplements devoted to such things as additional news commentary and the arts.

Articles in major newspapers tend to become a routine mix of such topics as major local and international events, local and international politics and crime, traffic other accidents, business news and sporting news

In most of these areas outcomes or results will be reported, along with editorial comment and discussion of coming events.

The many local and regional newspapers naturally focus more on events in their area so that, for example, plans for alterations to a local park might be a main article.

There are also many magazines which focus on news in special interest areas such as business, cars and computers.

For all newspapers and magazines advertisements are a major source of revenue. There are also a few newspapers and magazines devoted to advertising second hand goods for sale or to advertising products such as cars and computers.

As ever, editorial comment in the major newspapers is usually very guarded so that a rare hint of dissent with government policy is barely noticeable.

Ways in which editorial policy can influence politics, however, include:

➢ By simply giving less coverage to one party than another.

➢ By giving heavy coverage to a mistake or embarrassing incident involving a member of one party.

Over time, therefore, newspapers can have a considerable political effect and always have, so much so that they have often been subjected to government censorship.

Newspapers also play a cultural role, most obviously in discussing local arts and sporting events. The quotation that commences the next chapter is an excellent example of this role and the way in which advertisers can use newspapers to brainwash the young into becoming lifelong consumers of their products.

Radio

Radio has been one of the great advances in human life. It allows international communication of news, embraces the people of most cities and towns, and plays an important role in ambulance, police and other essential services.

Radio has evolved from a novelty in its early days to a habit of modern life. The first author recalls the first 24 hour broadcasting by a radio station in Melbourne taking place in the early 1960s. Since then radio has evolved in major cities to provide a wide variety of 24-hour AM and FM stations such as:

➢ 24 hour news.
➢ Classical music.
➢ Popular music.
➢ 'Old time' music.
➢ Talk-back.
➢ Sports.
➢ 'Traditional' radio: a mix of news, sport, music etc.

Most of these are supported by a good deal of advertising and it is often claimed that many people spend more time listening to radio than they do watching TV and that, therefore, radio ads are more effective.

Radio stations have much smaller audiences than prime time TV, however, though in Australia the government owned ABC radio sometimes has a good sized audience. No doubt, therefore, it will eventually be privatized!

Some of the talk-back stations cater for the sick, deranged, drunk and lonely in the later evening and throughout the early hours of the morning.

Whether radio has much effect politically is doubtful, TV playing a much greater role in this area.

Culturally, however, radio has great influence. The latest styles of pop music are played to the young and this has always had an effect on their behaviour.

Before the 1950s popular recording artists sang in a semi-classical style or were 'crooners' like Bing Crosby who only older people could identify with.

In the mid 1950s the young Elvis Presley was viewed as a potentially bad influence on the young. He was endorsed by such well-known TV personalities as Ed Sullivan, however, and that seemed to overcome early prejudice from the older generation, or at least guarantee the approval of the younger generation.

There is no doubt, however, that rock and roll music has had a bad effect on the young as its performers were often doubtful characters afflicted with all the vices. Inevitably a whole generation was influenced by such behaviour and began themselves to behave less politely and become a little more immoral. If the lyrics of a popular song talked about 'having it off' in the back seat of a car, then young people of that generation would do just that.

Currently we still have stylized singers who 'croon' a song and dress according to some current fashion. We also have bee-bop and other pop music styles that have become more and more 'in your face'. These sorts of songs are accompanied by music clips with scenes of dark alleys in the poor parts of major cities that project an image of loutish behaviour and crime that seems to rub off on young males in particular.

Popular music has occasionally had positive effects, for example through songs protesting war, and there are those that claim that the 'hippie' and 'flower power' movement in the USA of the late 1960s and early 1970s had through a few large pop concerts played an important role in galvanizing public opinion against the Vietnam war and bringing it to an end.

Evidence of the power of pop music is seen in the emergence of radio stations run by religious organizations that play 'nice' pop music for the young with only occasional interviews or ads concerning religious opinions and events.

Finally, some evidence of the power of radio is exemplified by Radio Vatican in Rome which can be heard globally on the Internet. This, no doubt, plays an integral part in the Vatican's ongoing task of propagating Catholic propaganda.

The 'brainwashing' role of radio, however, became relatively limited with the advent of TV because this became a far more potent medium for political and other propaganda.

Television

TV has an enormous impact on modern life and people typically watch TV for at least 3 or 4 hours on most days.

The wide variety of shows on TV includes news, current affairs, interviews, panel discussions, documentaries, movies, sitcoms, children's programs, live sport, sporting panels, quizzes, cooking, home renovation and reality shows.

Most of these types of shows play a cultural role and in Australia they are a mixture of US, British and local products, exactly in line with our traditional alliances.

Many documentary shows, particularly those about past wars and other events in history, tend to reinforce those alliances. A notable example are the almost weekly documentary shows concerning Adolph Hitler which seem designed to keep us 'conditioned' for the concept of justified war and the next 'villain' around the corner that our allies the US or UK want to denigrate as a lead-up to yet another war.

As with newspapers, TV news has editorial controls rarely allowing much criticism of the status quo. The many interviews on current affairs shows allow politicians and others to express a view, but only in short 'grabs' which have little impact.

Occasional panel discussion shows allow groups to express their views but again only in short grabs, a sequence of views contradicting each other having little influence on an audience.

As with any media, however, by judicious choice of material shown the public can be brainwashed most effectively.

In Australia, for example, recent Prime Ministers seem to have had a media team that even Hitler might have envied, one that has them seen on TV almost every day saying a few mindless words on some topic or engaged in some public event to identify themselves with the public. As a result, a typically unlikely politician becomes highly successful.

Children's shows on TV play a positive role. Early morning and afternoon shows help keep very young children occupied and entertained and also have some educational content. In the later afternoon shows which sometimes include quizzes help entertain older children and sometimes have significant educational content.

An example of TV brainwashing of the public

A fine example of TV brainwashing of the public in Western nations occurred before the 2003 invasion of Iraq when for months pictures of Sadam Hussein holding a rifle were shown almost daily, accompanied by misguided speculation on whether he possessed Weapons of Mass Destruction (WMDs).

This charade was so persistent as to make many viewers want to scream the next time they heard the term WMD. The purpose of this orchestrated litany of lies and deceit was clearly to 'condition' people into acceptance of the forthcoming military invasion of Iraq by the US and the few of its allies willing to assist it.

In fact, Iraq had been so severely weakened by the 1991 invasion and subsequent sanctions and continuous bombing in the broad 'no-fly' zone placed through it that is was incapable of anything but minimal resistance.

Religion and morality on TV

Religious shows on TV mainly appear in the early hours of Sunday morning. These are bible bashing US shows which cannot be watched and taken seriously by many.

In Australia there is an interview show that concerns itself with religion around midnight during the middle of the week and the government run ABC runs a program on Sunday evenings which shows documentaries on religious topics.

These few shows with a religious basis have little influence.

Many of the banal sitcoms and movies now involve high levels of foul language, violence and sex which should not be seen by anyone, let alone children.

Panel shows also involve plenty of poor language, somewhat stupid and loutish behaviour and too much joking about sexual matters.

Some of the ridiculous and voyeuristic reality shows are also completely tasteless. *Big Brother* was filled with bad language, silly behaviour and obscene talk on such absurd topics as farts.

To top it all off there are those ads shortly after midnight for sex shops and 'sex' chat lines for 'straight' and homosexual people which are a sad reflection on a sick society.

Worse still is the increasing level of violence on TV and at the movies. Inevitably the result is 'copy cat' behaviour in the society made audience to these movies (Cipolla, 1974):

> *It is disturbing to see that still today, even in the most advanced countries, in large sections of human society, aggressiveness is praised as a virtue - or at least as a valuable asset - and it is constantly advertised in the motion pictures and on television. We need - more than anything else - to educate people to tolerance and gentility.*

Only a few days ago there was yet more news of young woman being raped and killed in Melbourne one evening as she was walking home from working as stand-up comedienne. Melbourne used to be considered a quiet, if not dull city, and now it is developing a history of crime reminiscent of Chicago.

The mass media, particularly the many movies that glorify crime and violence play a large role in desensitizing people to violence to the point at which is comes almost naturally to them.

The final insult is not only the violence, but city half covered in graffiti painted by mindless louts who enjoy other irresponsible and dangerous practices such as throwing rocks and bottles at the windows of cars, trams and trains.

We need to draw a firm line quickly regarding mass media that encourages this sort of behaviour before life in this society becomes intolerable for decent people.

TV advertising

TV advertising has moved from the simple situation of a presenter reading a script while holding the product in question up in front of the camera to ads that have various styles such as:

➢ 'Basic' ads that mention the product and concentrate on telling you its name and where to get it. Sometimes these have no presenter and only text messages.

➢ Sophisticated ads that show the product in 'classy' surroundings.

➢ "Laid back' ads were the presenter extols the virtue of the product.

➢ Semi-humorous ads which sometimes use cartoon characters to present their message.

➢ Ads where the reader just about screams at you not to miss some bargain sale or to go to some cheap store.

➢ Ads targeting children which involve cuddly characters and fantasy scenes and the like.

More than other forms of advertising, TV advertising is sometimes very psychological. Many ads aimed at children, for example, are tested on young children who are asked whether they feel persuaded by them to pester their parents into buying the product.

Most important, however, is that ads only have to persuade a few children to try a product and they will spread the idea to their friends by the powerful pyramid effect of social learning which, unfortunately, is the main way in which children pick up bad habits like smoking and drugs.

Movies

An example of the Christian church using movies for brainwashing is a set of 5 movies of about 40 minutes duration and involving the following leading characters and languages:
1. Dini – Indonesian.
2. Khalil – Arabic.
3. Ali – Turkish.
4. Khosrow – Tarsi.
5. Mohammad – Hausa.

#3 is about a bossy, bad-tempered, alcoholic Muslim husband who beats his wife. He has a vision that leads him to Saudi Arabia and en route he has a vision of Jesus. Telling others it, his wife is doubtful, whilst his friends deride him. He hears the voice of Jesus again, however, and converts to Christianity, his wife doing the same, feeling it has saved them.

#5 is about a young African boy who while herding has a vision of Jesus, moving him to go to Saudi Arabia where he stays 18 months and learns Arabic. Returning home, his father pesters him about beginning to acquire wives but he has another vision, this of Jesus saving a man from attack by black-hooded men. He tells his father who sends him to a medicine man where he is given a potion without result. Another medicine man is tried before the boy has visions on six successive nights of Jesus defending him from the devil. A 7th dream promotes the Bible and the boy converts to Christianity. This upsets his father who calls him an "infidel" and the boy leaves home. Two years later, hearing his father to be ill, he returns to visit him, when his father forgives him, dying 3 hours later.

The Internet

The Internet has provided a new form of mass media which combines all the other mass media. Thus the now ubiquitous PC is linked by modem to the Internet and thence to web sites that link to newspapers, radio and TV, as well as to countless other information and advertising sites.

Through e-mail the Internet also provides an important new means of communication for both social and business purposes.

For business it also provides an alternative medium for both marketing and sales, as well as for other transactions such as bank account transactions and bill payments.

For children seeking information for school projects, for example, the Internet is often useful.

The widespread use of the Internet to present University courses, on the other hand, is deplorable and debases these greatly. Such a practice also tends to encourage lightweight courses like the absurd postgraduate courses in Sexology and Puppetry introduced at two Australian 'latter-day' Universities.

In recent years increasing numbers of people are becoming addicted to various 'social sites' such as Facebook and spend up to hours a day sharing mindless and useless gossip on them.

Undoubtedly the worst result of the Internet is the many sites devoted to sexual matters. Some of these involve the sex chat lines and dating services advertised in newspapers and on TV. Others involve pornography, including illegal child pornography, yet another indication of an increasingly sick society perhaps.

A recent news report said that "big data" gleaned by Google etc. from users "makes people more predictable" and helps make advertisements "more effective", noting that "Google alone makes 100 billion a year from ads".

This is because user website visits are 'tracked', allowing a profile of user needs to be formed and ads to be tailored to meet those needs

Thus big data from Facebook, Netflix etc. usage is "passed on to market researchers" who use software algorithms and "stream processing", but such data collection practices risk a potential "surveillance nightmare" in some countries.

Such date collection practices, however, have obvious applications in politics, for example to help decide on what might be the most effective campaign promises prior to an election (Deutsche Welle English News, SBS TV, 5.30 AM, 3/3/19).

Conclusion

The mass media play a great part in our lives. They 'condition' us to accept our culture and the attitudes of our government and society.

TV is perhaps the most potent of the mass media as it is the centrepiece of the modern home and often some of its bedrooms as well.

The Internet provides social, educational and business access via telephone links and also links to the other mass media.

TV programs and advertising, however, provide the most powerful means of brainwashing people politically and behaviourally, and advertising is the subject of the next chapter.

The major newspapers, however, have considerable political influence by way of frequent poll results and editorial comment, particularly in the weeks leading up to an election.

Chapter 13

ADVERTISING

> *The chief customers of the public house today are the elderly and middle-aged men. Unless you can attract the younger generation to take the place of the older men, there is no doubt that we shall have to face a steadily falling consumption.*
> *If we begin advertising in the press we shall see that the continuance of our advertising is contingent upon the fact that we get educational support as well in the same papers. In that way it is wonderful how you can educate public opinion, generally, without making it too obvious that there is a public campaign behind it all.*
> Sir Edgar Saunders, Director of the Brewers' Society, Birmingham, 1930 (Sargent, 1979).

The purpose of advertising

Nowadays, of course, there are massive media and advertising industries devoted to turning us into consumer zombies.

The main objectives of ads, in approximate order of priority, are to:

1. Make the brand name familiar.
2. To give the brand a distinct image.
3. Attribute at least one key attribute to that brand name.
4. Associate the product with certain usages.
5. To convince us that this brand is the best (for us).
6. To persuade us that we should buy the product.

To meet these objectives ads will involve:

slogans, demonstrations, comparisons, testimonials, and repetition.

Comparisons, of course, are usually of price, but sometimes also some sort of semi-official rating, for example safety ratings for cars.

By way of style ad types include basic facts, 'mood', feel-good, social setting, slice-of-life, humour, fantasy, hard-sell, and anxiety/danger/risk or 'fear' ads.

An example of fear type ads are those for household insect sprays, and the TV program *More Hidden Killers Of The Victorian Home* reminds us that fear ads have been around for a long time, ads in the Victorian era selling such products as poisonous Borax (sodium borate) as a household cleanser, the "new science of germs and microbes" helping promote a fear of myriad household 'bugs'.

To make ads more appealing attractive female models, smooth talkers, or sports and movie stars are often used to promote products.

To give ads more authority statements by 'experts' may be used to convince us of the merits of a product.

To make purchase more imperative ads will scream of huge bargains for as little as two days only, and buy on the never-never deals with no interest for a year or two, if not more.

Thus ads range from boring to extremely irritating, from dull and routine to the heights of excess and absurdity, from mere suggestion to downright pleading, and from slight desperation to screaming at us to buy the product.

More subtle are 'advertorials' of bought space in newspapers, conspicuous 'product placement' in movies, or internet sites. For maximum tedium there are half-hour infomercials on afternoon or late night TV which sometimes repeat night after night, week after week, and year after year. In these and most other types of ads there are often trial offers, bonus products for quick purchase etc.

In Equation 15.7 we equate aggregate demand and aggregate supply to obtain $MV = PQ$ where M is the amount of money in circulation, V is its velocity of circulation (in transactions per year), P is the price of goods in circulation, and Q is the quantity of goods in circulation per year.

Then if, for example, we increase Q we should advertise to ensure a corresponding increase in V or turnover. As the first author puts it, Mohr's First Law of Advertising is that we *'increase the velocity of bullshit in order to increase turnover.'*

As pointed out by Packard, one way of maintaining higher levels of production is through planned obsolescence of which there are three types (Packard, 1963):

[1] Quality: the product wears out in some planned manner.

[2] Function: a new product performs the function better.

[3] Desirability: the product is 'restyled', making the old version seem obsolete.

In case [1] we would hardly advertise product deficiencies. On the contrary we would do everything we could to prevent bad publicity and would always advertise claiming quality and reliability or at least ignoring these points. Cases [2] and [3] would be advertised as 'new, improved' and 'the new - - - .''

The psychology of attitudes

Attitude can be defined as 'psychological *tendency* expressed by *evaluating* a particular entity with some degree of favour or disfavour.'

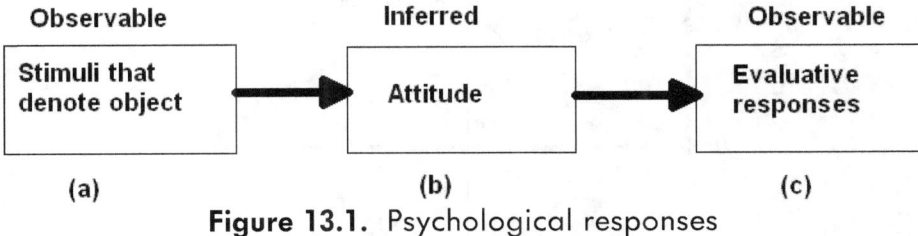

Figure 13.1. Psychological responses

Figure 13.1 illustrates the three types of response involved in attitudinal psychology. These are:

1. *Cognitive response.* This response is that of recognition of, for example, a name, a picture or other stimulus.

2. *Affective response.* This is a hypothetical construct and a latent variable. Here the sympathetic nervous system responds to (1) with feelings or emotions.

3. *Behavioural response.* This is the outward expression of (2) and may be a positive, neutral or negative response of some degree or intensity involving some observable action.

In this context conservatism, environmentalism or racism are objects. Then when we label a person a conservative, environmentalist or racist we infer an attitudinal position. Such attitudes are evidenced and also developed by the 'CAB' mechanism illustrated in Figure 13.1.

Schemas are cognitive structures that represent a person's past experience in a stimulus domain by a higher order or abstract cognitive structure. Then attitude is a subset of such a schema.

Schemas have a selective effect on the remembering of information so that people have a better remembrance of stimuli that 'fit' their schemas and also for those that 'oppose.' This same selectivity applies to the 'output' of information as well as its input.

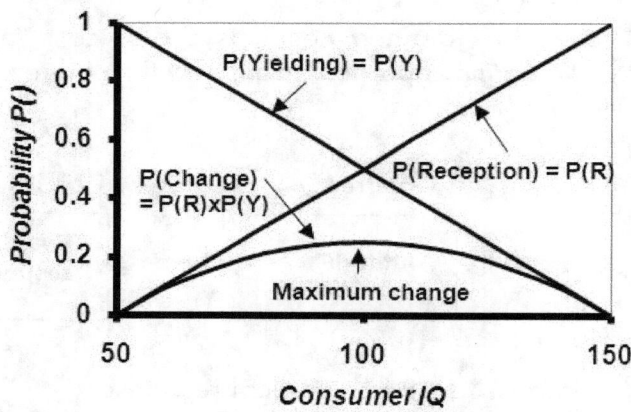

Figure 13.2.
Probability of reception, yielding and attitude change.

Figure 13.2 illustrates the reception-yielding model of attitude formation (Eagly & haiken, 1993). Here 'reception' refers to comprehending a 'message', for example an advertisement. This model postulates that the probability of attitude change is given by:

$$P(C) = P(R) \times P(Y)$$

so that a maximum change is obtained where the reception and yielding curves intersect, as shown in Figure 13.2.

180

One application of this idea is to 'get them young' so that advertising companies target the young and naive before they have the maturity or 'consumer intelligence' to develop resistance. Indeed, this is why the present authors believe that the horizontal axis in Fig. 13.2 should be labeled 'Consumer Intelligence' or 'Consumer IQ'.

The quotation that opens this chapter is an excellent example. Once an idea like 'beer is for men' is buried in a boy's brain he may become a beer drinker for life, the habit occasionally reinforced by ads that make the habit look completely appropriate.

The basic mechanism of persuasion, therefore, is to 'get them young' (and naive or 'less intelligent consumers') as Figure 13.2 suggests. To do this ads need only persuade/brainwash some of the target audience and then imitative or 'social' learning ensures that many of the rest follow them.

Advertisements having achieved this, regular advertising reminds the audience of a product. Then in Figure 13.1 the 'C' response will be one of recognition of your brand, the 'A' response will be one of approval of it, and the 'B' response will be to make a mental note to buy it.

Learning curves were discussed in Chapter 6 and in advertising it is important to have sufficient repetitions of an ad to ensure adequate average learning by the audience. The forgetting curves of Figure 13.3 also have important application in developing long-term marketing plans. Here curves A and B are for two messages and curve B* is the result after the second message is repeated.

Then, when time has elapsed after an advertisement its 'residual' effect depends upon both the *primacy* (strength) of the ad compared to others and its *recency.*

In Figure 13.3, after two weeks ad B* has greater recency than ad A, but less primacy so that they have nearly equal effect.

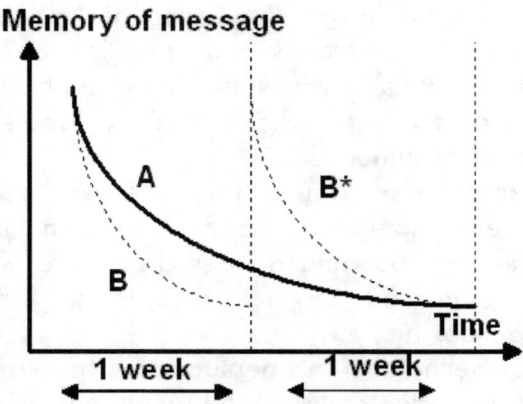

Figure 13.3. Forgetting curves.

Such repetition of ads will ensure long-term potentiation of the remembered message, an important objective (Vander et al., 1994). Correlation between retention and persuasion, however, is by no means guaranteed and ads can be tailored to these two ends.

Targeting advertising

Maslow defined two kinds of needs (Lindzey at all, 1978):

(a) *Basic needs* such as hunger, thirst, sex and security.

(b) *Metaneeds* such as achievement, beauty, goodness, justice, order and unity.

Maslow defines achievement as a basic need but the present authors prefer to classify it as a 'higher' or more human metaneed.

First, we must meet our basic or 'animal' needs. That done we can turn our attention to the higher 'human' metaneeds and thence Maslow's 'meaning of life' goal of 'self-actualization' as a human being.

These needs provide *primary goals* that may motivate us towards *secondary goals* such as money in order to achieve them.

Most of our basic needs are *intrinsic motivations* whereas most of our metaneeds are *learned goals*.

Advertising usually targets the metaneeds of your *ego*.

A Coke ad, for example, is not designed to remind you that you may be thirsty. If so, you might rush to the fridge and grab whatever drink you can find to satisfy that thirst. No, a Coke ad makes it look 'cool' to drink Coke with your friends and being 'cool' is a metaneed! So next day a young boy will want to be 'cool' when hanging out with his friends so they will all drink Coke and act foolishly, just like the actors in the Coke ads

Here again we see the down side of advertising, namely that increasingly ambitious executives will stop at nothing to sell their product, even if it has to brainwash the young into acquiring both bad behaviour and bad teeth.

In marketing to children, of course, familiar cuddly looking cartoon figures are often displayed on packaging and used to speak the lines of TV ads. Here, however, ads usually target the *Id,* the basic 'animal' personality that has basic needs like hunger. Young children tend to eat in smaller doses and often so that almost any time they are awake is a good one to put a picture of confectionery in front of them.

One of the best examples of brainwashing, however, is the use of *consumer panels* of children in marketing research. The children are often asked what they will say and do to persuade parents to buy them the product.

Finally, the extent to which children are exposed to advertising is incredible:

- - "*it is estimated that children between two and 11 years old may see over 20,000 advertisements in a year,*"
(O'Guinn et al., 2006).

Advertising, therefore, will brainwash someone in your family, even if it doesn't brainwash you!

In marketing to adults well known sporting identities are often used to market such things as golf clubs, household appliances and cars and houses. Indeed, this was the basis of Mark McCormack's very successful IMG (McCormack, 1986) and one of his earliest clients was Greg Norman who, marketed as 'The Shark', was made out to be a much better golfer than he was and made an awful lot of money from TV ads.

183

Addiction

There is no doubt that advertising has the effect of conditioning people. Just as Pavlov's dogs were conditioned to associate a bell with the appearance of food so that they then salivated when only given the stimulus of the bell, so too will a psychological 'trigger' be thrown in our minds when the 'CAB' responses to an ad are invoked.

In the same way advertising seeks to develop *habits*. Habits can be quickly formed and very hard to break. It only takes as little as one or two first exposures to learn something. Then only a few repetitions are needed for the memory to become *long-term potentiated* (Vander et al, 1994) and more easily recalled than most other memories in your brain.

In young children the result of confectionery advertising is often a virtual addiction to sugar. In teenagers this continues but junk food and Coke are added to their habits, soon followed by bourbon and Coke and then beer for the boys and perhaps some of the new vodka based mixed drinks for the girls.

Booze ads often *associate* booze with celebration so that at 'rave' parties for young people primeval music seems to go hand in hand with drugs and booze.

The psychology of this sort of behaviour is doubtless based on imitative learning from adults. In other words, as long as adults are stupid enough to drink booze children will too.

Since cigarettes are now discouraged in the media teenagers will smoke marijuana, arguing that it is not as harmful. This is not only an intoxicating drug but a hallucinogenic one as well. So, why not harder drugs like a little cocaine after that?

Then addiction quickly becomes likely. From booze to most other drugs, poisons have two problems:

(a) They don't really taste nice unless diluted enough by other things such as water and sugar in the case of booze.

(b) They alter the metabolic rate, resulting in changes in pulse rate and blood pressure, and contraction or dilation of blood vessels in the brain and elsewhere. Thus every fair sized dose of most drugs gives you withdrawal symptoms, whether you realize it or not.

If you have a booze overdose, for example, you might want some 'hair of the dog' (that bit you) as alcoholics call a dose of booze early in the day to help overcome a hangover.

Celebration is not the only excuse for booze. Wine goes well with food, it is said, so that is another.

The reality is that, because alcohol is a poison, wine will tend to eat at your stomach so it is best to line your stomach with a little food to ease the discomfort that you should be able to feel after a few glasses of wine.

This somewhat corrosive property of alcohol is the reason why it causes stomach ulcers and cancer of the oesophagus and stomach. It is also the reason why it was used to dissolve the connective tissue in the frontal lobes of the brain in the first lobotomy operations.

One way or the other, booze is inculcated as a daily habit, whether that be granny's tot of fortified wine, a bottle or two of wine with dinner or while watching TV afterwards, or a six pack of beer at a party or a sporting event.

In other words *advertising* does reduce us to brainwashed zombies who will enjoy drinking poison if told to. We will leap about to primitive music like savages if told to. Many of us still smoke because ads used to tell us to.

All too many of us take drugs like marijuana, heroin and cocaine. All these addictions are practices that supposedly more civilized European explorers learnt from primitive societies and took back to Europe with them.

Push and pull marketing

Some marketing campaigns use *push strategies* which concentrate on the availability of products. In this case the ads are 'basic' and concentrate on telling you the product name and where to get it. Examples of such ads on TV are

➢ A presenter reads a script while holding the product in question up in front of the camera.

➢ Ads with only text messages and a voice-over.

➢ Semi-humorous ads which sometimes use cartoon characters to present their message.

➢ Ads targeting children which involve cuddly characters and fantasy scenes and the like.

➢ Ads for junk food which play on having a high 'reward/effort' ratio (Govoni et al., 1988). That 50 million people a day eat McDonald's stuff is testament enough to the success of their advertising.

➢ Ads where the reader just about screams at you not to miss some bargain sale or to go to some cheap store.

Advertisements for 'basic' food, junk food, confectionery, clothing and home appliances are usually of the 'push' type.

Marketing campaigns often use *pull strategies* which promote the product in order to attract buyers. In this case the ads concentrate on 'image' to attract the audience to the product and the product name is secondary and *associated* with the imagery. Examples of this sort of ad on TV are:

➢ Sophisticated ads that show the product in 'classy' surroundings with actors dressed stylishly.

➢ "Laid back' ads were the presenter extols the virtue of the product with, for example, an island resort as a backdrop.

➢ Ads that use glamorous people such as movie stars as actors.

This type of advertising is usually used for higher priced or more 'up market' products, including fashion clothing, cosmetics, expensive furniture, luxury cars and overseas holidays.

One of the most important 'levers' in advertising, undoubtedly, is *keeping up with the Jones's*. This is exploited heavily in marketing cars and new gadgets of which the mobile phone is the supreme example at present.

Another powerful inducement is selling on the 'never-never', for example with no repayments for a year.

Ubiquitous advertising

Today advertising is literally everywhere.

On TV in Australia there used to be regulations limiting the amount of advertisements per hour to something bearable. Now there seem like 20 minutes or more of ads per hour at times. Worse still, owing to the increasing cost of TV advertising time a truly bewildering string of ads appears in each ad break, sometimes up to about a dozen.

It is almost as bad on radio where there are sometimes as many as half a dozen ads at once on the higher rating commercial stations.

Junk mail from supermarkets and other retail chains has reached epidemic proportions. Other 'direct marketing' is done by phone and is increasingly irritating, often involving requests to complete lengthy market research surveys over the phone.

In addition, free local papers almost totally full of advertisements are also stuffed into millions of letterboxes in major cities.

Trams, trains and buses carry plenty of ads, as do train stations and tram and bus stops.

Taxis and trucks all carry signage, as do many vehicles belonging to small businesses.

Shopping strips are becoming more and more cluttered with advertising signs above the shops, and sandwich boards and often products on the footpath.

More and more restaurants, coffee shops and juice bars have also spilled out onto footpaths, sometimes making little room for the pedestrians for which they were originally intended.

Shopping malls are filled with advertising and more and more stalls with spruikers have appeared in them.

Sporting grounds carry more and more advertising and sporting teams now carry prominent advertising on their clothing.

Casual clothing often comes complete with the brand name writ large upon it.

The Internet is full of advertising, of course, some of it of a lurid nature.

Then there is the despicable practice of placing confectionery and soft drinks near the checkouts at supermarkets, resulting in many a tantrum as young children taken shopping throw a tantrum to get another dose of perhaps the first 'drug' of addiction, sugar.

Perhaps the most predatory advertiser of all, Coca Cola, has its vending machines just about everywhere, including pubs and clubs, office buildings, stations and heaven knows where else (they are probably there too!).

Using religion

In the West Christianity has been heavily exploited in marketing for example by:

➢ The use of religious symbols such as stylized crosses in the jewelry business.

➢ The confectionery industry makes heavy use of Easter to sell chocolate. Bakeries join in by selling Easter buns and industries such as the entertainment and travel industries rely heavily on the Easter holiday period.

➢ Christmas, of course, is a bonanza for business and has become almost completely devoid of its original meaning. For example, the image of Santa is actually from a 19th century cartoon of a rich robber baron with some of *his* toys which he certainly isn't going to give away (Solomon, 1992).

➢ Not too distantly related to this are Mother's Day and Father's Day which are also exploited by, and were probably created by, big business.

As noted in Chapters 3 and 12, religion also makes increasing use of TV and radio programs for promotion and in the US some religious sects have also spent large sums of money to employ advertising companies to run PR campaigns to promote themselves.

New trends in marketing

Some of the many new trends of late include:
1. Healthy foods, for example low fat products.
2. Recycling.
3. Pollution free and environmentally friendly products.
4. Diets and weight watching.
5. Alternative therapies. Of these the list grows daily:
   a. Aromatherapy.
   b. Herbal remedies.
   c. Acupuncture and Chinese medicine.
   d. Group therapy.
   e. Exercise therapy, for example Yoga and Pilates.
   f. Transcendental meditation.
   g. Reflexology - and so on.

In many large cities where house prices have tended to become unaffordable to new entrants to the market there is a growing 'live for today' approach to consumer spending and this is seen in:
1. The growing fast food industry, including take-away food and packaged 'heat only' meals sold in grocery stores.
2. Increasing diversity in consumption of alcohol.
3. Increasing use of drugs which may perhaps be encouraged by the legalization of marijuana.
4. Increasing use of leisure industries such as gambling.
5. Increasing use of restaurants by young childless workers (who may remain childless).
6. Greater spending by young and independent working women on cosmetics, clothes, jewelry and other beauty and fashion products including hair dressing and magazines.
7. Greater spending on magazines, videos, books, computer games, music and other home entertainment products.
8. Greater spending on cars, holidays and other major items by young childless couples or unattached persons.

In these and many other areas there seems to be a growing market which advertisers are busy exploiting. In some communities, however, one or two of the foregoing examples may be on the wane.

The disastrous sociological results

The extent to which advertising has reduced us to zombies strolling around in uncomfortable jeans and carrying a mobile phone in one hand and a bottle of drink in the other is mind boggling.

An article in *The Australian* newspaper on 23 May 2005 reported that psychologists had found that regular use of text messaging on mobile phones could reduce IQ by as much as 10 points, a staggering outcome.

More important, advertising corrupts young minds by showing young people behaving irresponsibly, for example a recent Pepsi Cola ad showing a few youths riding a large wheeled garbage container down a steep street and into a harbour.

In the early 1960s a US Department of Justice official expressed alarm at the "startling" pace at which youthful lawlessness was increasing and concluded that by 1962 a million American teenagers would be arrested each year.

The same official remarked (Packard, 1963):

We seem to have misplaced the sense of values which made this a great nation. Self-indulgence and the principle of pleasure before duty on a vast and growing scale have become a phenomenon of the adult world. These are warning symptoms of the decadence disease which has contributed to the decay of so many civilizations throughout history.

The role that advertising has played in promoting decadent movies, music and behaviour has resulted in a more violent, lawless, indebted, miserable and brainwashed society.

Propaganda has always painted socialism as communism which permits little freedom. How free are we when we are all brainwashed to dress and behave in the same, often stupid way?

Advertising contributes heavily to the increasing debt levels carried by families in the West. Many people have half a dozen credit cards and get way above their heads in debt, often leading to family disunity and breakups.

The disastrous environmental results

Closely related to advertising is the slick packaging of many products, an example being the easy to use 'heat in the tray' packaging of frozen pizza and lasagna. The economic cost of such packaging is enormous and the environmental consequences drastic.

Another example of this are the thin plastic supermarket bags used in Australian supermarkets. Unbelievable numbers of these are used each year and many of them end up littering streets and parks and clogging creeks and storm water drainage systems, and only now (2019) is some action being taken on this issue.

Atmospheric pollution has reached serious levels in many large industrialized cities and global warming has already been significant not long after the term was first coined.

Parkinson's well known law *work expands so as to fill the time available for its completion* was mentioned in Chapter 6 where it is highly appropriate. The present authors prefer to generalize this to Mohr's Universal Law:

Junk fills the time and space available.

This covers a wide range of the problems of mankind including:

➤ Bureaucratic inefficiency, as in Parkinson's Law that work expands to fill the time available, when people are the junk.

➤ The Peter Principle problem of the most incompetent people being those that rise in hierarchies. Here those rising are the junk.

➤ The problems of pollution.

➤ The problems of resource depletion as a result of excessive consumption of 'junk products' which are unnecessary, extravagant and wasteful, and have planned obsolescence built into them.

Four wheel drives and other cars with massive engines are a good example of the latter issue.

The Club or Rome Report (Meadows et al., 1974) pointed out that we were then running out of chromium, once so heavily used by ostentatious American cars. That we are now running out of oil promises to be a major catastrophe because we have built our major cities around the car.

All this has occurred because we have long been brainwashed into becoming mindless zombies consuming not for our own benefit, but for the benefit of insanely greedy and highly overpaid executives whose motivation is an even bigger multimillion dollar bonus.

Though the world was already becoming overpopulated by then, "adman-columnist" E.B. Weiss commented in the 1950s (Packard, 1963):

> *Ever since I've been regaled with the current multitude*
> *of wonderful forecasts of a population future sparked by a*
> *remarkable growth of our population I have wondered about*
> *the magical powers of a large population automatically to*
> *assure eternal prosperity at successively higher peaks.*
> *The most populous regions of this mortal coil*
> *tend to be the most poverty-stricken.*

In other words, capitalist industry has been happy to brainwash us into mindless consumption and has even been happy to count on excessive population growth to help boost profits even further, all the while ignoring the finite nature of the world's resources and its finite capacity to absorb the waste products and pollution arising from extravagant consumption.

Chapter 14

ATTITUDE FORMATION AND MEASUREMENT

> *The body of science described in this book could only have been developed in democratic societies, where attitudinal influence is the form of control that is most often relied upon.*
> Alice H. Eagly & Shelly Chaiken, *The Psychology of Attitudes* (1993).

Introduction

The preceding chapter discussed conditioning which has important application in education where forcing pupils to sit out each day conditions them for productive life. Some aspects of conditioning are also involved, of course, in advertising and other forms of persuasion.

In the present chapter a brief introduction to the mechanics of attitude and belief formation is given. Of particular importance in advertising, *mere exposure research* and attitude measurement are also discussed.

Forbes' *contact hypothesis* regarding interactions between ethnic communities is briefly considered, this being of considerable importance in relation to religious persuasion, and, therefore, also having some relevance to advertising.

The formative years

The period from age 12 to 30 has been termed the *critical period* for formation of attitudes and it can be divided into two parts (Morgan et al., 1979):

(a) <u>Adolescence</u>, during which parental, educational, peer group, advertising and sociological influences are largely responsible for development of most of the attitudes a person will develop through life.

(b) <u>Young adulthood</u>, a time when commitments such as choosing a vocation and marriage occur, and one in which attitudes tend to *crystallize* or 'freeze' for life.

In part this crystallization may involve attempts at *cognitive consistency* in which we tend to make our attitudes relatively consistent with one another and thus avoid *cognitive dissonance* or conflicting attitudes.

An example of this might be that a person who goes to considerable effort to maintain good health, for example by exercising regularly and maintaining a healthy diet, is less likely to smoke or condone doing so.

Heider's *balance theory* is of the cognitive consistency type and assumes that we try to maintain consistent and balanced or harmonious relationships with other people and our environment. According to this theory we would not marry a person with whom we disagreed on major issues about which we felt strongly, such as abortion (Morgan et al., 1979).

That attitudes do indeed crystallize or 'firm up' in young adulthood was confirmed by a US survey of women college students in the 1930s which, when followed-up 20 years later, found that for most issues on the 'conservative-liberal' dimension the women's attitudes, except for a slight "conservative drift" typical of older people, remained the same as they had been in their twenties (Newcomb, 1963).

That attitudes tend to firm up in adolescence and young adulthood has, of course, important implication for marketing along the lines of 'get-em young and get-em for life,' an aim exemplified very well by the quotation that opens Chapter 13.

Expectancy-value models of attitude & belief formation

The most popular models of attitude formation towards an object, action, or event, are the expectancy-value models of attitude formation which are expressed as a summation of evaluations of each of several attributes of the object of the form:

Attitude, $A = \sum_{i=1}^{n} e_i \, v_i$ (14.1)

where e_i is the *expectancy* about the object for attribute i, that is its score on a simple scale as to the subjective probability or extent to which the object has this attribute,

v_i is the *value* or 'evaluation' of the attribute on a similar scale,

and n is the number of attributes considered (Eagly & Chaiken, 1993).

For example, a person is reasonably sure that a new soft drink Choke a Dope has nice taste and is trendy but considers that it is too expensive. Using scales of 0 to 10 for e_i and -10 to 10 for v_i he might thus rate the soft drink as follows:

Attribute 1 (taste): $e_1 = 5/10$, $v_1 = 7/10$

Attribute 2 (trendy): $e_2 = 6/10$, $v_2 = 5/10$

Attribute 3 (price): $e_3 = 10/10$, $v_3 = -5/10$

giving an attitude score

$A = (5 \times 7 + 6 \times 5 + 10 \times -5)/100 = 15/100 = 0.15$

whereas a 'moderately good' score in which 5/10 is given for each expectancy and value would yield $A = 0.75$, whilst a 'middling' score of zero for each rating v_i would, of course, yield $A = 0$.

In practice there might, of course, be many more attributes and, perhaps, we might average the score as $A = {}_{i=1}\Sigma^n\ e_i\ v_i\ /n$, giving 0.05 in the foregoing example, and such scores have been found to correlate well with attitudes assessed by evaluative semantic differential items (Eagly & Chaiken, 1993).

Information integration models of attitude formation

The information integration theory of attitude formation calculates the response to a series of stimuli i as

$$R = w_0\ s_0 + {}_{i=1}\Sigma^n\ w_i\ s_i \qquad (14.2)$$

where w_i and s_i are respectively the weight and scale of a person's attitude to a set of n items of information, and w_0 and s_0 are the weight and scale value of the person's initial attitude (Eagly & Chaiken, 1993).

Here the scale value of information is its location on the evaluative dimension and the weight is its *importance* or psychological impact in relation to the individual's judgment.

Simple summation models such as that of Equation 14.2 emphasize the importance of using multiple 'selling points' in advertising.

If the sum of the weights is required to be one then the model becomes an averaging model, but averaging models are more generally expressed as:

$$R = (w_0 \, s_0 + {}_{i=1}\Sigma^n \, w_i \, s_i)/(w_0 + {}_{i=1}\Sigma^n \, w_i) \qquad (14.3)$$

The initial attitude parameters w_0 and s_0 may in some instances, that of religion being perhaps the best example, represent 'intergenerational' attitudes acquired from a very early age from family and society at large.

Such initial attitudes, of course, may involve *prejudice*, for example ethnocentricity or racism, and, as history shows, such prejudices are often firmly rooted and perhaps could only be modeled by assigning them an exceptionally large weight.

More important in the modern consumer society, however, is social or imitative learning and in this context w_0 and s_0 represent initial attitude acquired by social learning from a peer or social group.

For example, a person believes that Christianity provides good moral codes (attribute 1) and that Christ did exist and provide a good exemplar of how we should live (attribute 2), but doubts that God really exists (attribute 3). Even if God did exist, however, in view of man's disastrous history he has a low evaluation of this last attribute, so that, using scales 0 to 10 for both w_i and s_i, he might thus rate Christianity as follows:

Attribute 0 (initial attitude): $w_0 = 5$, $s_0 = 5/10$ (i.e. 'halfway' values)

Attribute 1 (morality): $w_1 = 8/10$, $s_1 = 8/10$

Attribute 2 (good life model): $w_2 = 8/10$, $s_2 = 8/10$

Attribute 3 (God): $w_3 = 2/10$, $s_3 = 1/10$

giving a response score

$R = [(5 \times 5 + 8 \times 8 + 8 \times 8 + 2 \times 1)/100]/[(5 + 8 + 8 + 2)/10]$

$= [155/100]/[25/10] = 1.55/2.3 = 0.674$

whereas a 'middling evaluation score' with 5/10 for both the weights and scale values for attributes 0-3 would give $1/2 = 0.5$.

In contrast to simple summation models such as Equation 4.2, averaging models emphasize the need to have a limited number of effective selling points in advertising.

Set size effect can be demonstrated by assuming all weights $= 1$ and an initial attitude score of 50 on a scale of 0 to 100. Then if all further pieces of information have a score of 100 the resulting weighted average score for k additional attributes is

$$R = (50 + 100k)/(1 + k) \qquad (14.4)$$

giving the values 50, 75, 83.3, 87.5, . . . for 0, 1, 2, 3, . . . pieces of information, resulting in the hyperbola converging towards the asymptote $R = 100$ shown in Fig. 14.1.

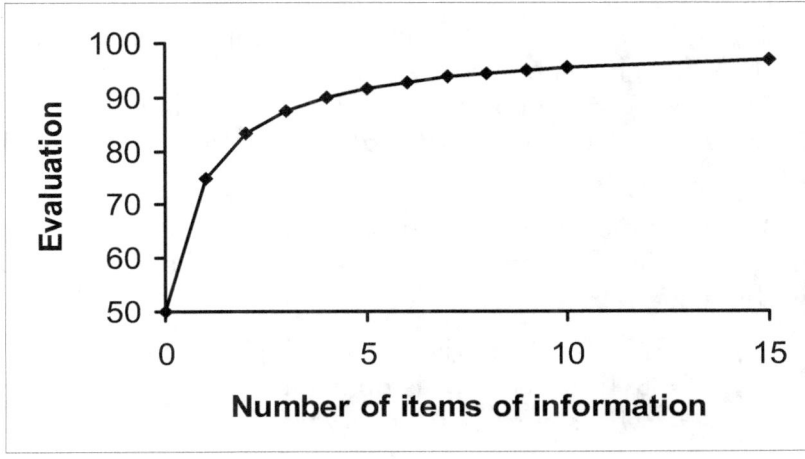

Figure 14.1. Theoretical set-size effect.

As might be expected, this hyperbolic result takes the same general shape as a learning curve, emphasizing that there is a diminishing return for each additional piece of information about a given subject, albeit with the unrealistic assumption that every piece of information has the same weight (w_i).

The *three hit theory* of advertising that three ads are needed to make people aware of a product, its relevance, and its benefits gives (with $k = 3$) $R = 87.5$ (on a scale 0 to 100) in Equation 14.4, or $R = 75$ if there is no initial attitude, i.e. $s_0 = 0$ so that the number 50 in the numerator is omitted.

This is a reasonably good result and, indeed, of some relevance, the present authors often find that it takes three goes to remember items of information, presumably because they were not retained in the short term memory register long enough in the first instance.

Three-value model

A more general 'three-value' model is obtained by combining the expectancy-value and information integration models to obtain

$$R = b_0\, w_0\, s_0 + {}_{i=1}\Sigma^n\, b_i\, w_i\, s_i \tag{14.5}$$

so that three ratings are associated with each attribute (Mohr & Fear, 2016):

(1) A *belief* b_i or subjective probability or extent to which the object has the attribute ($=e_i$ in Equation 14.1).
(2) A *weight* or importance rating w_i ($=w_i$ in Equation 14.2).
(3) An evaluation or *scale value* s_i ($=v_i$ in Equation 14.1 and s_i in Equation 14.2).

For example, a woman considers a dress that she has tried on in a ladies fashion shop is 'trendy' and her scores for this attribute might be:

(1) $b_i = 7/10$ (she is fairly sure that it possesses this attribute).
(2) $w_i = 8/10$ (trendiness is quite important for a new dress).
(3) $s_i = 9/10$ (she rates it as very trendy).

Whilst a good deal more difficult to use in practice, this model does emphasize that it is sometimes desirable to consider both *belief* and *importance* considerations in assessing attitudes.

Logical formation of attitudes

McGuire (1960) proposed that people maintain beliefs that are connected by the rules of formal logic. Whilst most of our early attitude formation is via parents, education, peer groups, advertising, etc., it is at least sometimes true that we take 'time out' to think about things and may reassess an attitude, trying to do so in a logical way.

As a simple example consider a confectionery product with the three attributes T = tastes OK, N = looks nice, and P = price is OK, and a positive attitude to the product is denoted as A.

Using a little symbolic logic in which $\rightarrow$ mean 'implies', $\wedge$ means 'and', $\sim$ means 'not', and denoting A = attitude to the product is OK, we can write $\sim P \rightarrow \sim A$
i.e. if the price is not OK then nor is attitude to it.

If $\vee$ means 'or' we might also write:

$$(T \wedge P) \vee (N \wedge P) \rightarrow A$$

i.e. if taste and price are OK, or if the product looks nice and the price is OK, then attitude is OK.

The example is a little trivial, however, but no doubt we do indeed sometimes reevaluate an attitude and use a little logic in doing so, but, generally, our attitudes are formed by the educational, imitative and information integration processes.

There is, however, scope for educators, religions, and advertisers to try and win us over with a little simple logic along the lines, for example, of: "You like to be comfortable so why not try - - -", an approach compatible with the cognitive consistency theory of attitude formation.

The contact hypothesis

Forbes (1977) proposed that ethnocentricity of different ethnic groups tended to be increased by cultural differences and (presumed negative) contact between them, expressing the ethnocentrism within two groups A and B as:

$$E_a = a_1 C_t D_t \tag{14.6a}$$

$$E_b = b_1 C_t D_t \tag{14.6b}$$

where a_1 and b_1 are assumed to be positive, and are measures of the latent tendency of each group to respond ethnocentrically to each other, C_t is the amount of contact between the two groups at time t and D_t is the magnitude of the cultural differences between the two groups at time t.

He then proposed that the amount of contact and the cultural differences between the groups depended upon their proximity, incentives for contact such as trade, and upon the ethnocentrism of the groups, expressing this as:

$$C_{t+1} = C_t (1 + g)/(1 + a_2 E_a + b_2 E_b) \tag{14.7}$$

$$D_{t+1} = D_t (1 + a_3 E_a + b_3 E_b)/(1 + h C_t) \tag{14.8}$$

where g is a factor that represents all the factors that determine growth or decline in contact other than the repulsive ethnocentrism and cultural differences of the two groups.

In equations 14.7 and 14.8 ethnocentricity decreases contact and increases cultural differences, as might be expected.

The denominator of the last equation ensures that cultural differences are reduced by contact so long as h is positive (the normal situation).

Contact theory has obvious application in marketing, PR and other activities involving persuasion, for example,

[1] It emphasizes that attitude changes with contact or, in general, information transfer, as we have already seen in Figure 14.1, for example.

If contact is 'positive', rather than negative as has generally been the case throughout man's sorry history, then equations 14.6 could be modified to reflect this by writing them in the form:

$$E_{a,t+1} = E_{a,t} - a_1 C_t + a_4 D_t$$

where a_1 and a_4 are positive. Indeed, it might be hoped that the latter situation might be more likely in today's age of electronic communication and high speed travel. Moreover, it is in this situation that such equations might be applicable to advertising with E = 'resistance.'

[2] It reminds us that ethnic or 'local' considerations are important in international marketing of a product.

[3] It reminds us of the importance of targeting advertising towards an appropriate demographic for a product, and that cultural differences exist between teenagers and their parents and, more so, their grandparents.

Mere exposure research

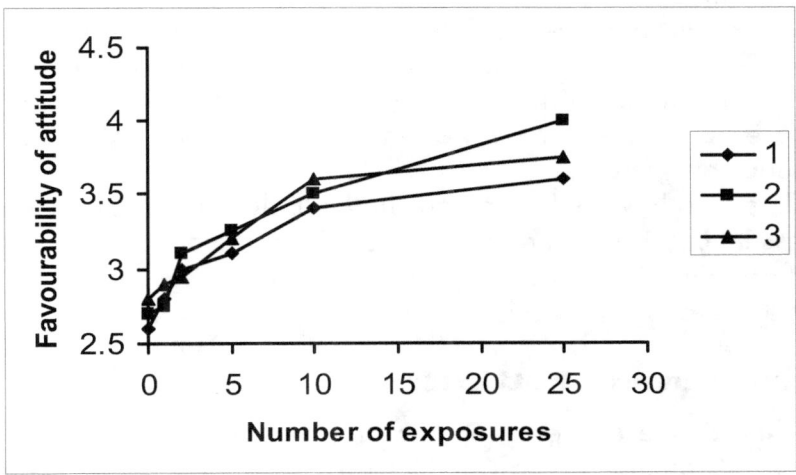

Figure 14.2. Increase in attitude favourability with increasing number of exposures to: 1. Turkish nonsense words. 2. Chinese-like characters. 3. Photographs.

Persuasion studies on message repetition usually focus on the effects of repeated exposure to *information* about attitude objects. In a classic monograph Zajonc dealt merely with the objects themselves. Figure 14.2 illustrates the increase in attitude favourability with repeated exposure to three types of stimuli, showing a somewhat asymptotic behaviour similar to that of learning curves (Eagly & Chaiken, 1993).

This result is comparable to the size effect seen in Figure 14.1 insofar as increasing response is seen with increasing amounts of information, albeit repetition of the same information in the case of mere exposure.

Contact hypothesis, however, should be remembered here because it reminds us that oft repeated attempts at persuasion can also be irritating and result in negative attitudes, and some especially loud, haranguing radio and TV advertisements are good examples of this.

Implications of mere exposure in education are obvious, principally that students grow accustomed to new and perhaps difficult at first subjects, if not blasé about them, given time and repeated classroom exposure to them.

The latter observations might remind us that with repeated exposure we become accustomed to, if not hardened to, 'bad things' in life. For example, this is how children endure an excessive number of hours and years in classes and how adults endure jobs which may be, in reality, exceedingly tedious, arduous and boring.

It is also how, unfortunately, individuals become accustomed to essentially bad things such as cigarettes, alcohol, and drugs, perhaps in that order. This is, of course, good news for purveyors of such products.

Measurement of attitudes

One of the earliest methods of psychophysical scaling was Thurston's *method of equal-appearing intervals.* In this a panel of judges rates each of a set of attributes of an object (for example a new product) according to an ascending scale such as 0 - 10. Then the mean value of the ratings of all judges is the scale value of the attribute on the attitude dimension. For example, Table 14.1 shows the scale values that might be established for a new soft drink Choke a Dope.

Then for surveys, the mean of the scale values of the attributes selected by respondents is their assessment of an object. To obtain more reliable results attributes that are rated inconsistently by the judging panel are not used for surveys.

Table 14.1.

Example scale values for new soft drink Choke a Dope.

Attribute	Value on scale 0 - 10
I don't like it.	0
It makes me feel ill.	1
It is very sweet and must have lots of sugar.	2
It has a nice colour.	3
The bottle looks nice	4
My friends like it.	5
it is trendy.	6
The price is good.	7
It tastes nice.	8

Likert's *method of summated ratings* was designed to be much easier to use than the method of equal-appearing intervals but to be at least as reliable. In this approach a large pool of items which are chosen intuitively for their relevance to the attitude object is used.

These items usually consist of statements of belief but statements about behaviours or affective reactions can also be used.

Typically each item is presented to respondents in a multiple-choice format such as:

1. Strongly disagree.
2. Disagree.
3. Undecided.
4. Agree.
5. Strongly agree.

Then, for example, a survey on attitudes towards women might contain questions like:

(a) Swearing is more objectionable from a woman.

(b) Intoxication in women is worse than in men.

With scores from 1 - 5 given to each of perhaps a dozen or so such questions the total score is then obtained for each respondent.

Desirably an initial pool of items should be pilot tested on a group of people to eliminate ambiguous and nondiscriminating items which tend to result in neutral responses.

This can be done by examining the *item-total score correlations*, each of which correlates the respondents' scores on an item with their scores summed over all the items. Then a good item will have a positive correlation and better items have higher correlations.

Likert Scaling is widely used, for example to assess the response to political advertising campaigns and a simple example of it is given in Chapter 17.

Guttman scaling

This approach gives stimulus-person scaling simultaneously and results in a matrix of data called the *Guttman scalogram*. For example, suppose we have five rods of from 5 to 7 feet in length (the exact lengths are not known) and ask each respondent to place a one in the Guttman scalogram matrix shown in Table 14.2 when they are taller than a particular rod. This raw data is then reorganized to give the result in Table 14.3.

Table 14.2. Guttman scalogram.

	Stimuli (rods)				
Persons	**C**	**E**	**B**	**D**	**A**
2	1	1	1	1	0
4	0	1	0	1	0
3	1	1	0	1	0
6	0	0	0	0	0
5	0	1	0	0	0
1	1	1	1	1	1
* e.g. person 2 is taller than C, E, B, D but not A					

Table 14.3 is obtained by placing the column with least ones at the left, the column with the most ones at the right, and so on. Then the row with the maximum number of ones is placed at the top (this is for person '1' in our example and hence this is the tallest person) and that with the least ones is placed at the bottom.

Table 14.3. Reordered Guttman scalogram.

Persons	Stimuli (rods)					Score
	A	**B**	**C**	**D**	**E**	**Score**
1	1	1	1	1	1	5
2	0	1	1	1	1	4
3	0	0	1	1	1	3
4	0	0	0	1	1	2
5	0	0	0	0	1	1
6	0	0	0	0	0	0

The result is an upper diagonal matrix, as shown in Table 14.3, resulting in a score for each person shown on the right side in Table 14.3, this giving the ordinal ranking for each person.

The preceding example of Guttman scaling was for physical stimuli, when a perfect upper triangular matrix resulted. Generally, however, this is not the case when attitudinal stimuli are considered.

An example is Bogardus' social stimulus scale, illustrated in Table 14.4, in which respondents are asked to judge how they would relate to people of various nationalities or races.

Table 14.4. Bogardus' social stimulus scale.

	Acceptance level					
	Would marry	As a friend	Would give a job	Allow as citizen	OK as visitor	No contact
Armenians						
Bulgarians						
Canadians						
etc.						

Such attitudinal stimuli do not yield a perfect upper triangular matrix but it has been suggested that when about 90% of the non-zero entries do appear on or above the diagonal that this *coefficient of reproducibility* value is acceptable (Eagly & Chaiken, 1993).

The Guttman scalogram has the advantage that the degree to which the reordered response matrix is 'triangularized' gives an immediate indication of the reliability of a survey. More complex to use, it is generally only usable for relatively small surveys, such as in-house surveys of consumer groups in advertising offices where it is an ideal tool.

Conclusion

Effective persuasion is all about changing attitude (where this, indeed, is necessary) so that some understanding of theories of attitude formation as cumulative or integrative processes is most important.

The preceding chapter on advertising (Chapter 13) discussed the important trio of cognitive, attitudinal, and behavioural responses and also McGuire's Reception-Yielding model of attitude formation, one that is particularly applicable in such contexts as advertising and religion.

Very relevant to attitude also is the vexatious question of ethnic conflict and, indeed, the equations of Forbes' contact hypothesis do emphasize that, over time, attitudes change. Moreover, models like that of contact hypothesis could be applied to the effects of advertising, and a recent book proposes a more comprehensive 'summation of scores' method of establishing attitudes towards societal groups (Mohr, 2014c).

The results of mere exposure research compellingly indicate how attitudes to new stimuli tend to improve given repeated exposure to them, the bottom line being that it is by such means that we are reduced to consumer zombies from cradle to grave.

Finally, measurement of attitudes is, of course, especially important in many areas such as consumer and political campaign surveys. Though perhaps only applicable to relatively small surveys, the Guttman scalogram is useful because the degree of triangularization of the reordered response matrix gives an immediate indication of the accuracy of a survey.

Chapter 15

ECONOBABBLE

> *Economics is as much a study in fantasy and aspirations*
> *as in hard numbers - maybe more so.*
> Theodore Roszak, *The Making of a Counter Culture* (1975).
>
> *The science* [economics] *hangs like a gathering fog in a valley, a fog*
> *which begins nowhere and goes nowhere, an incidental, unmeaning*
> *inconvenience to passers-by.* H. G. Wells, *A Modern Utopia* (1905).
>
> *If all economists were laid end to end, they would not reach a*
> *conclusion.* George Bernard Shaw (attributed to).

Financial jargon

One of the most unendurable things on TV is the slot in the evening news where a person with their finger on the economic pulse mumbles about the share market trends of the day, the exchange rate, and prognosticates about whether the central bank will alter its interest rates. This sort of waffle goes on day and night all over the world. Here we shall refer to it as *econobabble*.

Not long after this segment, which seems highly appropriate, the 'weather man' gives you the weather forecast. This is the main thing you watch the news for so they put it right at the very end so that you have to watch all the ads earlier in the news.

These days the weather forecasts are usually a lot more reliable than the econobabble.

As a brief introduction to financial jargon, however, one of the most important concepts is that of *compound interest*. A sum of money P (the principal) subjected to compound interest at an annual rate of i % has an accumulated value S after n years given by the formula:

$$S = P\,[1 + (i\,/100)]^n \tag{15.1}$$

Even more important is Mohr's Law of Money (Equation 8.4) as the exponential growth rate given by this is the fundamental principle of capitalism.

If you want to start a business and become a capitalist another simple but important concept is the *weighted average cost of capital* (WACC):

$$WACC = k_0 = k_e(E/V) + k_d(1 - t_c)(D/V) \qquad (15.2)$$

where k_e = WAC of equity, k_d = WAC of debt
E = monetary value of the company's equity
D = monetary value of the company's debt
$V = E + D$ = 'MV' of total capital
t_c = company tax rate

The *leverage* of a company is the ratio of D to the net worth of the company, whilst the OCS (optimal capital structure) is the optimum value of the ratio E/D.

Gross national product (GNP)

GNP is one of the most widely publicized economic yardsticks and is defined as the sum of several terms, namely:

$$GNP = C + G + I_g + X - M \qquad (15.3)$$

where
C = NP = private *consumption* and expenditures
G = government purchases of goods and services (not including transfer payments such as social security benefits)
I_g = gross domestic investment (plant and equipment, including inventories)
X = exports of goods and services
M = imports of goods and services

A net national product (NNP) can be calculated by adjusting I_g for depreciation but, because depreciation is difficult to estimate accurately, GNP is usually used.

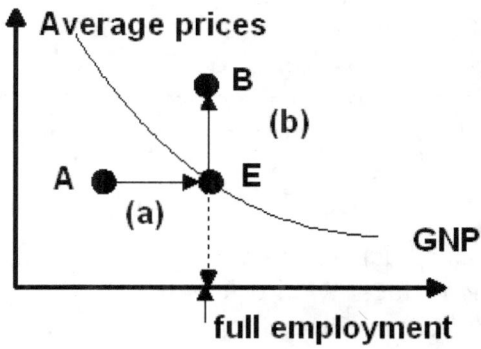

Figure 15.1. A Keynesian argument.

Keynes proposed that if government spending (G) is increased there is a *multiplier effect* which results in a much larger increase in GNP.

This is illustrated in Figure 15.1. Here, increased government spending has resulted in an increase in demand which shifts us from point A to an equilibrium point E (hence we have shifted to another demand curve).

There may then, however, be a further increase in demand as a result of increased competition (by those now employed etc.). This will result in an increase in price and we move to point B in Figure 15.1. Hence inflation has resulted and moves to curb this will reduce employment, the by now all too familiar cycle.

To give a measure of step (a) in Figure 15.1 Keynes defined a *marginal propensity to consume* (MPC) and a *marginal propensity to save* (MPS) as proportions of a change in disposable income *DI*:

$$MPC = \delta C/\delta DI, \quad MPS = \delta S/\delta DI \qquad (15.4)$$

and MPC is the slope of the consumption function whilst MPC + MPS = 1. Then, supposing we have MPC = 0.8, an increase in government spending (δG) of $M100 will, as recipients of spent money in turn spend 80% of it, result in a *multiplier effect* with the cumulative result:

$$\delta GNP (\$M) = 100 + 100(MPC) + 100(MPC)^2 + 100(MPC)^3 - -$$
$$= 100/(1 - MPC) = 100/MPS = \$500M$$

Note that the latter result is equivalent to that for bank lending and SRDs (statutory reserve deposits) in Equation 8.5.

The foregoing discussion of GNP considers only variation of G and its effect. To generalize how government *fiscal policy* affects the GNP we write the budget B in terms of revenue R and expenditure G as:

$$B = R - G \qquad\qquad (15.5)$$

and if $R > G$ (surplus), for example as a result of higher taxes, then demand is reduced and prices fall.

If $R < G$ (deficit), on the other hand, the deficit spending may stimulate the economy in the short term at the expense of greater government debt.

If this increase of $G = \delta G = \$M100$ and the tax rate is $t = 25\%$ we amend the multiplier effect calculated above to:

$$\delta GNP = \delta G \, / \, [MPS(1 - t) + t] = \$M250 \qquad (15.6)$$

so that inclusion of tax (or an increase therein) reduces the effect on the economy (this phenomenon is called *fiscal drag*).

Then in formulating *fiscal policy* the aim should be to 'juggle' R and G in such a way as to control unemployment and then balance the budget (so that $R = G$) when that objective has been attained.

The free market or monetary policy approach

Milton Friedman and other economists favour the free market or *monetarist* economic philosophy (Wonnacott & Wonnacott, 1979) given by the equation:

$$MV \text{ (aggregate demand)} = PQ \text{ (aggregate supply)} \quad (15.7)$$

where M = the amount of money in circulation (per year)
    V is its velocity of circulation (in transactions per year)
    P = the price of goods in circulation
    Q = the quantity of goods in circulation (per year)

Here V is the only relatively stable quantity and is based on the fact that, when you buy a product, the money you pay for it might be passed on quite soon as wages for somebody in the company you bought the product from.

Then that person spends his wages on food and other necessities, and so on. Typically V takes a value of around 4 in modern economies.

Monetarists argue that governments should increase M by between 2 and 4% each year to create a corresponding increase in Q and thence in GNP. This can be achieved simply by reducing interest rates.

This works because a reduction in interest rates increases the value of securities. This is because for a $100 bond with a yield of 8% the present value PV if it has a 10-year term is:

$$PV = 8/r + 8/r^2 + 8/r^3 + - - - - + (100 + 8)/r^{10}$$

where $r = 1+i$ and i is the market interest rate. From this it is clear that the PV increases when the market rate decreases.

In addition, reducing interest rates reduces the fiscal drag effect in Equation 15.6.

The trouble with the monetarist approach is that it favours rampant capitalism and spares little thought for the workers (= slaves), the environment or anything else except profits and huge executive salaries.

Two Pareto Problems

Two of the greatest problems Western economies face relate to Pareto's Law (Burch et al., 1983):

In most situations a relatively small percentage of certain objects contributes a relatively high percentage of output.

This is the basis of *contribution-by-value analysis* (also called ABC or Pareto analysis). For instance 15-30 percent of the population contributes 70-90 percent of the tax revenue, 20 percent of the employees in an office may do 80 percent of the work, or 20 percent of the items in inventory may account for 80 percent of the sales.

As an example of ABC analysis, the percentage of total dollar annual sales for each product are calculated and tabulated in descending order. Then the cumulative percentage contribution is added as a final column to show how much, say, the first 20% of products contributes.

The two great problems are:

[1] As a result of the Industrial Revolution, followed more recently by the Electronic Revolution (TV, PCs, mobile phones, the Internet etc.), an ever shrinking proportion of people *produce* anything tangible such as the three things essential for human life, that is food, clothing and shelter.

The rest of us are involved in *service industries* that are, for the most part, redundant. The rest of us sit and watch, reminding me of a good line by the singer Kamahl about critics:

They're like eunuchs, they like watching but they can't do it.

Thus, as the world's population continues to grow alarmingly, still fewer and fewer of us do the important work of farming.

[2] As a result of rampant capitalism a small proportion of the population has a large share of its wealth. In some countries the richest 5% of people have a 90% share of the wealth.

This situation has become so bad that in the US one in six children live in poverty and in the UK the poor have a life expectancy 11 years less than that of the rich.

Here we shall term such problems *Pareto Problems*.

Turning S&D around

The cornerstone of modern economics is the law of supply and demand. Some economics textbooks are so filled with obtuse S&D diagrams that they literally drive you mad.

Figure 15.2 shows typical supply and demand curves for which it is frequently assumed that there is *perfect competition*, that is there are many buyers and sellers and none are able to influence the price individually. Then the result is called a *competitive market*.

Here the supply goes up as the price goes up because the supplier is more motivated to produce more goods. The S curve, therefore, is drawn from the point of view of the *supplier*.

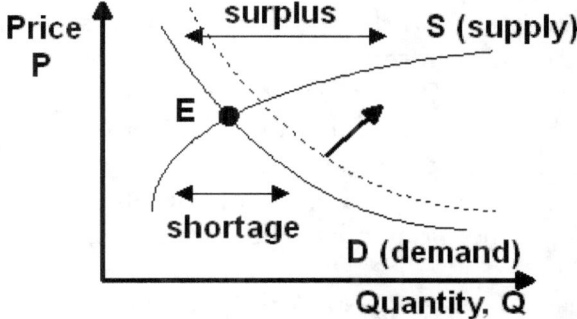

Figure 15.2. Traditional supply and demand curves.

The demand curve, on the other hand, goes down as the price goes down because with a greater quantity of goods available competition forces the price down (or conversely shortages result in increased prices). Hence the D curve is drawn from the point of view of the buyer.

The two curves intersect at point E, the equilibrium point at which supply equals demand.

That economists stick to the old fashioned S&D model of Figure 15.2 is a sure indication that they are behind the times. The model of Figure 15.2 applies well enough to agricultural or mineral products, for example, but not too heavily marketed products such Coke or McDonald's.

For these there is really no such thing as a shortage in supply, but, if there were to be such a shortage it would certainly reduce demand. No, these products have *created* a demand by using mass production to reduce costs and then advertising heavily.

The car industry, however, is perhaps the classic example. Australia, for example, is said to have begun to become 'motorized' in the mid 1950s. Before that relatively few people had cars and public transport was used to commute to work and school and holidays were taken by using buses, trains and, to a lesser extent, airplanes to get there.

Now, thanks to marketing, just about everybody has a car and, for example, dad parks his all day at the station and takes the train to the city to work, and mum uses hers to go shopping and pick up young children from the nearest school.

It was in the mid 1950s, however, that the world's population needed to reach a plateau fairly quickly. Then we wouldn't have such sprawling megacities and we wouldn't all need cars and the world wouldn't be on the verge of rapidly running out of oil and badly depleting many other vital resources.

Inverse law of supply and demand

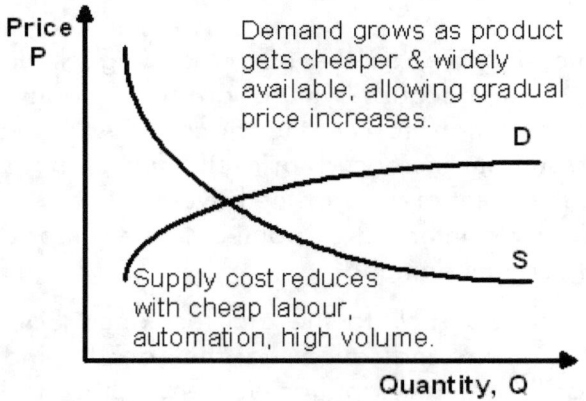

Figure 15.3. Inverse law of supply and demand, Mohr (2012a, 2012b, 2014b, 2017).

The cornerstone of modern economics is the law of supply and demand. In this the supply curve goes up as price increases, motivating greater production, and the demand curve goes down with increasing production, greater availability of goods decreasing their price. The two curves intersect at the equilibrium point at which supply equals demand.

The original 'D down' form applied OK in Adam Smith's day (1723 – 1790) but for today's global market S & D curves should often be the reverse, as shown in Figure 15.3, because:

(a) Economies of scale, use of casual labour, cheap labour in developing countries, etc. reduce cost.

(b) Mass marketing tends to sell as much as is produced.

214

The original 'D down' form still applies sometimes, for example in the case of food and commodities such as oil:

The first law of economics is that when the price goes up, consumption goes down. This is a divine law.
You cannot change it.
Sheikh Ahmed Yamani, Saudi Arabian Politician referring to OPEC's raising of oil prices in the early 1970s.

In modern global markets in which products are mass produced and heavily marketed the 'reversed' S&D model is that which applies and the massive growth in China's economy in recent decades is testament to this.

Some years ago the PC might have been a good example. The first microcomputers were tiny affairs suitable only for hobbyists but Clive Sinclair brought their price down to the point that they were affordable as toys for children. Then the first PCs suitable for business purposes, however, were quite expensive at first. Along came the IBM 'clone' from Asia, however, and that brought the price of PCs down to the affordable levels we still see today for 'bottom of the range' but extremely powerful PCs with dazzling clock speeds compared to those of yore.

The LM and IS curves

For decades central banks have counter-intuitively increased interest rates to, supposedly, control inflation, resulting in long periods of steadily increasing rates followed by a recession. Working with the simple equations of Jack Vernon's LM (liquid money supply) and IS (interest sensitive expenditure) curves it is not difficult to prove that, in fact, increasing interest rates increases inflation, as the 'man in the street' expects if you ask him (Vernon, 1980).

Indeed the first author e-mailed five pages on this matter to Australia's then Prime Minister few years ago, who acknowledged their receipt, but he assumes that little notice will be taken of them. As for the reader, the first author's modified/extended version of Vernon's LM/IS curve model in presented in the following section (Mohr, 2017).

Macroeconomic modelling

Many economists still mistakenly believe that increasing interest rates reduces inflation. Intuition suggests otherwise, as does Australia's economic history of the last 60 years, there having only been one instance of interest rates and inflation going in opposite directions, this being some time after the OPEC oil shocks of 1979/80 and the floating of the Australian dollar in 1983.

The proof is found using the equations of Jack Vernon's *liquid money supply* (LMS) and *interest sensitive expenditure* curves (ISE) given in his book *Macroeconomics* (Vernon, 1980).

Very concisely, with the modification transfer payments $D = f(r)$, the proof is as follows:

Real money supply = MS = M/P
= money demand = MD = $L + kQ - qr$

where P = price inflation = 1
M is non-inflation deflated money supply = 200
L is money demand constant = 50
Q is total output
r is the official interest rate
k is income responsiveness of money demand = 0.2
q is interest responsiveness of money demand = 1,000
giving

$$qr - kQ = L - M/P \tag{15.8}$$

and this is the LMS curve, an 'up' supply curve with r the up/rate axis and Q the across/quantity axis.

For demand, we have expenditure $E = C + I + G$

with C the consumption expenditure function = $a + bQ^* - sr$
where $a = 50$, $b = 0.8$, s = interest responsiveness of C = 1,000
so that $C = 50 + 0.8Q^* - 1,000r$
with $Q^* = Q(1 - t) - T + D$
where T is the tax constant, t is the tax rate,
D is the transfer payments,

216

and I is the investment expenditure function:

$$= I^* - ir = 200 - 1{,}000r$$

where i is interest responsiveness of I and $i = 1{,}000$ (early versions of the Fed-MIT model take s approx. $= i$) and G is equal to 230 (government spending)

so that $E = E^* + b(1 - t)Q - (i + s)r$

with $E^* = a - bT + bD + I^* + G$

where $a = 50$, $b = 0.8$, $t = 0.25$, $T = 50$, $I^* = 200$, $G = 230$

Now let D = transfer payments $= D^* + yU$ with $D^* = 25$, $y = 1{,}000$

where U = unemployment rate $= U^* + r/2$ with $U^* = 0.025$

so that $E^* = a - bT + bD^* + byU^* + byr/2 + I^* + G$

Then $E = Q$ for equilibrium gives

$$Q = a - bT + bD^* + byU^* + byr/2 + I^* + G + b(1 - t)Q - (i + s)r$$

or

$$(i + s - by/2)r + [1 - b(1 - t)]Q = a - bT + bD^* + byU^* + I^* + G$$
$$(15.9)$$

and this is the ISE curve, a 'down' demand curve.

Solving Equations (15.8) and (15.9) gives the equilibrium values of r and Q (and thence U).
With the values of constants stated above, we obtain

$$1{,}000r - 0.2Q = -150 \qquad (15.10a)$$

$$1{,}600r + 0.4Q = 480 \qquad (15.10b)$$

Adding twice the first to the second gives $r = 0.05$ and thence $Q = 1{,}000$ and $U = 0.05$.

With inflation $P = 1.1$, however, the solution is

$$r = 0.0601, \qquad Q = 959.6, \qquad \text{and } U = 0.0551.$$

Looking in reverse, this shows that increasing interest rates to 6% will cause 10% inflation, increase unemployment by 0.5%, and reduce total output by 4%.

To prove this beyond doubt, put $r = 0.0601$ in Equation 15.10b [not Equation 15.10a as this originally involved P which is now taken unknown], giving $Q = 959.6$ and put these values of r and Q (and $L = 50$, $M = 200$, $q = 1,000$, $k = 0.2$) in Equation 15.8, giving $P = 1.10$.

The bottom line is that increasing official interest rates increases inflation. This is because greater interest rates increase company debt repayments, leading to higher costs which are passed on to the consumer and the economy at large.

China's economic boom

Since 1980 China has transitioned from a command economy to a market economy with economic growth rates of up to 9%. In 2009, China overtook Germany to become the world's 3rd largest economy.

We believe that China has, at least in effect, reversed the Keynes multiplier effect. That is, they have allowed private capital from the major capitalist countries such as the US to stimulate their economy. The imported capital investment came from greedy American companies that set up in China to exploit their cheap labour and have helped kick-start China into an economic boom.

In addition, the Chinese government has supported over 20 major Chinese companies so that they could grow into major multinational operations, a practice more like the conventional Keynes effect.

The result has been that Chinese companies now dominate the global market for household electrical goods and have also became major players in the PC business and in the huge white goods business. In addition, cheap Chinese clothing and $2+ shop products are sold globally and priced so low that nobody else can compete. In addition Chinese government companies now own, for example, much of Australia's electricity network.

Some of us remember, however, that some Japanese products such as cars were viewed as being somewhat cheap and nasty in the mid 1960s. That certainly changed a great deal and their product quality in some areas is undoubtedly unsurpassable.

In the fullness of time the cheaper Chinese products will improve in quality and increase in price, further swelling their trade surplus with countries like the US.

Thus, as Heywood (2011) says:

Although the notion of US decline had been fashionable during the 1970s and 1980s, it returned with greater force in the early years of the twenty-first century, usually linked to the idea that the world was witnessing a general shift in power from the US-led West to Asia, and especially China.

The US is already seeing red (ink) about this and suggesting that China should devalue its currency which it pegs and does not float.

Pegging a currency, in fact, does have some advantages, for example that occasional adjustments, rather than constant daily fluctuations, tend to have more effect so that the government has much more control over its economy and importers and exporters have much greater certainty.

Australia floated its currency around 1970 but perhaps should not have:

If traded goods with prices determined exogenously on world markets constitute a large proportion of the economy, then exchange rate uncertainty translates into a high degree of uncertainty in the economy's overall price level. Such an economy may be too small and too open to have an independently floating currency.

Caves et al., *World Trade and Payments* (1990).

As for the econobabblers, they always sound like a record stuck in the same damaged groove when exchange rates alter significantly. If our currency goes down they say that it will be good for the economy because exports will be cheaper and will therefore increase in quantity. If it goes up they say that it will be good for the economy because exports will be dearer and earn us more money, neglecting to point out that the quantity of exports should be expected to fall.

In other words, they don't know what they are talking about.

Conclusions

One great mistake made by economists is that they don't see that S&D diagrams should have two alternative forms, depending upon whether:

(a) One is dealing with agricultural or mineral products prone to supply variations depending on such factors as the weather or discovery of new deposits.

(b) One is dealing with nonessential mass produced products for which large scale production reduces unit costs and for which the demand is stimulated by advertising.

Another is failing to see that the monetarist free market approach applied globally must eventually favour countries like China with stable governments, low labour costs and large populations.

Furthermore, in contrast to the laissez faire perfect competition notions of the monetarists, the Chinese government has very considerable influence over Chinese companies and this is having positive results.

In addition, China has not floated its currency, allowing even greater government control. Indeed, in 2016 Republican Presidential Nominee Donald Trump spent of lot of campaigning time raving about China, and in particular it's pegged exchange rate, threatening to impose 45% tariffs on Chinese imports to the USA to help rebuild US manufacturing.

Up until the last few years, during which China's economy has slowed considerably, the results have been spectacular with double digit growth rates reminiscent of those in the USSR in the 1960s and Germany in the 1930s. In July 2016, for example, China's English TV news service said that thousands of "new corporate entities" were registering themselves in the city of Chengoua because it was much cheaper to operate there than in China's largest cities such as Beijing.

The US, on the other hand, has rarely been in surplus over the last two or three decades and has had to increase its agreed limits of accumulated foreign debt several times.

Thus, according to Heywood (2011):

Finally, Kagan (2008) sought to revise the optimism embodied in the 'end of history' thesis by announcing the 'return of history'. This suggests that twenty-first century global politics will be characterized not by a democratic peace, but by rivalry between democratic states (especially the USA) and authoritarian states (notably China and Russia).

Such rivalry has indeed been hotting up recently between the US and China, with Donald Trump increasing tariffs on a wide range of Chinese imports, and China retaliating with like measures.

As for political and economic farce in Australia in the last decade or two, we have had our own Abbot and Costello comedy, with treasurer Peter Costello playing a role in introducing the GST in the 1990s, after PM John Howard had prior to his election promised not to have a GST.

Then in the 2000s Costello crowed that he could reduce the budget deficit by selling Telstra, the government-owned telecommunications 'giant'.

Having sold just about everything possible now, we wonder why the government is not privatized. It might be an improvement!

Then, we had Tony Abbott as PM for a while, with as unlikely a background as might be possible for a PM, and, having been deposed in a LNP coup by Malcolm Turnbull (who has since then also been deposed), he remains a somewhat comical figure in parliament, being laughed at by the opposition for changing his mind several times over key issues.

The bottom line is: are all the ideas and econobabble of the economic experts and textbooks in the USA full of hot flammable air and ready to explode in their face sometime soon? It sure looks like it.

[15] Econobabble

Chapter 16

THE PSYCHOLOGY OF CONFLICT

> *It is disturbing to see that still today, even in the most*
> *advanced countries, in large sections of human society,*
> *aggressiveness is praised as a virtue - or at least as a valuable asset -*
> *and it is constantly advertised in the motion pictures and on television.*
> *We need - more than anything else -*
> *to educate people to tolerance and gentility.*
> Carlo Cipolla, *The Economic History of World Population* (1974).

An attitudinal model of conflict

An alternative to well-known 'contact hypothesis' models such as that of Forbes discussed in Chapter 14, this simple summation model of attitude formation is a very simple 'first approximation' formula for assessing the potential for conflict between a person or group assessed and another person or group.

The basic formula takes the form:

$$A^* = A + xB + yC + zD \qquad (16.1)$$

where A^* = current 'overall' attitude,
A = initial or 'basic' attitude (based on 'known history'),
B = attitudes towards behaviours of the second party,
C = contact history between the two parties,
D = degree of difference between the parties considered,
and x, y, z are scaling factors that indicate the relative importance of the terms and here these will be assumed unity for simplicity.

Equation 10.1 can, of course, be used to assess the attitude of both parties involved in the assessment.

Here attitude is assessed in the same way as attitude is measured by the information integration model of Equation14.2 but for simplicity only scale values (but not weights) will be given to a small set of items in measuring *A*.

Similarly, only scale values are used in assessing *B, C* and *D*. These extra terms add a great deal to the 'basic' *A* assessment to give a 'picture' of the 'overall' attitude.

Example application

As an example of application of the simple model of Equation 16.1 the attitude of a typical individual towards a hypothetical terrorist organization 'HTO' is considered.

To assess this only five items are assessed by simple questions for the initial attitude, behavioural, contact and difference terms in Equation 161. Assessment is similar to that used for the 'five-factor' model of personality (Larsen & Buss, 2002) and uses five possible scores:

+2 = strongly like/very similar etc.
+1 = like/similar etc.
0 = neutral
-1 = dislike/different etc.
-2 = strongly dislike/very different etc.

Table 16.1 gives an example assessment for a hypothetical individual.

Here total scores less than -30 are 'very negative', -10 to -20 'negative', -10 to +10 are moderate, +10 to +20 'positive', and more than +20 'very positive'.

Thus the results of Table 16.1 are 'negative', the total of -22 indicating a considerable degree of disapproval. It is only very negative scores of less than -30 that might be a cause for concern if they were obtained for a significant percentage of a population.

Table 16.1. Person's hypothetical attitude towards 'HTO'.

SCORE:	-2	-1	0	1	2
A, initial/basic attitude	Dislike/Like				
The people			0		
Their government(s)		-1			
How they look		-1			
What they say	-2				
What they do	-2				
B, group behaviour	Dislike/Like				
Sectarian conflict		-1			
Negative rhetoric		-1			
'Pushing' their religion	-2				
Threats	-2				
Terrorism	-2				
C, contact history	Uncomfortable/Comfortable				
See on TV			0		
See on street			0		
Close to		-1			
Talk to		-1			
Socialize	-2				
D, differences	Different/Similar				
Language		-1			
Economic				1	
Culture		-1			
Religion	-2				
History		-1			
TOTAL SCORE, A*:	-22				

Weighting factors can be assigned to items in Table 16.1 to reflect differing importance associated with them, for example the 9th and 10th items might have weights >1.

Effect of Societal views

The effect of the views of society on individuals and groups can be included in Equation 16.1 by adding an extra term comparable to the inclusion of 'social norms':

$$A^{**} = A^* + fS = A + xB + yC + zD + fS$$

where *f is a scaling factor* here assumed = 1 for simplicity, and the factors *x, y, z* are also assumed =1 so that:

$$A^{**} = A + B + C + D + S \qquad (16.2)$$

and *S* is the person or group's assessment of the attitude or 'position' of society, society here including the media, politicians, religious leaders, the public, friends and family.

Then measurement of *S* is done in the same way as for *A, B, C* and *D* in Table 16.1.

Table 16.2. Person's assessment of society's attitude.

SCORE:	-2	-1	0	1	2
S, perceived society view	Negative/Positive				
TV/radio/papers		-1			
Politicians			0		
Religious leaders		-1			
The public		-1			
Friends & family		-1			
TOTAL SCORE:	-4				

For the views of a typical person regarding society's attitude towards 'HTO' the result might be that shown in Table 16.2. Adding this result to that of Table 16.1 the aggregate score is -26, a 'negative' overall result.

A 'very negative' score would be less than -30, so the combined result of Tables 16.1 and 16.2 (i.e. -26) for an individual or a group is not of concern but worth taking some notice of.

Responses to conflict

When the group, attitudes towards which are sought, is in some form of dispute or conflict, whether this be economic, concerning mistreatment of a few people, or armed conflict on any scale, the attitudes concerning what measures should be taken against the group can also be measured in like fashion to Table 16.1.

Table 16.3. Attitudes towards measures against group.

SCORE:	0	1	2	3	4
	Level of support for action				
Government condemns					4
Cut diplomatic ties				3	
Trade embargo			2		
Public demonstrations				3	
UN sanctions		1			
War	0				-
TOTAL SCORE:	13				

Table 16.3 shows an example of such an assessment for a hypothetical individual concerning his or her views towards HTO's terrorism around the world. The total score is R = 13 out of a possible 24, perhaps a 'fail' mark by way of assessment of the group in question, but not an extremely bad score. Total scores of close to 20, on the other hand, would indicate very strong feelings of which, perhaps, considerable notice should be taken should they be found to apply to a significant number of people.

The results of Tables 16.1 – 16.3 can be combined as:

$$A^{***} = A + B + C + D + S - (R - 12)$$

with the last term adjusted to allow for its different scale of measurement, giving A^{***} = -27 for the present example case. When the results of Table 16.3 are included, measure of positive attitudes towards the group in question should also be added for 'balance' (Mohr, 2014c; Mohr et al., 2018c).

Other factors affecting attitudes & conflict

[1] Hierarchical influences.

These include the influence of strongly hierarchical organizations that have very great influence on society and its individual people, some of these being:

(a) Governments of any type, whether they be monarchies or dictatorships have considerable influence on the populace by way of propaganda and enforceable laws, for example those of conscription.

(b) Political parties. Even when they are not in government, supporters of political parties are often considerably influenced by their views.

(c) Religions. These, of course, have had great influence throughout history but have less influence in the West now, whilst in contrast Muslim sects still have great influence on many of the world's 1.5 billion Muslims.

(d) TV, radio and print media also tend to come from 'on high' and also have considerable influence.

[2] Social norms.

Social norms have a great influence on the thinking of individuals and groups within any society, for example the wearing of scarves, veils and burkas by Muslim women is still very widely practiced.

The structure of society has also been an important factor. Fairly soon after the Agricultural Revolution and the formation of man's first permanent towns and farms the first small armies would have been formed to defend them, at first only temporarily.

Indeed, with the diversification of occupations that the Agricultural Revolution brought, permanent armies were one eventual result, notably in the Rome and its empire, for example. Then, of course, given the availability of armies, there has always been a tendency to use them sooner or later, most obviously as the 'external police force' to deal with external problems, albeit a very large force all too often in history.

[3] Economic factors.

Economic considerations have often been the cause of human conflict, for example competition for resources, a good historical example being the Spanish Empire's enthusiastic search for gold in the Americas.

Man has always been inventing new tools and weapons, particularly since the Industrial Revolution. Now the arms industries have become massive and are able to considerably influence government policy in many countries whose economies have suffered a steep decline in their manufacturing industries in recent decades (Sampson, 1977; Thomas, 2006).

An example of the absurdity of it all, the CIA knew that chemical weapons were pouring into Iraq from Chile and South Africa in the 1980s. Cardoen industries in Santiago, for example, sent its chemical weapons, and the German-made artillery 'cups' or shells to contain them, to Iraq (Ben-Menashe, 1992). Then, the US later condemned Iraq for using these weapons on the Kurds and used this as an excuse for their first invasion of Iraq early in 1991.

[4] Growing populations.

Even as far back as early man's troglodyte days it is not hard to imagine an extended family group growing to the point at which a second cave was needed.

Similarly, when man had towns and then cities these too grew in size, needing ever more space and, more importantly, resources, particularly food.

This, coupled with man's habit of exploration, which no doubt dates back to his hunter-gatherer days and thence the hunt for food, has led man to engage in conflict with neighbouring populations.

Conflicts may have arisen simply out of the suspicion that the sight of strangers aroused when they suddenly appeared. Perhaps, for example, a spear might be thrown to scare them away. Then, of course, there might be retaliation and thus conflict.

As man's population continued to increase, of course, the tendency for migration and thence conflict must have increased, for example people leaving crowded and disease-ridden cities in Europe to colonize the 'New World' from the 16th to 19th centuries.

[5] Proximity.

For tribal man, as with his chimpanzee relatives, proximity was a key factor in regular tribal conflicts.

Indeed, until only about two thousand years ago, human conflicts were only between neighbouring cities, regions, or countries. With the building of ships capable of sailing hundreds of miles, however, came the ability to explore more widely, and human conflict began to occur over greater distances and on a greater scale.

Eventually ships travelled even greater distances and great empires were built, notably the Roman Empire and the Spanish and British Empires.

As noted in the section on Contact Hypothesis in Chapter 14, proximity also affects people's attitudes as does contact which, of course, is facilitated by proximity, the more 'negative' the contact the more negative the attitude formed.

[6] Competitiveness.

In the Roman Empire, for example, there was a competitiveness in its governments, an obvious drive that made it wish to become 'bigger and grander' and go out and conquer other lands to achieve that end.

This obsession with competition runs all through the history and cultures of Homo sapiens, an example being our obsession with sport, or any kind of competition even if it is called a 'game.' It seems fundamentally related to the alpha-male behaviour of several other animal species.

Man, however, takes the alpha-male issue to absurd lengths, for example the original Olympic Games in Ancient Greece being conducted in the nude and, indeed, it seems to be returning slowly towards that situation now.

Equally, man has often indulged in war without good reason, usually because some loony leader and his acolytes want to 'beat' some other foe.

Conclusions

The simple formula of Equation 16.1 combines the measurement techniques of attitudinal psychology with the concepts of the contact hypothesis to assess the attitudes of individuals and groups of people to other groups of people. The point of this exercise is that, when the attitude of one group to another is very negative, then conflict between the groups is, of course, more likely.

The attitudes of leaders are of particular importance, as it is these that may lead to conflict and war. The attitudes of leaders will, of course, be influenced by many of the same factors and stimuli that affect the public.

There are many other factors that affect modern human conflict. For example, particularly in modern times, alliances between nations have played a part in many wars, World War 1 and World War 2 being notable examples.

One difficulty is that, if two groups of 4 nations are allied, then a single nation attacking some part of another may quickly result in 8 nations being at war. In other words, the larger the parties involved, the bigger the conflict.

One fear for the future, therefore, is the increasing power of such huge nations as China and India, and also of the 1.5 billion Muslims around the world. The numbers involved here are an order of magnitude greater than those involved in the two world wars of the last century and war between any of these three entities and another of perhaps similar size could well be the war to end all wars.

Chapter 17

So Have You Been Brainwashed?

> *An asylum for the sane would be empty in America.*
> George Bernard Shaw, attributed.
>
> *Fools are in a terrible, overwhelming majority,*
> *all the wide world over.*
> Henrik Ibsen, *An Enemy of the People* (1882).

Few, if any, escape for long

Few of us get wise to the fact that we have been brainwashed almost from birth so that by the age of 20 or 30 or so we end up zombies more defined by the products and habits we have been brainwashed into than anything else.

This is illustrated appropriately on the cover of a book on consumer behaviour which shows people in a city street dressed according to some product they indulge, for example a man 'dressed' in a Coke can (Solomon, 1992).

If you have already realized what a brainwashed mess you have become then you are one of the few people coming to their senses. You might, for example, have given up smoking, remembering with regret the 'bullshit' that brainwashed you into taking up such a disgusting and unhealthy habit.

You may not be the typical brainwashed zombie with mobile phone in one hand, drink bottle or cigarette in the other, uncomfortable jeans, baseball hat and perhaps a 4WD if you are old enough and affluent enough to waste that much money on a heap of gas-guzzling metallic junk.

Chances are, however, that you still have other behaviours that are the result of brainwashing earlier in life and which you would be better off without.

How we are brainwashed

We are brought up and educated with a lot of conditioning in which various kinds of rewards and punishments, most of them verbal, are dished out along the way.

As part of that education moral, religious, ethical and legal arguments will be brought to our notice to influence and control our behaviour.

Nowadays, people spend much of their lives absorbing TV and other media bullshit half full of repetitive advertising and, consequently, they also spend a lot of time at sporting venues or in pubs and clubs where they are indulging some brand or other, whether it be a sporting team or a brand of beer.

At work, as at school, we are likely to be at the bottom end of a hierarchical system of 'top-down one-way' (TDOW) communication which treats us no better than slaves or lab rats.

The result is that our behaviour at times can often be likened to that of animals in conditioning experiments, for example:

(a) Rats in a Skinner box pushing a lever to receive food pellets [c.f. working in a production line to receive pay and thence food].

(b) Pigs using their snouts to push the right spot on a PC screen to receive a food reward [c.f. gambling machines].

(c) Rats in 'running wheels' etc. [c.f. humans with their myriad of usually ridiculous sports].

(d) Pavlov's dogs salivating at the sight of food [c.f. humans doing likewise over food or wine].

Humans at times, however, are far more ridiculous than animals could ever be, for example how we carry on and 'perv' over sex and now have our media littered with it. We have no doubt that a good deal of *social learning* that is very equatable with conditioning is associated with that sort of behaviour.

Social learning and *imitative learning* (IL) are much the same thing but we associate IL more with infants who at the outset imitate their parents with whom they have *imprinted*. People of all ages, however, imprint a group of friends or role models whose behaviours they imitate.

How brainwashed a consumer are you?

The simple test of Table 17.1 uses Likert scaling (much used in market research) to rate your consumption habits.

Give scores to each item (RH column) according to whether you consume/indulge the particular item to the following levels:

1 = Not at all or minimally
2 = To some extent/a little
3 = Moderately
4 = Quite a lot/a bit too much
5 = Much too much

Table 17.1. Survey of consumption habits.

#	Item	Score
1	Soft drinks, confectionery and snack 'foods'.	
2	Fast food	
3	Booze	
4	Smoking	
5	Drugs - illegal or unnecessary prescription drugs	
6	Jeans, baseball hat or other originally foreign clothes	
7	Cosmetics	
8	The fitness industry: gyms and fitness equipment	
9	Do you indulge in insane activities like skate boarding, rollerblading, bowls or golf?	
10	How much attention do you pay to TV ads?	
11	Do you buy the latest pop music?	
12	Do you go to restaurants and pubs?	
13	Do you go to the movies?	
14	Do you gamble (pokies, horses etc.)?	
15	Do you pay to attend commercialized sporting events?	
16	How much do you use your mobile phone?	
17	Do you have a 4WD or other 'fashionable' car?	
18	Do you have domestic pets?	
19	Do you take holiday trips?	
20	Do you buy things just because they are 'on special' and supposedly a bargain?	
	Total	

If your total score (/100) is greater than 20 you are fairly badly brainwashed. If your total score exceeds 30 you are a hopeless case! [The first author's score at an earlier age would have been about 20].

Of course countless other questions could have been included in Table 17.1, for example:

(a) Do you give regular allegiance to a particular political party?

(b) Do you 'consume' sex products, that is, prostitution, pornography, sex chat lines etc.?

Do you really believe the bullshit?

The foregoing crude quantitative test is of consumption habits. At a more qualitative level the following subjects are areas in which your views may have resulted from brainwashing, that is, mere acceptance of the bullshit given on the topic in the media.

➤ Propaganda has always painted socialism as communism which permits little freedom. How free are we when we are brainwashed to dress and behave in the same stupid way?

➤ How free are we in schools, Universities, workplaces and hospitals increasingly operated like assembly lines and in which our roles are reduced to those of mere automatons?

➤ How free are we when increasing numbers of us spend time in jail or psychiatric institutions, many children are doped to help them tolerate an educational process that becomes more and more meaningless, massive numbers of us take to booze and other drugs, and massive numbers of us commit suicide or simply drop out of society?

➤ How secure are we when 50% of marriages end in divorce, we have to work longer and longer hours, children are sent to long-day-care almost at birth and women have to work as well when once they didn't?

➤ How free are we when there is less and less job security and the idea of one career or occupation for life has vanished? Now you are expected to change jobs 3+ times which cannot be a reasonable or economically efficient way of life.

➢ Do you really believe in God or that Jesus Christ did the definitively impossible and rose from the dead? Do you really think it is right that religious sects throughout history have kept on killing each other, as they still are right now in many parts of the world, most of them encouraged by the BS in the Koran?

➢ Do you really believe that Coke or booze, or whatever junk is pushed at you by advertising, is a smart and healthy thing to consume?

➢ Do you really believe locking infants up in day care is right?

➢ Do you really believe 12 years at school is necessary when Francis Bacon left Cambridge at age 14 and Michelangelo and da Vinci were apprenticed at that age?

➢ Do you believe that increasingly corporatized Universities should be able to con people with ridiculous courses like postgraduate courses in Sexology and Puppetry?

➢ Do you really believe it is sensible that Australian Unis increased their output of PhDs by 85% between 1996 and 2006 (the increase in the USA was only 15% in that time)?

➢ Do you really believe the Westminster 'revolving door' two-party system is anything like halfway democratic?

➢ Do you really believe that 'she'll be right' and the pollies and other leaders who have always led us into wars or profited from them will fix everything when we have just about bred ourselves out of existence and ruined and depleted the planet beyond repair?

Just what then is sensible?

If one wishes to avoid being a sucker for advertising and other bullshit one should do almost nothing. There are, however, a few necessities of life such as:

[1] **Food:** obviously one should try and develop a healthy diet which has minimal fat and sugar, plenty of complex carbohydrate, and sufficient protein, fibre and essential nutrients. To that end, therefore, junk food, fatty snack foods and confectionery should be largely avoided.

[2] Clothing: Neat, well fitting and practical clothing at modest prices should be sufficient for all but those with too much money. Other money spent on appearances should be minimal, for example, in the 'old days' women did their own hair.

[3] Shelter: Modest, practical and not too cramped housing should be all that we need. Indeed, with our collapsing standards of living and everybody but the children needing to work at often menial jobs most young families can barely afford that or pay at least double or triple in the long run to a greedy bank.

[4] A partner: It is difficult to do or achieve much in life alone. A writer such as I, for example, needs above all else a publisher, and preferably an agent also to get publishers interested in the first place.

[5] A job: As with the hunter-gatherers, society needs people to produce food, clothing, shelter and many other things, their production involving countless 'service' occupations such as selling products. Whether one needs the money or not, however, some sort of occupation is needed to pass the time so that, for example, geriatrics are given OT or *occupational therapy*.

[6] Exercise: Most of us have relatively sedentary occupations so that we need healthy exercise such as walking, running, calisthenics and weights training.

[7] Relaxation and sleep: Rest and sleep are, of course, absolutely necessary and for good health one must make sure of getting enough of both.

[8] Pastimes and entertainment: After the foregoing essential activities have been done one normally still has spare time each day as well as days off from work. To fill the gaps we need 'pastimes' which for most people include watching TV, listening to music, interacting with family or friends, or going out to dinner or the movies.

In most of the foregoing there is considerable scope for excess. In the last, for example, it is possible to spend a fortune on restaurants, pubs, and gambling over a lifetime.

If we consider needless habits such as smoking, booze and expensive clothes and cosmetics, however, then even the average married couple can spend the price of a halfway decent house (two if they were still fairly priced!) on such habits over a lifetime.

Conclusions

Most of we ordinary peasants can greatly improve our lives by being careful and economical in our consumption practices and habits, in turn improving the prospects of the planet as a whole. Not least of these, of course, is making every effort not to have more than a couple of children, if that. In addition, we should not waste precious time and resources on keeping unhygienic household pets and it would be a great deal saner to instead spend a few dollars supporting a starving child in Africa, or better still, supporting population reduction programs in such countries.

We can also make a difference by actively supporting ethical and sustainable business practices, perhaps by joining organizations that push for sustainable practices and conservation.

Most of all, however, people should push for real democracy that might limit wasteful global marketing and reduce the greed and influence of ruthless transnational companies.

The bottom line, therefore, is that both at a personal and public level we should do what we can to reverse the power and influence of the 'brainwashers'.

[17] So Have You Been Brainwashed?

PART 4
REAL DEMOCRACY

Chapter 18

REAL DEMOCRACY

> *A democracy exists whenever those who are free and are not well-off, being in the majority, are in sovereign control of government, an oligarchy when control lies with the rich and better-born, these being few.* Aristotle, *The Politics*, 343 B.C.
>
> *All inequality that has no special utility to justify it is injustice.* Jeremy Bentham, British jurist and philosopher (1748 - 1832). *Writings* (W Stark ed.), 1952.

Parliamentary democracy

Aristotle's remark about oligarchy which opens this chapter is an important reminder that, as then, we do not have *real* democracy today. In fact the better-off Greeks voted with black and white stones on the questions of the day in open forum. Aristotle's complaint was that it was only the men, and then those of commerce, who had such a say in things.

In other words they had a mildly capitalist society which the Romans savagely improved upon in even greater style, enslaving most of the population.

In most of the world today we do not have anything like real democracy. We have, in fact, Westminster type *parliamentary democracy,* a very brief history of which is (Mackenzie, 1950):

1. Pre 1066 (Saxon times). The barons and King met each year at Easter, Whitsun and Christmas.

2. 1258 (in the reign of Henry III). A meeting of the barons of England at Oxford was the origin of the *House of Lords.*

3. 1264. Simon de Montfort, on the King's behalf, organized a meeting of two knights from each county.

4. 1265. Two citizens from each county were included in the latter meeting, constituting the origin of the *House of Commons*.

5. In the reign of Elizabeth I the puritans became the first party and were the opposition to the crown.

6. In the reign of James I the cavaliers and roundheads emerged as two opposing political forces.

7. 1681. The origin of the names *Whig* and *Tory*.

This system has evolved in England, Australia and New Zealand into the two main parties being a conservative party, which supports the capitalist ruling class, and a Labour Party which traditionally supported the workers or modern-day slaves.

The conservative party is said to be *right wing* and the Labour Party *left wing*, a fine example of the power of emotive language.

Now, however, big business has considerable influence over both parties and the policies of the Labour Party are sometimes more conservative than those of its opposition conservative party.

The result is a revolving door parody of democracy in which stooges become our leaders for relatively brief periods but their policies are greatly influenced by the business sector and the economic imperialism of traditional allies in war, in Australia these being the US and UK.

In this parody the 'fat cats' of the public service wield more influence in policy-making than do average members of parliament (Self, 1977).

In the USA and like countries, however, it is an inner core of rich and powerful families that endures long after any one politician's term of office and which runs the country.

An example of this was the call by David Rockefeller's Trilateral Commission to quell the "excess of democracy" in advanced capitalist countries and to "rationalize the US economy through capitalist dominated planning and in conjunction with other leading capitalist nations to reassert US authority on a world scale" (Crough et al., 1980).

We don't need to remind the reader of the influence of the Kennedy family in the 1960s, nor of that of the Bush family in the 1990s and beyond. In each case the results were disastrous, John Kennedy having involved the USA in the disastrous Vietnam War, it is said partly because of his Catholic background, and the Bush family having involved it in two unjustified conflicts in Iraq, presumably to please Saudi Arabia where they have strong connections.

Capitalism vs Socialism

In the western world unrestrained capitalism is rampant and these days commentators sometimes talk of the "triumph of capitalism." The pros and cons of capitalism and socialism were discussed very briefly in Chapter 6, where it was concluded that capitalism was inherently unfair and that under it living standards of all but the richest are rapidly declining in the developed world.

The first author asked the somewhat famous John Argyris just before he died: *Is the problem of the human race anthropology?* He immediately replied: *Of course.*

As Cipolla (1974) put it:

> *There is no escaping man's origin - a carnivorous and cannibalistic animal - and disgustingly so.*

On another occasion he asked Argyris:
"Are real democracy and communism the same thing?"
He replied immediately: *"Of course!"*

Here we should quickly remind the reader that socialism involves state ownership and control of almost everything whereas true communism is only practical in small groups of people.

243

In such groups each person would have an equal say on each and every issue, though hopefully views that most thought too extreme, illogical or even 'mad', would be discounted by the group. That might prevent little Hilters from having much influence or even developing at all.

As for extremes regarding socialism, according to PBS News Hour:

North Korea has elections every five years. Voters in each electorate are presented with a single box on the election slip and they tick it (Australian SBS TV news, 1 PM, 9/3/19).

But what form then would the real democracy that we so urgently need take in our modern and immensely overpopulated world?

Real democracy

The Concise Oxford Dictionary defines democracy as

1 a a system of government by the whole population, usu. through elected representatives.
   b a state so governed.
   c any organization governed on democratic principles.
2 an egalitarian and tolerant form of society.

Key words seem to be *whole population* and *egalitarian*. We have the 'usual' elected representatives and the Westminster system of two main parties which take it in turns to govern the country.

What they govern, however, is a capitalist society. Indeed, powerful capitalists who run transnational companies hold considerable sway over our so-called democratic governments. In Australia and most developed countries they have, for example, taken over the government owned banks, airlines and utilities.

Capitalism is the furthest thing possible from egalitarian and the increasing gaps between the rich and poor in developed countries bear testimony to this.

Real democracy, therefore, should have the following features:

[1] Each *eligible* citizen (e.g., older than, say, 14, and not in jail) should be able to vote to elect members of parliament.

[2] Members of parliament should be independent and represent only the interests of their constituency, not those of any other organization.

[3] All citizens should be allowed to vote on key issues such as significant changes in taxation, not just on referenda relating to proposals for changes in the constitution. This issue is discussed further in the following chapter.

There is nothing new in [1] but penalize members of parliament who collude with each other or with external organizations to influence parliamentary outcomes should be penalized.

Currently our main parties are given much of the funding with which they contest elections by the federal government, this perpetuating the status quo of the 'revolving door' two party system. Proposal [2] requires that *eligible* individuals seeking election should receive such funding, presumably a modest amount. To make it effective rules could be put in place to help ensure that candidates are given equal publicity, for example by printing and posting similar 'flyers' for each candidate.

Proposal [3] could be easily implemented using modern information technology, for example via the Internet or the phone, providing one or more sites for Internet or phone voting in each electorate.

Preferential voting

Australia is one of the few countries that have a preferential voting system for state and federal elections.

In this, voters are given a list of candidates standing for elections and they must place a 1, 2 and 3 in three of the boxes to represent their first, second and third preferences.

When votes are tallied and two candidates have similar primary vote totals, preferences are 'distributed' between the candidates to decide the final vote.

The latter situation applies for the 'lower house', the House of Representatives, but for the 'upper house' or Senate preferential voting has a much greater effect.

Voting for this is on a second quite large form with many candidates, with several parties listed above 'the line', a line across the form at about mid-height, and then several more 'independent' candidates listed below that line.

Voters then simply place 1, 2 and 3 in boxes for parties above the line, or they must place sequential numbers in all the boxes below the line to vote for particular candidates.

Then the total sum of above the line 'party votes' for each party determines how many of their senate candidates are elected, the party having allocated them an 'order' on the senate ballot paper, only the first few in that order being elected.

The preferential voting above the line, however, allows candidates for minor parties with very few primary votes to be elected 'on preferences' when major parties recommend them to voters as second or third preference vote, rather than recommend the major party they usually do battle with for control of the country.

Similarly, the preferential voting below the line then allows independent candidates with very few first preference votes but numerous second and third preference votes to be elected.

A recent example is the small One Nation party, one of whose candidates for the 2016 Australian Federal Election was elected with only 19 first preference votes, and this is the reason that there are now almost half a dozen small parties in Australia which get one, two, or three members elected to the senate.

In the recent years there have been occasional objections in the media to such outcomes as the latter example, however, and it is quite likely that one day some changes might be made to Australia's preferential voting system, though it is unlikely to be abandoned altogether.

Democratic rights

In a country like Australia, for example, we would like to see every young citizen given *land rights* when they reach a certain age, perhaps 25 or thereabouts. Thus, rather than pay now absurdly inflated prices for a home, they would be able to obtain land for it as a birthright.

To this we must quickly add the proviso that this 'free' land would not be in the inner areas of major cities but in outer suburban areas of them, or in regional towns or cities.

Then they would still have to find the money to build on this land. One solution would be to lend them a modest amount of money to place a cheap temporary housing unit on the site.

Another birthright should be suitable employment. By suitable we simply mean that we wouldn't give somebody with physical disabilities, for example, the dangerous job of roof tiling, a job we would rather not give anyone.

Alternatively, young people should be encouraged to start their own businesses. They must, of course, be allowed to build their business so that accumulation of assets or capitalism must be permitted to a limited extent.

Disabled people, for example those injured in industrial accidents, must be supported by society so taxes must always be levied for this and many other purposes.

In Australia and like countries, the issue of women's rights has been growing for a couple of decades, and recently there have been calls for "gender equality" in the main political parties.

Certainly men and women are different in many respects, and though research has sometimes indicated that men are better at more mathematical subjects (Vernon, 1960), the fact that there are now more women studying at University than men now in Australia and elsewhere suggests that women are, at least overall, doing better academically.

As for behavioural differences, most these are doubtless learned, a classic example being one of two identical male twin infants, one of whom traumatically lost his penis at 7 months and was thus raised as a girl after surgical "sex reassignment".

At age 7 there was reportedly:

"a tremendous difference in the behavior of the two. The little girl likes to dress nicely, dislikes being dirty, loves to have her hair set, help with the housework, plays with dolls, and wants to be a doctor or teacher when she grows up. Her brother plays in the dirt, helps his father fix things, and wants to be a policeman or fireman. These children, in spite of having exactly the same genes, conform perfectly to the traditional American sex roles. Learning is evidently of great importance" (Weiss & Mann, 1978).

So it is in Australia's parliament that the male leaders of the government and opposition constantly yell at each other from the two opposing sides of parliament in the lunatic fashion typical of the antiquated Westminster system, whereas the women members of parliament usually behave in a much more civilized and less anthropoidal manner.

Taxation

It is in the interests of the people that companies and individuals with large incomes should be taxed more heavily because their wealth was derived from the population at large in the first place, that is, their wealth came from the 'common pool' of money in circulation. If they had dipped more heavily into this pool than others this could almost be called a form of theft but, whatever 'excess wealth' might be called, it should be taxed more heavily than average incomes.

As part of this policy, therefore, those who inherit large fortunes should be required to pay 'inheritance duties' on them. This is a preferable approach to that of 'death duties' as it taxes a form of income, the usual purpose of taxes.

Some authors suggest that inequality in capitalist societies should be reduced by reducing the inheritability of wealth, in other words by increasing death duties (Broom et al., 1980).

This is an unpopular proposal to both the rich and the middle class. As a result the Australian State of Queensland abolished death duties many years ago and other States only apply them to large fortunes.

Freedom and the law

Real democracy would, of course, allow freedom of speech and numerous other freedoms. An example might be freedom of association which might be taken to include religious affiliations.

As for political affiliations, real democracy should make these unnecessary because society would be concerned with 'one issue at a time' so that political 'creeds' that involved a collective approach to a 'raft' of issues would seem comparatively useless.

People should also have freedom of action, for example they should be allowed to go wheresoever they please.

There must be legal constraints and limits on society, however, to limit such clearly immoral and unacceptable actions as murder, rape, incest, theft, slander, and the like.

Indeed, one would hope that a decent legal system would replace the need for religion and 'cover' such issues as laid down by the Ten Commandments of Christianity and similar codes in other religions.

Work and welfare

Just as the Neanderthals looked after their elders up to a point, at least, any just society would have a welfare system that supported disabled and elderly people. This would be funded, of course, by taxation, or as Karl Marx put it:

From each according to his abilities,
to each according to his needs.

If, furthermore, the education and employment systems saw to it that those who worked were always doing jobs with which they were content then, indeed, they should not mind paying 'reasonable' taxes to support, for example, people who might have been disabled by serious workplace accidents.

249

Conclusion

Real democracy is urgently needed in this world, not the sham of government run by wealthy capitalist families, by the 'revolving' door approach of the Westminster system, or by dictators and authoritarian 'socialist' governments.

Real democracy should involve election of ordinary people representative of the fullest possible cross section of society in order to represent the broad mass of the people equitably. It should also allow all the people to vote on important, not just constitutional, issues.

It could then be hoped that:

(a) Our societies might become less sectarian.
(b) A fairer and more just society would result.
(c) Society would be more prosperous.
(d) The crucial population, resource depletion, pollution issues threatening us now would be dealt with far more promptly and effectively.
(e) Truly representative and independent governments would not get involved in wars and would not provoke or promote terrorism.

Finally, it should be noted that in Australia it is likely that eventually changes will be made to its preferential voting system to prevent candidates for the Senate being elected with very few primary votes.

Australia's compulsory voting system seems likely to remain, however, and the poor voter turnouts in other countries such as the USA may, indeed, one day encourage them to adopt compulsory voting.

Chapter 19

PARLIAMENTARY PROCESS

> *The ballot is stronger than the bullet.*
> Abraham Lincoln, speech, 19 May 1856, Bloomington, Illinois.
>
> *Constantly choosing the lesser of two evils is still choosing evil.*
> Jerry Garcia, *Rolling Stone*, New York, 30 Nov. 1989.

Introduction

Many negative comments have been made about meetings, often in humour, for example (Hodgson & Hodgson, 1992):

➤ *The length of a meeting rises with the square of the number of people present.*

➤ *A meeting is a group of people that keeps the minutes and loses the hours.*

➤ *What is a committee? A group of unwilling, picked from the unfit to do the unnecessary.*

There are many ways to in which one can wreck a meeting, and many of these are seen often in Australia's state and federal parliaments, and also in Westminster:

➤ *Distract and disrupt* by making loud noises, talking off point or about irrelevant subjects, and giving unwanted advice.

➤ *Disagree* with any argument put forward, politely or otherwise.

➤ *Defend* your proposals strongly and *attack* proposals of the opposition party.

➤ *Dominate* the scene with loud voice, waving of arms and take up as much time as the chairperson of the meeting will allow.

- ➤ *Deviate* from the point at hand, for example by saying that a proposal reminds you of some bad outcome in the past.
- ➤ *Divide* opinion by lobbying different groups before the meeting and saying different things to each one, trying to set one group against another.
- ➤ *Deride* opposing people and views by suggesting that they are dishonest, silly etc.
- ➤ Question the accuracy or validity of the *data* cited by a person making a proposition.

Politics and power

In a classic study French and Raven (1959) discussed five main types of power:

(1) **Reward power** when a person can reward people for compliance with their instructions. These rewards might include promotion, money or support for some project financially or publicly.

(2) **Coercive power** where the person in power has the ability to punish, kinds of punishment including withdrawal of favours, humiliation, withdrawal of friendship and support, reduction of promotional opportunities, delayed pay rises etc.

Here an important factor is the receiver's perception of coercive power being applied negatively to them, when sometimes the person threatening them may not have that power.

(3) **Referent power** when people follow an individual, believing that they have characteristics that are desirable etc.

An unusual example was Gandhi whose "lack of other forms of power (his powerless-ness) was itself attractive to many of his followers ((Hodgson & Hodgson, 1992).

(4) **Connection power** is important in politics and involves a person being known to be friendly or connected in some way to prominent and powerful people.

(5) **Information power** when a person is known to have information that may be negative about other people, and which could be used to harm them legally, reputationally etc.

Referent power is important when it comes to elections, and may considerably influence which person a voter votes for. Connection power may also be important in this context.

Information power is also important in politics, and Wikileaks 'leaking' thousands of Hilary Clinton's emails may have been the reason she lost the 2016 US Presidential election.

Similarly, negative information and gossip about President Trump since that time, particularly about whether his connections and dealings with Russia may have played a part in the Wikileaks and other negative information about Clinton in 2016, and may have involved him in illegal business dealings with Russia after being elected, have considerably reduced his chances of re-election in 2020.

The Westminster & US parliamentary systems

England, the rest of the UK, and Australia have the Westminster system of government with three branches of government: legislative, executive and judicial. In addition to these is the administrative apparatus of government and the various government agencies over whose operations government has a substantial degree of control, for example determining how much funding they have.

In the American 'presidential' system, these three branches of government are separated, with the executive branch directly elected and entirely separate from the legislature. Thus policy cannot be imposed unilaterally, but must be arrived through multilateral bargaining between the competing centres of power. Even when they are attached to the same party, executive and legislative branches often take opposing views over important issues. Congress thus has a powerful role to play in policy-making, which it does through its well-established committee system, but congress is deliberately fragmented, whilst the legislature is divided into two houses, neither dominant, with different (and for the Senate divided) terms of office.

Table 19.1. Australia's cabinet and outer ministry in 1996+.

Cabinet	Outer Ministry
Prime Minister	Aboriginal and Torres Strait Islander Affairs
Trade	
Treasurer	
Foreign Affairs	
Finance	Administrative Services
Primary Industries and Energy	Resources and Energy
Defence	Defence Industry, Science and Personnel, Veteran's Affairs
Employment, Education, Training & Youth Affairs	Schools, Vocational Education and Training
Health & Family Services	Family Services
Social Security	
Industrial Relations	
	Immigration and Multicultural Affairs
	Attorney-General

For many years in Australia the Ministry has been separated into a 'Cabinet' and an 'Outer Ministry', and as an example Table 19.1 shows the ministry of 28 with 15 cabinet positions, with several of the cabinet positions linked to junior ministers, established by John Howard after the 1996 general election (Fenna, 1998).

Here the Department of Employment, Education, Training & Youth Affairs (DEETYA) combines what were once separate departments, as do a couple of other departments.

The interaction-influence systems

Organizations are human enterprises, their success depending upon the coordinated efforts of their members. Organizations have several important characteristics and processes:

> ➢ They have organizational structures within which there are communication processes through which information flows.
> ➢ They have observational and measurement processes that collect information about the internal state of the organization and its external success in financial terms. For political organizations the key measures of performance are regular surveys of public opinion and, of course, the results of elections.
> ➢ They have decision-making processes, for political parties these being local branch meetings in each electorate, branch meetings in each state, and meetings of the MP's of the party at both state and national level.
> ➢ They have resources to carry out decisions, such as the personnel of the organization, the various premises they occupy, and the equipment and funding required for the organization to operate.
> ➢ They have influence processes.
> ➢ They have attitudinal dimensions and motivational characteristics, such as the basic motivational forces they seek to draw upon in using the efforts of their members, and the positivity or negativity of attitudes and loyalties towards the organization, their component parts, and their members (Likert, 1961).

Research has found that organizations that allow greater influence from all their levels tend to be more productive and successful, contrary to what most managers believe (Likert, 1961; Mohr, 2017).

Real democracy, as proposed in this book, therefore, should be more productive/effective than current political systems because members of local electoral branches chose the person to represent them at parliamentary elections, and candidates for these elections must be *independent* and not 'attached' to any special interest group or political party.

In addition, we propose that, except for routine issues such as that of 'supply', members of parliament should put submissions tabled for parliamentary voting to their local branch members for them to vote 'yea or nay' on it, and then take that result, the *electorate members vote* or EMV, to parliament when it is voted upon there.

Conclusion

In the all too often farcical Westminster system that we have in Australia, members of the governing party and the opposition yell and abuse each other from opposite sides of the house of parliament and use some of the negative techniques outlined in the first section of this chapter.

In this largely senseless process the real decisions are usually made by just a few members of the 'inner cabinet' of the governing party.

Then, on average, at every second election the other major party is elected, then undoing much of the work of the preceding parliamentary term.

With the *real democracy* we propose, there would be no parties and thus the 'revolving door' farce of the Westminster system would be avoided.

In addition, on most issues members would vote in parliaments according how the members of their constituency decided by an *electorate members vote.*

Chapter 20

MARKET RESEARCH AND REFERENDA

> *The market came with the dawn of civilization*
> *and is not capitalism's invention.*
> Mikhail Gorbachev, speaking of substandard manufacturing practices
> in the Soviet Union, TV documentary, March 23, 1987.
>
> *Market fundamentalism undermines the democratic political process*
> *and the inefficiency of the political process*
> *is a powerful argument in favour of market fundamentalism.*
> George Soros, *The Crisis of Global Capitalism* (1998).

SURVEYS OF PUBLIC OPINION

Surveys are the only effective way of gauging public opinion and are much used in market research.

On a smaller scale, questionnaires can be used to gauge student opinions in schools and Universities or customer satisfaction with a small business.

A special case, perhaps, elections are the cornerstone of parliamentary democracy. At the beginning of Chapter 1 Aristotle's views on so-called democracy actually being oligarchy in his time were quoted, the point being that real democracy would allow us to vote on every major issue rather than have politicians do it for us (Buchanan & Tullock, 1965).

Voting, however, is a simple form of survey and is used to reach decisions on company boards and at meetings of shareholders to elect board members.

In this chapter we consider market research and examples of survey techniques.

MARKET RESEARCH

The purpose of market research is to collect data upon which to base marketing decisions which may range from ad hoc decisions on how to market a new product to fine tuning the operational routine for long term advertising of a product. Some of the stages of a market research campaign and the techniques that may be employed in these stages are:

[1] Problem awareness and conceptualization. This may include monitoring of trade press, appraisal of current marketing practice, feedback from marketing efforts and 'related-area' reading in newspapers and magazines.

[2] Hypothesizing and qualitative problem refinement. This may include:
- ➤ Group discussions
- ➤ Motivational research
- ➤ Unstructured interviews
- ➤ Recorded observations
- ➤ Laboratory experiments
- ➤ Consumer 'clinics'

[3] Validation and quantification of marketing program. This may include:
- ➤ Market surveys
- ➤ Retail audits
- ➤ Consumer panels

Considering these in order:

Market surveys

Market surveys are to determine the situation in a market at present, the performance of the competitors in the market and likely future trends. This may involve:
- ➤ Collecting existing data ('desk research').
- ➤ Collecting new data, for example official figures such as trade statistics.
- ➤ Usually a census of part of the relevant population is conducted.

> ➤ Structured questionnaires may be used and the results collated to provide a final report.
> ➤ Reports should include details of the sample, the time and the method by which the survey was conducted.

Retail audits

These involve regularly checking stock levels at selected sites to give a measure of the effectiveness of distribution and sales for these sites.

Consumer panels

These are representative groups of people who provide continuous data, for example via a diary provided for this purpose. This approach is often used to test brand loyalty and switching.

MARKET RESEARCH SAMPLING

Sampling may be by characteristics such as gender or variable features such as weight where matters of diet are concerned, for example. Some of the simple procedures of selection commonly used include:

> ➤ Random sampling using random numbers, for example when the sample size is 1,000 out of a total population of 100,000 then the chance of selection is 1/100.
> ➤ Systematic sampling, for example every n^{th} person is chosen, for example from the phone book.
> ➤ Stratified sampling where a quota for each stratum of the population, for example for middle and low incomes, is set.
> ➤ Cluster sampling. An example of this would be choosing a street at random and then interviewing everybody in it.

Accuracy

If we are seeking data on population age distribution, for example, the preferred source would be birth records but generally verbal data is gathered for such purposes and this may involve error and bias.

Sampling errors
These diminish with the size of the sample (whereas bias does not) and are measured by the *standard deviation* or error S (which is the square root of the variance) which is calculated as

$$S = \sqrt{\Sigma(x - x_{av})^2/(n - 1)} = \sqrt{(\Sigma x^2 - (\Sigma x)^2/n)/(n - 1)}$$

the second formula being called the *raw score formula.*

POLITICAL SURVEYS

Political surveys of voter intentions are conducted regularly in most countries by both media organizations and political parties themselves, in Australia one of the best-known polls being NewsPoll which is conducted by media giant News Corporation.

Usually these are conducted on a national or statewide basis, using random sampling to select which voters to contact seeking their opinion, contact usually being made by phone or email.

The results of these polls are of special interest, of course, prior to elections, poor results for a particular party perhaps motivating them to change their campaign promises etc.

Occasional polls by political parties often seek to ascertain voter attitudes to some of their key policies, negative results, of course, giving some encouragement to change them.

MEASUREMENT OF ATTITUDES

Psychophysical scaling, or the measurement of reactions to a stimulus, is sometimes referred to as 'stimulus-person scaling'. This is related to the 'CAB' mechanism introduced in Figure 13.1 and is not to be confused with *psychometrics* or 'person scaling' which deals with IQ and like tests.

Scales of measurement
First it is useful to consider different types of scales of measurement that might be used to measure attitudes:

➤ 'Nominal' measurement. This simply differentiates items, for example the numbers given to members of a sporting team.

➤ Ordinal measurement. Here, for example, we simply establish an order such as A > B > C. Such scales can be subjected to a *monotonic transformation* when the relative positions on the scale are altered but they remain in the same order.

➤ Interval scales. For these a *unit* is needed. When such scales undergo *linear transformation*, for example, the values on the scale might, say, be doubled, but points on the scale remain in the same relative positions.

➤ Ratio scales. For these we need a fixed origin relative to which points are some ratio to each other.

Ordinal scales are much used in measuring attitudes and sometimes, once these are established, interval scales can be formed.

Psychophysical scaling

Some of the more notable techniques developed for psychophysical scaling include (Eagly & Chaiken, 1993):

[1] Method of successive intervals. This was proposed by Thurston in 1937 and involves assuming reactions to stimuli are equivalent to a distance on the 'psychological scale' which assumes normally distributed responses and measures distance on this scale in terms of the standard deviation *S*.

[2] Method of equal-appearing intervals.

This was proposed by Thurston in 1929. In this approach responses are divided into 11 intervals each of size one. Then respondents are asked to place an item, for example the statement "I like - - " or item A, into one of the intervals. If the interval 5 is chosen this gives a score of 5 for A. Then the mean score for the item A is its scale value.

This procedure establishes a scale which is then used to measure attitudes by using a subset of the items scaled by the first (scaling) pool of judges.

These items are presented in random order to persons to be tested and they are asked to place them on the scale, not according to their attitude, but according to their view of the score deserved by the item.

Then the resulting test score is the sum of the scale values selected and this can be compared to the 'standard' values selected by the first pool of judges to measure the attitude of individual persons.

[3] Method of paired comparisons.

This approach was proposed by Thurston in 1928. In this approach the statements or stimuli are presented in pairs and placed in order. Hence the process is comparable to a 'bubble sort' and results in an ordinal scale. Then the number of times options A, B, C etc. were favoured is summed for each and the resulting score yields a scale. This process, however, requires very large numbers of judgments and is impractical except for a relatively small number of items requiring scaling.

[4] Guttman scaling.

This approach gives stimulus-person scaling simultaneously and results in a matrix of data called the *Guttman scalogram*, and details of this method were given in Chapter 14.

Conclusion

In attitude scaling stimuli should not be ambiguous or irrelevant and responses to them should approximate a 'parabola distribution'. In psychological research electricity, light and sound have been used as stimuli. As we have noted, however, it is attitudinal stimuli of the type shown in Table 17.1 which are most relevant in market research.

PERSON SCALING

Unlike stimulus-person scaling techniques, person scaling techniques make no attempt to locate responses on a scale and they are classified *a priori* as either favourable or unfavourable toward the attitude object. Then the location of persons on the attitude dimension is determined by the number of stimuli with which they agree and the extent of their agreement.

These person scaling methods are derivatives of the psychometric model traditionally much used for ability or IQ tests in which responses to items are viewed as indicators of a common latent ability.

Likert's *method of summated ratings* was designed to be much easier to use than the method of equal-appearing intervals but to be at least as reliable. In this approach a large pool of items which are chosen intuitively for their relevance to the attitude object is used. These items usually consist of statements of belief, but statements about behaviours or affective reactions can also be used.

Typically, in Likert scaling each item is presented to respondents in a multiple-choice format such as:

1. Strongly disagree.
2. Disagree.
3. Undecided.
4. Agree.
5. Strongly agree.

Then the response to each item is given a score such as 5 for strongly agree.

Then, for example, a survey on attitudes towards women might contain questions like:

(a) Swearing is more objectionable from a woman.
(b) Intoxication in women is worse than in men.

With scores from 1 - 5 given to each of perhaps a dozen or so such questions the total score is then obtained for each respondent.

Such a survey is much simpler than Thurston's method of equal-appearing intervals but usually the initial pool of items should be pilot tested on a group of people to eliminate ambiguous and nondiscriminating items which tend to result in neutral responses. This can be done by examining the *item-total score correlations*, each of which correlates the respondents' scores on an item with their scores summed over all the items. Then a good item will have a positive correlation and generally better items have higher correlations.

Likert scaling, in addition to the method of equal-appearing intervals and Guttman scaling are all of interest and the reader will probably recognize at least the description of Likert scaling.

EXAMPLE OF LIKERT SCALING

Table 20.1. Questionnaire using Likert scaling.

Circle the appropriate number:	Very good	Good	Aver-age	Fair	Poor
Rate your lecturer's:					
1. Choice of material	5	4	3	2	1
2. Performance generally	5	4	3	2	1
3. Explanations of the theory	5	4	3	2	1
4. Use of practical examples	5	4	3	2	1
5. Development of theory	5	4	3	2	1
6. Stressing important points	5	4	3	2	1
7. Choice of tutorial examples	5	4	3	2	1
8. Time given to individuals	5	4	3	2	1
9. Choice of lab. experiments	5	4	3	2	1
10. Helping understand subject	5	4	3	2	1
11. Useful in its own right	5	4	3	2	1
12. Teaching report writing	5	4	3	2	1
How well does the lecturer do in:					
13. Getting you interested	5	4	3	2	1
14. Knowledge of subject	5	4	3	2	1
15. Motivating you	5	4	3	2	1
16. Giving clear explanations	5	4	3	2	1
17. Lecturing at followable rate	5	4	3	2	1
18. Giving good lecture notes	5	4	3	2	1
Other:					
19. Are the tests useful?	5	4	3	2	1
20. Course relevant to needs?	5	4	3	2	1
Add the numbers you circled:	**Score/100:**				

The foregoing table gives an example of a type of questionnaire which the author once found useful for class evaluation of teaching. The approach is, in fact, reminiscent of Likert scaling and students enjoyed the revenge of giving a mark out of 100, especially as I asked them to also give marks (with different colour pen or ringed etc.) to the HOD who shared teaching of the subject with me. He scored pretty badly!

Though it looks a little formidable this survey worked well and I was pleased with the results.

In hindsight, however, I should point out that in most cases only a few questions should be used and perhaps never more than ten, and preferably five for most purposes. In the case of Table 20.1, however, I had a captive class happy to fill out the longish questionnaire as a change from the usual lecture scenario.

Conclusions

Market research campaigns require a good deal of planning if the results are to be meaningful, let alone accurate.

Attitude measurement or psychophysical scaling plays an important role in market research and the Guttman scalogram is an appealing method for this.

Likert scaling is a simple and widely used method of 'person scaling,' that is, determination of people's attitudes to a product or service.

Market research and polling, of course, play an important role in politics, and we would like to see more polls on important issues and governments taking more notice of the results of these.

We propose that on major issues referenda should be held to allow the people to directly decide them, a good example being the Brexit referendum in the UK a couple of years ago.

Indeed, it is now looking quite likely in the middle of March 2019 that another referendum maybe held on this important issue because of difficulties in getting a UK-EU 'deal' on Brexit approved by parliament.

❖ ❖ ❖ ❖ ❖ ❖ ❖ ❖ ❖ ❖ ❖ ❖ ❖ ❖

Chapter 21

CONCLUSIONS

> *The average man votes below himself; he votes with half a mind or a hundredth part of one. A man ought to vote with the whole of himself, as he worships or gets married. A man ought to vote with his head and heart, his soul and stomach, his eye for faces and his ear for music; also (when sufficiently provoked) with his hands and feet. If he has ever seen a fine sunset, the crimson colour of it should creep into his vote. . . . The question is not so much whether only a minority of the electorate votes. The point is that only a minority of the voter votes.*
> G. K. Chesterton, Tremendous Trifles, *A Glimpse of My Country* 1909.

Combating the many global problems

Problems such as population explosion, resource depletion, pollution, global warming, growing income inequality, corporate and political corruption are a growing threat globally, some of these being largely the result of the greed of a few powerful and wealthy people.

Some of the things we that might help ameliorate our already catastrophic situation are:

➤ Make the 4 day working week the standard.

➤ Allow families with a single breadwinner to split their income before tax with their spouse to help reduce the need for women with children of preschool age, if not any age, to work.

➤ To help reduce our excessive population women should be encouraged to consider having only one child by being reminded that it has often been found that only children tend to have higher IQs and do better academically (Vernon, 1960).

➤ Improve our education system by cutting school back to 10 years and using on the job training as we used to do for nursing and many other occupations. The remaining sensible University courses would be more responsibly run by separate professional colleges.

➤ Encourage a return to small 'local' businesses and reverse the trend to globalization and industries run by heartless and overpaid executives who are nothing more than little Hitlers.

➤ Reduce the hierarchical nature of our society so that young people in their 20s and 30s and at their productive and imaginative peak are not lived off by these little Hitlers. In other words, create a *fairer society,* the topic of the next section of this chapter.

➤ Raise minimum wages and put a ceiling on executive salaries. Remove *all* executive perks and bonuses.

➤ Decentralize industry so that vast countries like Australia do not have nearly all their population crammed into huge megacities more like large scale ant hills than anything sane people should want to live in. To encourage this, rail networks should be extended and precious oil used to run these in remote areas, not absurdly wasteful cars with huge engines used as shopping buggies.

➤ Encourage a return back to farming by family concerns and not big business to help revitalize decaying rural communities.

➤ Government bodies should be established to see to it that people are not brainwashed into buying unnecessary and wasteful products like junk food, four-wheel drive city cars and swimming pools. A society in which we are brainwashed into becoming zombies that wear uncomfortable jeans and carry a mobile phone in one hand and a bottle of drink in the other is not really free, quite the opposite.

Examples of actions taken on advertising include:

(a) Restriction of and compulsory warnings on tobacco products in most countries.

(b) At one time, at least, TV commercials in Italy were limited to 10 showings a year with no two showings closer than 10 days apart (Cateora, 1996).

➢ Increase efforts at developing sustainable energy sources such as wind, solar and tidal.

➢ Legislate against planned obsolescence in cars, electrical, building and other products.

➢ Encourage electric cars, especially small personal transport vehicles that might be an improved form of Clive Sinclair's £400 (1975) tricycle using nickel cadmium batteries.

➢ Create a society in which housing stock is affordable to those beginning careers and family. This could be done by appropriate legislation setting land values at prescribed rather than market values. Young families might also be allowed free land for a house on the fringe of cities and rural towns.

➢ Return to government economic management that protects those governed by the use of fixed currency rates and at least modest tariffs in places like Australia.

➢ Introduce *real democracy* allowing everybody to vote on major issues. This could easily be accomplished using the Internet and polling stations like bank ATMs in all shopping centres. Voting could also be accessible free of charge via all public telephones.

Parliament should be composed of *independent* members of the various electoral regions and collusion by them should be illegal.

➢ The UN should be provided with a large and sophisticated army to help maintain peace and combat terrorism.

➢ Religions and sects responsible, directly or indirectly, for terrorism and war should be outlawed and their religious sites and offices around the world should be closed down by the UN.

➢ A UN funded organization should be established to educate people around the world that God does not exist so that people cannot be duped by self-serving religions and sects.

➢ Ban nuclear and biochemical weapons. Ban land mines.

➢ Take steps to ban war and limit all weapons.

➢ Reduce unemployment levels which in almost every country are too high, and in many countries they are far too high. This issue is discussed in the following section.

Reducing unemployment levels

In Australia and many like countries the 'official' unemployment level has been circa 5% for many years, having been an unacceptable 7.7% in 1998, and 4.4% in 2007.

The 'real' level of unemployment is, in fact, far higher, if one includes people who have given up looking for work and retired, people who are working part-time but want full-time work etc.

More important, this 5% official level corresponds to the level of unemployment that Marx suggested was what Big Business likes to restrict wage growth, and certainly wage growth has stalled somewhat for several years now in Australia, and gone 'backwards' in a few recent years, i.e., been less than the rate of inflation (Marx, 1933).

In fact, a desirable target for the official unemployment rate is circa 2%, and the first author recalls such rates in Australia when he was young, that is, circa 50 years ago.

In periods of economic downturn, of course, 'UE' levels will increase, of course, being a disastrous 24.9% in the U.S. in 1933 as a result of the Great Depression. During WW2, on the other hand, the UE rate fell to 1.9, 1.2, 1.9% respectively in 1943, 1944, 1945, illustrating the truth of Keynes' famous statement that: *war is like digging a hole and pouring money into it.*

Since then in several single years that were declared recessions, the US UE rate was generally between 6 and 7%, whilst after the 'GFC' of 2008 it was 9.9% in 2009.

Presently, in many countries such as some in Africa and a couple in South America, UE rates are circa 20% as a result of financial crises, Venezuela being a notable example.

To reduce UE rates for the 'new normal' of 5% we would propose many measures which are, in any case, desirable, for example:

➤ Make a 4 day, 35 hour week standard practice. Indeed, with such a reduction no reduction in overall productivity was experienced in Norway as workers worked more efficiently in their reduced hours.

➢ Encourage couples with children of pre-school age to have one parent stay at home to look after children and perhaps give some home schooling which has been found immensely effective in increasing the learning ability and IQ of young children.

➢ Keep the retiring age at 65, bearing in mind that in most physically demanding occupations this is perhaps too high, whilst for office jobs such as teaching performance will be in decline by 65, 'real IQ' having declined substantially by then, both as a result of 'normal aging', and sometimes as a result of health problems such as SDAT (Senile Dementia of the Alzheimer Type).

➢ Encourage early retirement when people have enough money to retire, or when they have health issues that make work difficult. In such cases they could be encouraged to do some sort of voluntary work for a couple of days a week, and this still contribute to society and the economy.

The minimum wage

As noted above, in Australia the government-legislated minimum wage has stagnated and sometimes fallen below the level of inflation in recent years.

From 1907 to 2010 GDP per capita increased by 454% and average weekly earnings by 394%, but the 'real minimum wage' increased by only 214%.

The 'wage bite', that is, the minimum wage compared to average weekly earnings has reduced from 0.85 in 1907 to only 0.46 in 2010, largely because, of course, the rich are now getting still richer at a greater rate than ever, whilst the minimum wage has stagnated.

In addition, many part-time workers, and workers in such industries as those restaurants of fast-food outlets, are paid substantially less than the minimum wage.

Some legislative action is needed, therefore, to deal with the minimum wage issue, whilst action is also needed to increase the Newstart allowance which for the long-term unemployed is too low.

Don't become a consumer zombie

Those of us who cannot accept that we are in reverse evolution and getting even more stupid should at least realize that we are animals after all and were never all that clever to begin with.

An article in *The Australian* on December 5, 2007, was nicely headed:

Chimps make monkeys of humans

and went on to say that Japanese researchers had found that, overall, chimpanzees outscored humans on two tests of short-term memory. The tests involved quickly remembering and reproducing a sequence of 5 or 9 numbers on a PC touch screen, the chimps having been taught the order of the Arabic numerals 1 to 9.

Today, indeed, the human race spends an inordinate amount of its time in front of TV screens, PC screens, mobile phone screens, movie screens and so on, thus having been reduced to little better than lab rats constantly brainwashed by the often ridiculous bullshit produced by advertising weirdos.

The ratbags in big biz who have us brainwashed with ads are also those almost entirely responsible for looting the planet and then making it a polluted rubbish dump. For them the exploding population has been a huge bonus but it is already proving to be a terminal disaster in the making for mankind.

Politicians have said and done little or nothing on the population issue over decades and have for the most part been very slow on the uptake concerning pollution, resource depletion and GW, preferring to kowtow to big biz instead, as usual.

On the issue of unnecessary consumption, the first author's late father's dictum

"It's not a bargain/cheap if you don't need it"

applies awfully well to 'junk products' like fast foods, confectionery, booze, cigarettes and overseas holidays. *To add insult to injury, advertising is a large chunk of the cost of most 'junk products.'*

In other words we need to 'get wise' and realize that the bullshit and brainwashing we are subjected to so constantly is, as the rat race intensifies, more and more a form of bullying and something that we should do our utmost to resist.

We must also realize that to be truly free we must be cautious about imitative and social learning which mostly involves *copying* others.

In summary, we need both personally and collectively to:

[1] Largely ignore advertising, only taking notice of the rare ad that may promote something we actually do need at a good price.

[2] Ignore other bullshit from business, political and religious organizations, only taking notice if, after careful analysis and thought, we can judge that a particular message is worth taking some notice of.

[3] Push for consumer education programs relatively early on in schools, including in these cautions about avoiding thoughtless imitative and social learning.

[4] Push for decent products rather than junk, for example healthy food, affordable not 'showy' housing, and sensible, economical cars like a new supposedly US$2000+ petrol engine car released in India recently, prompting people interviewed in the street on TV to say: "Now I can afford a car."

[5] Push for reversal of the growth of wasteful and greedy trends of globalization in business.

[6] Push for reductions in pollution, including greenhouse gasses.

[7] Push for reduced consumption of fast disappearing fossil fuel resources such as oil.

[8] Push for conservation of other precious resources, particularly water, farming land, forests and natural habitats for threatened wild life species.

[9] Push for plans to reduce our population to levels at which a reasonable standard of living is sustainable for all.

Push for better government and less corruption

A 2004 academic analysis of consumption concluded:
"It is trickling into all aspects of being an individual.

It is – for good or bad – the foundation of human existence" (*The Australian,* 3rd Aug. 2005).

Indeed, pretentious persuasion by bullshit artists has been at the core of the ongoing disaster of human history. Now the resulting combination of excessive population and excessive per capita consumption is inevitably leading us towards catastrophe and we consumer zombies, like the earth itself, are deteriorating along the way.

The bottom line, therefore, is that we should:

(1) Largely ignore the bullshit and brainwashing efforts of business, political and other organizations seeking only to improve their situation and, in most cases, make our situation and that of the planet worse.

(2) Insist on eliminating corruption and greed in our societies as far as possible. To that end we should ensure, for example:

(a) Rational limits on executive salaries.

(b) Profit proportional company tax.

(3) Campaign to replace the outdated and farcical Westminster 'revolving door' two party system with *real democracy* in which electorates are represented by truly independent people not influenced by big business or any other section of the community.

An example might be Iceland which, mired in government debt to the unprecedented extent of 10 times GDP, established a "Constitutional Assembly" of people in Reykjavik and a social network Internet site on which the public suggest reforms, soon resulting in 300 amendments to the constitution.

(4) Insist on sensible economic management, for example:

(a) The inverse law of supply and demand and the LM and IS curves noted in Chapter 15 should be understood to avoid the cycles of boom and bust caused by incorrect fiscal fiddling.

(b) A least limited tariffs should be the norm to protect local industries and jobs.

274

(5) Greater efforts must be made to solve the many problems such as overpopulation, resource depletion and pollution that threaten both our quality of life and survival.

(6) Be more careful in choosing who runs what.

Noting that circa 50% of personality may be genetic (Galton, 2001), 'Mohr's Morphology,' postulates three personality types based on a scale of aggressiveness:

(a) Placid (the meek).

(b) Neutral (the OK guys).

(c) Aggressive/assertive (the bossy types).

The meek do not inherit the earth, as The Bible has it, for the bossy little Hitler types usually end up as boss. These bossy types typically have 'type A' behaviour associated with stress. Research has found that, contrary to popular belief enshrined in such terms as "executive stress," being boss involves less work stress and it is the slaves, of course, that really are stressed, and perhaps never more so than in today's consumer society.

Human history might not have been so catastrophic, in fact, had quieter, less aggressive, more intelligent, more honest, and harder working people been leading us.

(7) We must solve the global 'Muslim conflicts' problem almost invariably instigated by Islamic terrorists, an exception being the TAMIL Tigers of Sri Lanka who effect ethnic cleansing of Sinhalese and Muslim inhabitants from areas under their control. Indeed, increasingly commentators now refer to global Islamic terrorism and the fight against it as 'World War 3.'

(8) New privacy laws are needed to restrict data collection from Internet users by Facebook, Google etc. for, as noted in Chapter 12, in some countries such data collection poses a potential 'surveillance nightmare'.

Recently, however, Facebook threatened to reduce "funding" in countries that place restrictions on their date and information collection (ABC New Breakfast, 7 AM, 3/3/19).

Real democracy

The first author used to talk to a famous Greek engineer, John Argyris, in Stuttgart who had done much to pioneer a major field he had spent much of his adult life working in (Argyris, 1960). This went on happily for 10 years and Argyris was always very complimentary about the first author's abilities and work and very modest about his own, for example saying one night:

> "I have no great intelligence, I have imagination."

He used to go to his University office every weekday until he was almost 90 years old. Then his health took a turn for the worse which he had foreseen a couple of years earlier when going off to have his second cataract operation.

Then, he said: *"You are now number one."*

He could still read the writing on the wall!

The last time he spoke to the phone the first author a walking frame could be heard. Clearly the end was nigh: when you are no longer ambulatory and are 90 the prognosis is poor.

On different occasions, the first author asked him two questions:

(a) *"Is the problem of the human race anthropology?"*

(b) *"Are real democracy and socialism the same?"*

Two quick and identical answers as always from a quick mind: ***"Of course!"***

In other words:

(a) The chief apes, whether of religion, politics or business, that have led us to the brink of extinction have a lot to answer for.

(b) Don't be brainwashed by bullshit about products of any kind, including religion, politics or whatsoever. We are all animals with a halfway well developed cerebral cortex and yet are so stupid that we continually make a mess of nearly everything, including ourselves.

We are slow learners, however, and have a very hard time learning to walk, let alone talk sense. We can't be born knowing the answers or being wise to the wiles of unscrupulous old men and women trying to push their products at us.

We need new, more responsible forms of government that don't build up industrial-military states and kowtow to big business but represent *our interests*. All of us should have a *direct* and democratic voice in major decisions at all levels of government and, for that matter, in the running of the organizations that we work for if we are not self-employed.

In other words we should have *freedom*. Specifically, we should have freedom of:

➢ **Speech:** we should be allowed to express our views.

➢ **Opinion:** we should be allowed to democratically express our opinion on *all* major issues.

➢ **Association:** we should be able to meet with and talk to whoever we choose.

➢ **Education:** we should have more educational paths, some of them with faster pacing and shortcuts for example.

➢ **Careers:** we should have a society in which children develop a vocational idea relatively early in life, rather than a lottery process based on a few marks 'either way' in just one set of exams.

➢ **Employment:** we need a return to the 'a career for life' approach so that people in the work force are committed to and good at what they do.

➢ **Choice:** industry should make a reasonable effort to provide us with responsible and genuinely innovative and beneficial products which do not have obsolescence built into them.

➢ **Power:** we should have a truly democratic system in which all eligible voters are able to vote on all major issues.

➢ - - and so on, but with some restrictions, of course, and this is always a difficult question. Most obviously these would preclude violations of common law.

As Martin Luther King put it during his famous 'I have a dream' speech: **" LET FREEDOM REIGN !! "**

That sounds fine to us. Just so long as the bullshit of the brain washers does not rain down upon us quite so heavily, whether that be via advertising, the lectern or the pulpit, and that we can make some progress towards *real democracy* so that the wishes of the people can be heard, not the BS artists.

Conclusions

In conclusion, some of the key aspects of *real democracy* as we envisage it include:

[1] Each *eligible* citizen (e.g., older than, say, 14, and not in jail) should be able to vote to elect members of parliament.

[2] Members of parliament should be independent and represent only the interests of their constituency, not those of any other organization.

[3] All citizens should be allowed to vote on key issues such as significant changes in taxation, not just on referenda relating to proposals for changes in the constitution.

Thus, we propose that, except for routine issues such as that of 'supply', members of parliament should put submissions tabled for parliamentary voting to their local branch members for them to vote 'yea or nay' on it, and then take that result, the *electorate members vote* or EMV, to parliament when it is voted upon there.

There has been some evidence in recent years of a slight voter swing towards independent candidates in Australia, and on a couple of occasions of late a small group of about half a dozen independents have united to defeat the governing party proposals in the Federal Parliament.

More spectacular, when the leader of the governing Liberal-National Party (LNP) coalition was dumped by internal party 'machinations' in August 2018, an independent candidate won the following by-election in what had until then been a safe seat for the LNP.

In addition, in the last two decades a few very small 'minor parties' have emerged, most spectacularly Pauline Hansen's One Nation party which 'came from nowhere' to win half a dozen seats in a Queensland state election in 1996.

❖ ❖ ❖ ❖ ❖ ❖ **THE END** ❖ ❖ ❖ ❖ ❖ ❖

References

Aarons M, Loftus B, *The Secret War Against the Jews,* Mandarin Press, Melbourne (1999).

Adams, J, *The Next World War,* Simon & Schuster, New York (1998).

Adamson I, Kennedy R, *Sinclair and the 'Sunrise' Technology,* Penguin, Harmondsworth (1986).

Alder B, Fernbach S, Rotenberg M, *Methods in Computational Physics,* Academic Press, New York (1963).

Alexander W, *Future War,* Thomas Dunne Books, New York (1999).

Alibek, K, *Biohazard*, Arrow, London (2000).

Argyris JH, *Energy Theorems and Structural Analysis,* Butterworth, London (1960, reprinted from *Aircraft Engineering* 1954 - 55).

Batra R, *Surviving the Great Depression of 1990,* Bantam/Schartz, Sydney (1988).

Bell R, Hall, R, *Impacts: Contemporary Issues & Global Problems,* The Jacaranda Press, Milton QLD (1991).

Ben-Menashe A, *Profits of War, The Sensational Story of the World-Wide Arms Conspiracy,* Allen & Unwin, Sydney (1992).

Bethe HA, *The Road from Los Alamos,* Touchstone Books, New York NY (1991).

Black E, *IBM and the Holocaust,* Little Brown, London (2001).

Blondel J, *Voters, Parties, and Leaders,* Penguin, Harmondsworth (1963).

Blundell, Nigel, *The World's Greatest Crooks and Conmen and other mischievous malefactors,* Octopus Books, London (1982).

Brook-Shepherd G, *Iron Maze, The Western Secret Services and the Bolsheviks,* Pan, London (1998).

Broom L, Jones FL, McDonnell P, Williams T, *The Inheritance of Inequality,* Routledge & Kegan Paul, London (1980).

Buchanan JM, Tullock G, *The Calculus of Consent,* The University of Michigan Press, Ann Arbor (1974).

Burch JG, Strater FR, Grudnitski, *Information Theory and Practice,* 3rd edn, Wiley, New York (1983).

Cateora, PR, *International Marketing,* 9th edn, Irwin, Chicago (1996).

Carey J (ed.), *The Faber Book of Science,* Faber and Faber, London (1995).

Caves RE, Frankel JA, Jones RW, *World Trade and Payments: An Introduction,* Scott Foresman/Little Brown, Glenview IL (1990).

Chambers Dictionary of World History, Chambers Harrap, Edinburgh, 1993.

Churchill WS, *My Early Life, A Roving Commission,* Fontana, London (1959).

Churchill WS, *Churchill in His Own Words*, Capricorn Books, New York (1966).

Cipolla, CM, *The Economic History of World Population,* 6th edn, Penguin, London (1974).

Clark G, *In Fear of China,* Lansdowne Press, Melbourne (1967).

Collins AM, Quillian MR, Retrieval time from semantic memory, *Journal of Verbal Learning and Verbal Behaviour* 8 (1969) 240-247.

Cooke JP, Zimmer J, *The Cardiovascular Cure,* Broadway Books, New York (2002).

Cornwell J, *Hitler's Scientists, Science, War and the Devil's Pact,* Viking, London (2003).

Cowie HR, Collins MB, Ryan DB, *Imperialism, Racism and Re-Assessments,* Nelson, Melbourne (1994).

Crough G, Wheelwright T, Wilshire T (editors), *Australia and World Capitalism,* Penguin (1980).

Davis JW, *An Introduction to Public Administration,* The Free Press, New York (1974).

Dees M, *Gathering Storm, America's Militia Threat,* Harper Perennial, New York (1996).

Delgado JMR, *Physical Control of the Mind: Towards a Psychocivilized Society,* Colophon Books (Harper & Row), New York (1971).

Doyle D, *Inside Espionage, A Memoir of True Men and Traitors,* St Ermin's Press, London (2000).

Eagly AH, Chaiken S, *The Psychology of Attitudes,* Harcourt Brace Jovanovich, Orlando FL (1993).

Egerton Eastwick RW (ed.), *The Oracle Encyclopaedia,* George Newnes, London (1896).

Fancher RE, *The intelligence men: Makers of the IQ Controversy,* WW Norton, New York (1985).

Fenna, Alan, *Introduction to Australian Public Policy,* Addison Wesley Longman, South Melbourne (1998).

Forbes HD, *Ethnic Conflict: Commerce, Culture, and the Contact Hypothesis,* Yale University Press, New Haven (1997).

Galton D, *In Our Own Image, Eugenics and the Genetic Modification of People,* Little Brown & Co, London (2001).

Gillespie, David, *Taming Toxic People, The science of identifying & dealing with psychopaths at work & at home,* Pan MacMillan Australia, Sydney (2017).

Goodwin S, *Hubble's Universe, A New Picture of Space,* Constable, London (1996).

REFERENCES

Govoni N, Eng R, Morton G, *Promotional Management: Issues and Perspectives,* Prentice-Hall, Englewood Cliffs NJ (1988).

Hall, T, *White Collar Crime in Australia,* Harper & Row, Sydney (1979).

Hersha C, Hersha L, Griffis D, *Secret Weapons, Two Sisters' Terrifying Story of Sex, Spies and Sabotage,* New Horizon Press, Far Hills NJ (2001).

Heywood, Andrew, *Global Politics,* Palgrave-Macmillan, New York (2011).

Hilmer FG, Donalson L, *Management Redeemed: Debunking the Fads that Undermine Corporate Performance,* The Free Press, East Roseville NSW (1996).

Hodgson P, Hodgson J, *Effective Meetings,* Century Business/Random House, London (1993).

Holland Jack, *Hope Against History, The Course of Conflict in Northern Ireland,* Hodder & Stoughton, London (1999).

Hollingsworth M, Fielding N, *Defending the Realm, MI5 and the Shayler Affair,* André Deutsch, London (1999).

Hughes-Wilson J, *Military Intelligence Blunders,* Carroll & Graf, New York (1999).

Jay P, *The Crisis of Western Political Economy,* The Australian Broadcasting Commission, Sydney (1981).

Jencks C, Smith M, Acland H, Bane MJ, Cohen D, Gintis H, Heyns B, Michelson S, *Inequality: A Reassessment of the Effect of Family and Schooling in America,* Penguin, Harmondsworth (1975).

Jonas G, Into the brain, *New Yorker,* July 1, 1974, p 57.

Jones S, Israel P, *Others Unknown: The Oklahoma City Bombing Case and Conspiracy,* Public Affairs, New York (1998).

Kagan R, *Paradise and Power: America and Europe in the New World Order,* Atlantic Books, London (2008).

Kissinger H, *Years of Renewal,* Simon & Schuster, New York (1999).

Knightley P, *Philby, KGB Masterspy.* Andre Deutsch, London (1988).

Lifton RJ, *Destroying the World to Save It: Aum Shinrikyo, Apocalyptic Violence, and the New Global Terrorism,* Metropolitan Books, New York (1999).

Likert R, *New Patterns of Management,* McGraw-Hill, New York (1961).

Lindzey G, Hall CS, Thompson RF, *Psychology*, 2nd edn, Worth, New York (1978).

Lynne R, Vanhanen T, *IQ and The Wealth of Nations,* Praeger, Westport CT (2002).

Mackenzie KR, *The English Parliament*, Penguin, Harmondsworth (1950).

Marx K, *Capital,* Dent & Sons, London (1933, first published 1867).

Maxwell N, Yahuda M, Wheelwright T, Jayawardena C, The Chinese model: politics in command, in *Political Economy of Development,* Australian Broadcasting Commission, Sydney (1977).

McCormack MH, *What They Don't Teach You at Harvard Business School,* Fontana/Collins, London (1986).

McGuire WJ, A syllogistic analysis of cognitive relationships, in *Attitude Organization And Change,* CI Hovland & MJ Rosenberg (eds.), Yale University Press, New Haven (1960).

Meadows DH, Meadows DL, Randers J, Behrens WW, *The Limits to Growth,* Pan, London (1974).

Miller J, Engelbert S, Broad W, *Germs, The Ultimate Weapon,* Simon & Schuster, New York (2001).

Mohr GA, *The Finite Element Method for Solids, Fluids, and Optimization,* Oxford University Press, Oxford (1992).

REFERENCES

Mohr GA, *The Pretentious Persuaders,* Horizon, Sydney (2012, 2014 – 2nd edition).

Mohr GA, *The Doomsday Calculation,* Xlibris, Sydney (2012b).

Mohr GA, *2045, A Small Town Survives Global Nuclear Holocaust,* Xlibris, Bloomington, IN (2014a).

Mohr GA, *Elementary Thinking,* Xlibris, Sydney (2014b).

Mohr GA, *The History & Psychology of Human Conflict,* Horizon, Sydney (2014c).

Mohr GA, Richard Sinclair & Edwin Fear, *The Evolving Universe: Relativity, Redshift, and Life From Space,* Xlibris, Sydney (2014).

Mohr GA, Fear E, *World Religions, The History, Issues & Truth,* Xlibris, Sydney (2015).

Mohr GA, Edwin Fear & Richard Sinclair, *World War 3: When and How Will It End?,* Inspiring Publishers (2015).

Mohr GA, Fear E, *The Brainwashed: From Consumer Zombies to Islamism and Jihad,* Inspiring Publishers (2016).

Mohr GA, *The Scientific MBA,* Balboa Press, Bloomington IN (2017).

Mohr GA, R. Sinclair, E. Fear, Mohr PE, *Human Intelligence, Learning, and Behaviour,* Inspiring Publishers, Canberra (1917).

Mohr GA, *The DIY Cardiovascular Cure, A Comprehensive Program to Reverse Atherosclerosis,* Amazon-Kindle (2018).

Mohr GA, *Mohr's Law of Hierarchies and many other Mohr's Laws,* Amazon-Kindle (2018b).

Mohr GA, *The Psychology of Life, A practical introduction to psychology,* Amazon-Kindle (2018c).

Mohr GA, *The Psychology of Depression, Developmental, attitudinal & lifestyle factors* (2018d).

Mohr GA, Mohr RS, Mohr PE, *New Theories of The Universe, Evolution, and Relativity,* Amazon-Kindle (2018).

REFERENCES

Mohr GA, Mohr RS, Mohr PE, *Human Psychology, Learning and Intelligence,* Amazon-Kindle (2018b).

Mohr GA, Mohr RS, Mohr PE, *Human Conflict: An Attitudinal Psychology Model,* Amazon-Kindle (2018c).

Morgan CT, King RA, Robinson NM, *Introduction to Psychology,* 6th edn, McGraw-Hill, Tokyo (1979).

Newcomb TM, Persistence and regression of changed attitudes, *Journal of Sociological Issues* 19 (1963) 3-14.

Niblett WR (ed.), *Higher Education: Demand and Response,* Tavistock Publications, London (1969).

Nicholas M, *The World's Greatest Cranks and Crackpots,* Exeter Books, New York (1984).

Nojumi N, *The Rise of the Taliban in Afghanistan,* Palgrave, New York (2002).

Odle F, *The Picture Story of British Inventions,* World Distributors, Manchester (1966).

O'Guinn TC, Allen CT, Semenik RJ, *Advertising and Integrated Brand Promotion.* Thomson South-Western, Mason OH 2006.

Packard V, *The Status Seeks,* Pelican, Harmondsworth, London (1961).

Packard V, *The Waste Makers,* Pelican, Harmondsworth, London (1963).

Packard V, *The People Shapers,* Nelson, Melbourne (1978).

Parkinson CN, *Parkinson's Law, or the Pursuit of Progress* (1958).

Parkinson CN, *The Law,* Schwartz, Melbourne (1980).

Peter LJ, Hull R, *The Peter Principle,* Souvenir Press, London (1969).

Philby R, Lyubimov M, Peake H, *The Private Life of Kim Philby,* Fromm International, New York (2000).

Pringle P, Spigelman J, *The Nuclear Barons,* Holt, Rinehart and Winston, New York (1981).

REFERENCES

Przemieniecki JS, *Theory of Matrix Structural Analysis,* McGraw-Hill, New York (1968).

Regis, *The Biology of Doom, The History of America's Secret Germ Warfare Project,* Henry Holt, New York (1999).

Ripps LJ, Schoben EJ, Smith EE, Semantic distance and the verification of semantic relations, *Journal of Verbal Learning and Verbal Behaviour* 12 (1973) 203-210.

Robertson I, *Sociology*, 2nd edn, Worth, New York (1981).

Robertson TS, *Consumer Behaviour,* Scott Foresman, Glenview IL (1970).

Sampson A, *The Arms Bazaar,* Coronet Books, London (1977).

Sargent M, *Drinking and Alcoholism in Australia: A Power Relations Theory,* Longman Cheshire, Melbourne (1979).

Sauerbruch F, *A Surgeon's Life,* André Deutsch, London (1953).

Schmidt-Nielsen K, *Animal Physiology: Adaptation and Environment,* 2nd edn, Cambridge University Press, Cambridge (1979),

Self P, *Administrative Theories and Policies,* 2nd edn, George Allen & Unwin, London (1977).

Silber L, Little A, *Yugoslavia: Death of a Nation,* TV Books, New York (1995).

Smith A, *Paper Money,* Summit Books, New York (1981).

Snow RL, *Terrorists Amongst Us, The Militia Threat,* Perseus Publishing, Cambridge MA (1999).

Solomon MR, *Consumer Behaviour: Buying, Having and Being,* Allyn and Bacon, Boston (1992).

Sweezy PM, *The Theory of Capitalist Development*, Dennis Dobson, London (1946).

Sykes CJ, *Dumbing Down Our Kids: Why American Children Feel Good About Themselves But Can't Read, Write or Add,* St Martin's Griffin, New York (1995).

Thomas, Keith (ed.), *The Oxford Book of Work,* Oxford University Press, Oxford (1999).

Thomas M, *As Used on the Famous Nelson Mandela, Underground Adventures in the Arms and Torture Trade,* Ebury Press, London (2006).

Townsend P (ed.), *The Concept of Poverty,* Heinemann, London (1970).

Ungar G, Desidero DM, Parr W, Isolation, identification and synthesis of a specific behaviour inducing brain peptide, *Nature* 238 (1972) 198-202.

Vander AJ, Sherman JH, Luciano DS, *Human Physiology,* 6th edn, McGraw-Hill, New York (1994).

van Lawick-Goodall, Jane, *In the Shadow of Man*, Houghton Mifflin, Boston (1971).

Vernon, Jack, *Macroeconomics* (2nd end), The Dryden Press, Hinsdale IL (1980).

Vernon PE, *Intelligence and Attainment Tests,* University of London Press, London (1960).

Wagner RH, *Environment and Man,* 3rd edn, W.W. Norton, New York (1978)

Weiss ML, Mann AE, *Human Biology and Behaviour, An Anthropological Perspective*, 2nd edn, Little Brown, Boston MA (1978).

Wolfe L, Brainwashing: How the British Use The Media For Mass Psychological Warfare Brainwashing. Internet posting - originally printed in *The American Almanac,* May 5, 1997.

Wolfe L, Americans Target Of Largest Media Brainwashing Campaign In History. Posted on the Internet and originally in *Executive Intelligence Review*, 16/10/01.

Wonnacott P, Wonnacott R, *Economics,* McGraw-Hill, New York (1979).

REAL DEMOCRACY

This book discusses the evolution of today's various systems of government, the problems associated with them, how modern persuasion techniques are used to 'brainwash' us, and proposes *Real Democracy,* detailing how this might be implemented.

Key topics in the book thus include:

> Evolution of the consumer society and consumer zombies.
> Religion and Islamism and Islamic Jihad.
> Major problems such as global warming and widespread conflict.
> A highly detailed numerical attitudinal model of conflict.
> Hierarchies and the psychology of psychopaths
> Big Business and 'econobabble'.
> War and terrorism.
> Details of how to implement *Real Democracy.*

G. A. Mohr did his PhD at Churchill College, Cambridge. He published circa 60 papers for 20 international journals and more than 30 books, including:
A Microcomputer Introduction to the Finite Element Method
Finite Elements for Solids, Fluids, and Optimization
The Pretentious Persuaders, A Brief History & Science of Mass Persuasion
Curing Cancer & Heart Disease
The Variant Virus;   2045: A Remote Town Survives Global Holocaust
The Doomsday Calculation: The End Of The Human Race
Heart Disease, Cancer, & Ageing: Proven Neutraceutical & Lifestyle Solutions
The History & Psychology of Human Conflict;   The War of the Sexes
Elementary Thinking for the 21st Century;   Mohr's Law of Hierarchies
The 8-Week+ Program to Reverse Cardiovascular Disease
The DIY Cardiovascular Cure;   Combating Cancer
Elementary Thinking for Modern Management;   The Scientific MBA
The Psychology of Life;   The Psychology of Depression

Also with R.S. Mohr/Richard Sinclair & P.E. Mohr/Edwin Fear:
The Evolving Universe: Relativity, Redshift and Life from Space
World Religions: The History, Psychology, Issues & Truth
World War 3, When & How Will It End?
The Brainwashed, From Consumer Zombies to Islamic Jihad
Human Intelligence, Learning & Behaviour
New Theories of The Universe, Evolution, and Relativity
The Population Explosion;   World Religions: From Animism to Mohronism;
Brainwashed Zombies: Religious, Political & Consumer Persuasion
Human Conflict: An Attitudinal Psychology Model
The Psychology of Hope;   The Psychology of Success
World War 3: Global Islamic Jihad
Human Psychology, Learning and Intelligence

www.ingramcontent.com/pod-product-compliance
Lightning Source LLC
Chambersburg PA
CBHW062128280526
45788CB00001B/98